John Dryden

A CRITICAL BIOGRAPHY

by

Kenneth Young

SYLVAN PRESS

First Published 1954

Printed by Hollen Street Press Ltd.,
for Sylvan Press Ltd, Museum
House, Museum St., London W.C.1

MADE IN GREAT BRITAIN

for

BONAMY DOBRÉE

affectionately

John Dryden
A CRITICAL BIOGRAPHY

CONTENTS

ERRATA

page 121 line 7   Dryden's cleverness appears not
                 only as a political writer
page 151 last line   last word   The
page 166 line 10   it was as a translator
       line 21   we have at length
page 191 line 31   those men
page 234 line 20   The Mourning Bride

John Dryden
A CRITICAL BIOGRAPHY

CONTENTS

Preface

WRITING a life of John Dryden is like trying to carve in solid rock with a tablespoon. The difficulty is not accidental ; Dryden himself wished it to be so. He said : " Anything, though never so little, which a man speaks of himself, in my opinion is still too much ". Aubrey intended Dryden to write an autobiographical sketch for him, leaving a blank space for it in his MSS with the note " He will write it for me himself ". It was blank still at Aubrey's death.

Of course, Dryden does reveal his opinions, particularly his literary opinions, not merely by his choice of theme and treatment, but also directly in asides and personal remarks in his prose prefaces and discourses. In two poems, *Religio Laici* and *The Hind and the Panther,* he goes further still, relaxing his rule to allow direct autobiographical statements about his mind and—it is no exaggeration—his soul. It is incidentally strange that his remark in his address to the reader at the beginning of *The Hind and the Panther*—" What I desire the reader should know concerning me, he will find in the body of the poem "— has had so little weight attached to it by those who have written about him : the passages he refers to, after all, contain considered statements by the poet about his own deepest nature—a nature no less deep than that of Wordsworth, statements no less considered than those made in *The Prelude* to which so much dogged attention has been paid, and upon which, naturally, our whole view of Wordsworth is based. So I have tried to give full weight to what Dryden allows us to know of himself.

Apart from that, no writer of Dryden's eminence can hope to keep his private life private ; it is natural and proper that those who admire his works should want to know about the man who wrote them, and should delve into the past to find out about him. Yet in fact Dryden has had his desire for privacy largely granted, for in spite of all the painstaking, if not altogether scientific, inquiries in the eighteenth century by such men as Samuel Derrick and Edward Malone, surprisingly little of first-rate personal data has turned up. The bare events of his life, from at least 1668 when be became Poet Laureate and a public figure, were already well enough known ; but where is the revealing anecdote, the family recollection, the diary, or the personal reminiscence by friends and acquaintances of the man who met almost every notable person of his time ? Stray remarks, stray references, a delightful tribute by Congreve—these can be found, but they tell us really very little. The eighteenth century concluded, not unreasonably, that little had been discovered about Dryden because there was little to discover; that Dryden was a very ordinary person who happened to be a master of his craft, and that was all.

That conclusion is still generally accepted, particularly since the romantic and typically nineteenth-century efforts of Macaulay and Christie to paint a portrait of a sordid, villain poet, unscrupulous and two-faced, have been discounted.

That he was the supreme craftsman is true, as it is true of other great artists such as Bach and Haydn ; that he was not a romantic figure in the nineteenth-century manner, a Byron or even a Coleridge, nor even in the seventeenth-century manner of Donne or Rochester is equally true. But the man who wrote *Religio Laici*, who passed through stages of vaingloriousness and fought with his pride, who came to consider the sources of life and death in his Lucretius, who emerged from the spiritual doubt of Anglicanism into the calm waters of faith, a faith he stuck to in spite of all blandishments and pressing needs,— this was no *homme moyen sensuel*, dull, phlegmatic, material to stuff churchyards with, as Ford Madox Ford used to say. The quiet front may have been successfully presented to his world over seventy long years, but Dryden was a person susceptible to the terrors, doubts and strange joys of the sensitive intellect, now the calculating businessman, now the open-handed, open-hearted *bon viveur* ; now the good parent, now the lover of actresses. He is a lover of good company whose greatest delight is the quiet retirement of country life, a playwright happy in " bold bawdry " who is intensely occupied with religion— a man in fact worth knowing more about, because it is seldom that a great poet is also such a complete human being, so balanced, so coherent, knowing the terrors, supping freely with them, but refusing to succumb to their menacing.

This is what makes him so interesting, and why I have written this book. Yet from one point of view it has been an unnecessary labour : there already exists one life—and only one—in which the real John Dryden is portrayed. That is the life by Sir Walter Scott. I have read it many times, and never yet turned the last page without being near tears—the tears forced from one by the presence of genius. Here is one great writer devoting himself to another, not imposing himself but for a brief space living himself into the other.

One further observation about this magnificent Life, which shame-fully is unobtainable save in very large libraries : that is that the observations Scott makes about Dryden, his shots in the dark, have been in many instances fully substantiated by the researches of the last forty years.

But it is those researches that have fortified me in the hopeless endeavour of " improving " on Scott ; for when we know things for hard fact rather than as brilliant *aperçus*, the picture shifts slightly and a new pattern imposes itself on the material, and so on the works themselves. Moreover, each age—it is a mere truism—must look for itself at the great figures of the past, must find for itself what is most valuable and significant to it in the work of a great writer—without, however, abdicating from the historian's duty of trying to see what the writer was to himself, to his contemporaries, and they to him, and of trying also to see him and his age *sub specie aeternitatis*. On this, the deepest level, the biographer's attitude to his subject must be the same as the humanist's to his fellow men, the position being, as Cyril Connolly has well expressed it : "Every human being enjoys an exquisite privilege, that of being alive, and suffers, in the knowledge that he must die, an unbearable torture. To all those so privileged we owe respect and honour, to all those under that common death sentence pity and love . . . . . the sum of human consciousness is what is loaned to the living for the appreciation of the world and should be handed on in better shape to those who follow ".

The researches of the last forty years, to which I referred, and without which my attempt would have been impossible and otiose, have been carried out almost entirely by Americans, for reasons on which this is not the place to speculate. Indeed after the eighteenth century singularly little real research took place until twentieth-century American scholars took a hand : Macaulay and Christie, although the latter was a trained historian and an expert on the Restoration period which he heartily disliked, produced little in the way of new facts ; Saintsbury, though his Life has a fair claim to be considered the second best in existence, seems never to have moved from his study. But in 1909, the American Professor George R. Noyes brought out his complete, annotated edition of the poems and translations, everything Dryden wrote in verse except the plays. This edition, in its 1950 revised form, is a magnificent piece of scholarship and a gold mine for the biographer. It has, too, an excellent short life—and, I must regretfully add, it is difficult to obtain in this country, never having been handled by an English publisher. It is, therefore, good news that Dr. James Kinsley of the University of Wales is working on a complete three-volume edition of all Dryden's poetry, except the plays, for the Oxford English Texts series.

Two other outstanding American studies must be mentioned. One is Professor Louis I. Bredvold's *The Intellectual Milieu of John Dryden*, published by the University of Michigan Press in 1934, in which the contents of a mind steeped in seventeenth-century philosophical, religious and political writing are devoted to revealing the origin and development of the ideas in Dryden's mind. The second is Mr. James M. Osborn's *John Dryden : Some Biographical Facts and Problems,* published by Columbia University Press in 1940. This is a sort of omnibus volume summarising the most recent research under various headings, with some shorter studies and six most illuminating though academic examinations of earlier biographies—those by Birch, Derrick, Dr. Johnson, Malone, Scott, and the nineteenth-century writers.

One further and invaluable book must be mentioned, and it is by an Englishman : Hugh Macdonald's *John Dryden, a bibliography*, published by the Oxford University Press in 1939. The many other books I have found valuable are mentioned in my notes on sources at the end of this book.

One word about my method. I have had sometimes to guess about certain things, sometimes to follow up and elaborate a mere hint ; but in no case is a statement of fact made without evidence, and in no case is any single detail highly coloured to support any theory about Dryden. I have no theory, except that he was a human being and a great writer, and worthy of as intelligent and instructed approach as can be mustered by a biographer.

There are three people whom I wish especially to thank for their help to me in writing this book ; they are my teacher and friend, Professor Bonamy Dobrée ; my publisher, Mr. Charles Rosner ; and my wife, for her unfailing forbearance, kindness, and willingness to listen to chunks of this book being read out to her—chunks like new-born puppies before they are licked into shape.

London, 1954   KENNETH YOUNG

Prologue

THE PICTURE of Dryden we all remember best is of the great poet and Man of Letters in the ripeness of age sitting in his arm-chair at Will's Coffee House, in the winter by the fire, in the summer on the balcony overlooking the bustle of Covent Garden. He is florid, rather plump in the face, and his wavy grey hair falls untidily round his neck and ears ; his mouth with its thin upper and thick lower lip is agreeably touched with irony, and it can break into a charming smile ; but usually he has a " down " look for he is shy, incredibly shy for a man of his fame and distinction. There is " something slow and, as it were, diffident in his advances to others ", and the first token of his regard to the chattering young poets and writers around him— Southerne, or the dandy and critic, William Walsh, or dearest of all, Congreve—is likely to be an offer of a pinch from an enormous snuff-box.

This, at the end of the seventeenth century, is England's most famous author, at the forefront of literature for thirty years, now about to succumb to the gout that gave him " St. Anthony's fires " ; mortal, yet leaving immortality behind him in the glow of poetry behind lines of satire, or ratiocination, or translation, in plays and naughty lyrics, in resounding odes and witty prologues, leaving behind him, too, friendly, thoughtful prose, and homely letters about marrow puddings, and a gold clock for his son, and a fat woman in the North-ampton coach, and the irritating habits of his publisher, Jacob Tonson.

It is a pleasant, happy picture, like a still from a film of action caught and held in mid-air, and it is valid enough of a moment in time—but that moment has come between us and the truth about an extraordinary human being, just as Macaulay's sketch of Dryden's life of " mendicancy and adulation " came between the Victorians and the truth, or just as a new theory of poetry blinded Wordsworth to the fact that Dryden, too, was a poet.

Swing the camera away from the coffee house, and we see Dryden, this poet of the town and of politics, in the country, in the Nene valley of his Northamptonshire birthplace, or at the houses of his

patrons, or in Wiltshire at the house of his father-in-law, the Earl of
Berkshire. It has been estimated that he spent at least two months of
every year away from London ; even when he was in London, there
are so many records of his being at home, in Long Acre, or later in
Gerrard Street, working in the morning and lunching *en famille*, so
many dinners with Pepys and Evelyn and the Earl of Dorset, that his
time at Will's must have been comparatively short.

This is a small point, but already our impression of Dryden begins
to change. Look again and we see his grey straggly hair of one
portrait dissolve into the neat, brown curls of another, the pleasant
irony give way to the rather superior lift of the lip, the precise fingers
on the cheek, the air of " I am an important person so don't keep
me sitting here long ". Nor can we in honesty say that this is the
picture of a shy phlegmatic man—as the original often insisted—
nor of a modest one, as Congreve asserted. The answer is, of
course, that Dryden, like every other man ever born, did change in
the course of his life. He *was* shy and the slightest bit dull when he
first came to London ; he was shy, modest and unassuming in later
years. But the younger portrait is also correct, for at about the time
when Kneller must have painted it Dryden, as Sir Walter Scott and
Professor Saintsbury observed, was passing through a period of
arrogance. That we can see in his superior comments on the older
English writers. Success in the theatre, friendship with noblemen and
at least acquaintance with His clever, jovial, shrewd Majesty Charles II
had, temporarily, gone to his head, and he was cock-a-hoop.

But the complication does not end there. Can a shy or modest
man be a satirist of Dryden's type, seeing his victims from an Olympian
height :

> Sons of a day just buoyant on the flood,
> Then numbered with the puppies in the mud.

or dealing with such powerful men as Shaftesbury and Buckingham so
disdainfully ? Psycho-analysis has taught us that, in fact, shyness is
often a sign of a great superiority complex, one's idea of oneself being
so inflated that the outer world cannot possibly measure up to it.
But Dryden himself has given a more certain clue in a famous couplet :

> My pride struck out new sparkles of her own.
> Such was I, *and by nature still I am.*

In other words, Dryden *was* filled with self-pride but he believed that he had conquered it. Nor was this a delusion considering his kindness latterly to young poets, his high regard for earlier writers and his low opinion of his own productions.

Already the picture of Dryden of " Old Will's " has dissolved, like a cinematic fade-out, into something, not contradictory, but more complex—and the curious Romantic idea that poets who used regular metres were simple people has dissolved with it. Complex, indeed, Dryden was, and therefore the more human, and being human basically mysterious—the mystery being deepened by his belief that " anything, though never so little which a man speaks of himself, in my opinion is still too much ". He is, indeed, complex to the point of paradox, and on the surface " everything by starts and nothing long " like his own Zimri. Born a Puritan, or at least into strictly Puritan circles, he became an Anglican and ended a Roman Catholic ; he wrote a poem in praise of Oliver Cromwell, and one in praise of King Charles ; he was a fond father who kept a mistress, a religious poet who wrote bawdy plays, for which he later apologised, but which he clearly enjoyed writing for they remain *amusing* smut (*pace* his nineteenth-century apologists) ; a keen fisherman who loved town society ; one of the most original poets who ever wrote in English, but who believed that " innovation " was " the blow of fate ", and was, as Professor Bredvold has said, the first English Conservative. And paradox has haunted him in the centuries since his death, for this great poet who taught not only his contemporaries how to write but whose direct influence stretched even to Keats, was dismissed by Matthew Arnold as not really a poet at all.

There are, of course, keys to this mystery, and the unlocking of the box within the box ,which is Dryden, is immensely exciting, not only for itself, but also since we know that in the very last box is the kernel of genius, irreducible though that may be. Here I will suggest only one or two of the keys as an appetiser. Dryden was complicated at least partly because he lived in a highly complicated time, a time rather like our own, and he was forever worried by ideas. Then the mind-shattering notions were those revealed by the experimental scientists—the Harveys, Ents and Boyles ; now it is the atom and its extraordinary powers of good and evil. The political ideas, too, were no less complicated ; a certain ideology, as we should now call it, had riven the country and brought bloodshed, destruction and cessation of civilised pursuits. But were the ideas wrong ? Could war be justified in defence of them ? The upshot of such doubts, and the collapse of opinions once fiercely held, led to scepticism, which Dryden said was natural to him, as he believed it was to his age. But, peace above all was what was needed, in his view, and a régime that could bring peace had his support. We can, indeed, trace in Dryden a slow growth of thought, which led finally to Toryism and Roman Catholicism ; and having got to that point, Dryden remained in his beliefs, though to do so meant hardship and shortage of money in his declining years. But he mastered his intellectual difficulties as he had his self-pride, and the cadences of the couplet ; and slow mastery of difficulties is a key-word in the political and intellectual biography of the poet. He was a Conservative in politics and an innovator in poetry ; but the one explains the other, for Conservatism brought peace, and only in peace could the pursuit of poetry be successfully undertaken.

There is another key to Dryden worth mentioning here : the fact that not only have ideas vastly changed since the seventeenth century, but also the *way* of thinking. The modes of scholasticism were then still in operation and are visible in Dryden's work from the first to last, although he was a member of the Royal Society. One of the results of this was that the men of the seventeenth century, like the Elizabethans, could be at once astrologers (as Dryden was) and believers in experimental science, seriously interested in religious questions and at the same time keepers of mistresses and lovers of bawdy plays. The *weltanschauung* was totally different from our own ; and appreciation of that fact will also help to open one of the boxes. The others will, I hope, open themselves in the course of this essay.

CHAPTER ONE

An Education in Doubt

IN A QUIET glade along the banks of the river Nene in Northampton-shire, a boy of about fourteen sits fishing.   He is chubby, pink-cheeked and his auburn hair is close-cropped in the Puritan style ; there is a slightly arrogant lift to his upper lip ; his brow is creased with thought beyond his years.   As he casts his line over the slow-running, rank stream, his expression relaxes ; he is turning over some lines from a book he has been reading, Sylvester's *Divine Weeks and Works*, a translation of Dubartas, which has " rapt him into ecstasy " :

> Now when the winter's keener breath began,
> To crystallise the Baltic ocean ;
> To glaze the lakes, to bridle up the floods,
> And periwig with snow the bald-pate woods.

" Periwig with snow " !   Surely that was almost as good as many of Mr. Cowley's verses in his *Poetic Blossoms* ?   And a great deal better than old Spenser's long-drawn-out, sleepy lines.   But not, of course, the equal of Dr. Donne with his twists and turns, his enormous clever-ness, and his words that, though one didn't always quite understand them, left one trembling.   What a pity he had no one to discuss him with, except of course little cousin Honor over at Canon's Ashby, and she only listened round-eyed as he read to her.

That was the trouble : no one would talk to him about poetry. Indeed, his grown-up cousin, Sir Gilbert Pickering, took a positive pleasure in teasing him about reading poetry, telling him that it was a waste of time and a lot of lies, and anyhow people like Abraham Cowley were papist rogues.   How he despised Gilbert with his red face and foxy eye and blind hatred of the King and his supporters ! Now, thank goodness, he was away in London pushing himself forward with the Parliament people, for it was the year 1645.

But it was the same thing with all his family—nothing but talk about the wickedness of the Royalists, the drunkenness and debauchery of their soldiers, and how the King had been misled by evil counsellors. He remembered how his grandfather, the Rev. Henry Pickering, had told him tales of Archbishop Laud sending spies into his church to hear what words he used in the services, to see what position he took up at the altar, whether he had removed any of the images of the saints ; and behind it all the dreaded Star Chamber. The boy's father on walks from his home at Titchmarsh manor had pointed out to him the grim old pile of Fotheringay castle and bidden him remember " Mary Queen of Scots ". He had been told, too, how his other grandfather, Sir Erasmus Dryden, had gone to prison at the age of 70 rather than pay loan-money to the King.

Just tales they had seemed ; but now the tales had come to life ; the King had raised his standard at Nottingham pledged to overthrow Parliament, and men were fighting about the tales. Young men had gone off from Titchmarsh and would not come back ; there had been a battle near his uncle's house at Canon's Ashby when he had been staying there. His uncle, it seemed, had gone quite mad, for he had turned his little church into a quartermaster's store for the Parliament troops. Even his father was mixed up in the turmoil, for he was what they called a " committee-man ", and he went round the district turning out parsons from their livings because they persisted in the old order of service.

The boy on the river-bank sighed. His father must be right, but it made things very dull ; were such things as maypoles, and Church Ales, and dancing and singing really so very wrong ? They said such things led to drunkenness and immorality, but the old books and ballads he read did not speak of those things, only of :

> When Tom came home from labour,
> Or Cis to milking rose,
> Then merrily went the tabour,
> And nimbly went their toes.

Nor did the life and talk at Titchmarsh seem to have any place for the vistas opened up by Dr. Donne's poetry ; they did not fit at all. Perhaps, though, it was he himself who did not fit ; they were always telling him he was too shy, and so he was except with Honor and the old schoolmaster who lent him books which sometimes he had to hide. For the books did not fit in either. It was all very puzzling, and—ah, that was a bite, by Jove ! And then young John bit his lip, for Jove was not a word to use ; Jove was part of classical paganism, of the " nowhere feigned acts " that Roger Ascham wrote about in *The Schoolmaster,* the book he sometimes read—to please his parents.

It is in some such way as this that John Dryden comes into view in the early forties of the seventeenth century, living with his father and mother and their ever-increasing family at Titchmarsh manor, where " dreaming saints of the old Enthusiastic breed " flitted in and out like pained ghosts. John, the eldest, had been born in August, 1631, just across the river in his grandfather's rectory, a long, low building with thatched gables (still standing) at Aldwinkle All Saints. Both sides of his family, who came from the north in Tudor times, were small landowners, and John's father, Erasmus, had a small estate at Blakesley near Canon's Ashby, where lived the eldest brother, Sir John. Both families had long histories of Puritanism, and bitter opposition to the Anglican aristocracy ; neither family had ever before bred a poet.

So it was a grim enough boyhood, as John will remember :

> Youth that with joys had unacquainted been,
> Envy'd grey hairs that once good days had seen ;
> We thought our sires, not with their own content,
> Had ere we came to age our portion spent.

And he will go on being shy, for hard dogma is not for the imaginative, at least until it becomes, through trial and error, imaginative dogma. The intellectual, sensitive spirit revolts, but because the opposition is too bigotedly unanimous, and also too emotionally close, it will take refuge in silence, and secret reading, and fishing. The enemy will say that the silence is that of stupidity, broken only when " the bottle goes round ". The friend will refer to it as " something slow and, as it were, diffident ".

Shy, yes, but John Dryden will often return to this valley, the seat of his shyness, and to his relatives at Cotterstock and Oundle. He will fish in the Nene when his auburn hair has grown long again, and later still when it has turned to grey ; there he will always happily read and work, scribble, scribble, and doubt will pursue him to the end : " always a poet and never a good one ". Until, when he is dead, his cousin, Elizabeth Creed, will inscribe some words under the wooden bust of the poet in Titchmarsh church, and the secret will be out ; for in this short tribute, she refers particularly to his " most delightful conversation ". It seems that only here, by some process the psychologists call " compensation ", would Dryden unpurse his lips ; and perhaps especially in the company of Mrs. Creed, who was the daughter of his early tantaliser, Sir Gilbert Pickering.

ii

But now it is London, war time London, full of alarms and the tread of armed men ; and the schoolboy is dizzy for a moment with the noise and bustle. Then the extraordinary quiet of the big class-room as the awe-inspiring Dr. Robert Busby, headmaster of West-minster School, raises his cane and points to a boy to construe his Virgil. " Arma virumque cano . . . I sing of arms and the man . . .", the voice drones on. For a time the narrow world of Titchmarsh is forgotten ; and Sir Gilbert, the fox, the " fiery, furious and implac-able ", becomes smaller and smaller until he is no bigger in the mind than a pinhead. He will reappear in the highest counsels of the nation, and in the small fortunes of his young cousin ; but never again in the same magisterial way. For at Westminster School the apron strings are being cut ; and against that " moody, murmurous race " with no time for poetry, a carapace is being grown.

Just as Sylvester and Cowley had done, Dr. Busby is opening up new horizons where there is no place for doubt about the value of poetry and writing. The whole world of the ancient school revolves round the study of words and their meaning and their use by the great line of poets from Homer down. Even grammar helps, boring though it sometimes is ; and rhetoric, which some boys find dull, bears on writing since it concerns the shaping of phrases, maxims, epigrams, all the tricks to adorn and fill out the flat, common speech. But it is the classics, Homer and Virgil, Ovid, Juvenal, Persius, that bring most delight, with their wonderful stories and their air of authority and their superb manner which seems to take for granted that nothing else in the world matters except poetry. John Dryden will always remember his " Thursday night exercise " translating a satire of Persius and will publicly recall it in dedicating a poem to his old master. All his life, too, he will find it easier to put his thoughts first into Latin before making them into English poetry.

Dr. Busby is interested also in modern writers, and recommends the study of a translation of the *Metamorphoses* made by George Sandys during a trip to America ; printer Ogilby's Homer with the amusing pictures by Hollar is in the school library, as is Francis Quarles's *Divine Emblems*—poor Quarles who died of a broken heart because the Parliament soldiers burned his books. All these writers are a help, as another master Charles Hoole said, to finding " Flourishes of wit, which you think will more delight them and help their fancies ".

Dr. Busby enjoys " wit ", but he is also a stickler for decorum and thoroughness ; he has the sharpest eye for slovenly work, and his wrath is petrifying. How he whacked little Robbie South for his insolent humour ! He is proud and severe, and in a few years time, he will refuse to take off his hat when the King visits the school, " Because, Your Majesty, no boy must think there is anyone higher than his Master ". Yet he is also just and convinced that learning is more important than dogma or such passing nuisances as civil war. To a shy, but conscientious boy, with a soft face and a liquid eye, and a facility for Latin verses, he is, indeed, a god, but one ready to praise and stimulate. When that boy's sons are at Westminster, and he believes they have been unjustly treated by an usher, he will still address Dr. Busby as " Honoured Sir ", and he will at all costs avoid " disrespect to my old master, of which I will not be guilty, if at all possible ".

But, as with all young poets, it was what he read out of class that had the deepest effect. Cowley's variety and experiment still held him, and he widened his knowledge of the metaphysical school, which in a few years he was to reject so vehemently. But now the metaphysicals were the " thing ", at least to schoolboys who did not know that over in France such men as the " plotter ", Edmund Waller, were plotting the reform of English poetry, and the relegation of extravagance and harshness and obscurity, which was all they saw in the poetry of Donne and King and even Herbert. Nor could a schoolboy, just finding his poetic feet, imagine that old George Wither, who for a satire had been put in the Marshalsea by James I, and who was still plunging about the country commanding a troop of Parliamentary horse, was really speaking to him when, in the preface of his *Halelviah* he condemned " verball, or literall Conceits as delight Schoolboys and pedanticall wits ". It was as though an old Victorian poet were to warn a boy today that Dylan Thomas's verse is kindergarten stuff.

Conceits and cleverness fill John Dryden's first published poem, an elegy he wrote on the death of his schoolfellow, Henry Lord Hastings, son of the Earl of Huntingdon. Henry died of smallpox, and this awkward piece demonstrates Dryden's close knowledge of the verses of such forgotten writers as Thomas Jordan, Cartwright, Alexander Brome and Shipman. It is tortured like the poetry of Donne, but to no end at all :

> A young apostle ; and (with reverence may
> I speak it ?) inspired with gifts as they.

It has the lush unpleasantness of Crashaw at his worst when it is considered that these words refer to the physical manifestations of smallpox :

> Blisters with pride swelled, which through his flesh did sprout,
> Like rosebuds, stuck in the lily-skin about.
> Each little pimple had a tear in it,
> To wail the fault its rising did commit . . .

But its appearance in 1649 with 32 other poems on young Hastings's death was a great matter to the schoolboy poet ; for the volume, *Lachrymae Musarum*, also contained work by such comparatively established poets as the Yorkshire M.P., Andrew Marvell, the architect author of *Cooper's Hill*, Sir John Denham, and the Rev. Robert Herrick, a reformed " spark " recently ejected from his Devonshire rectory and now living in Westminster.

Herrick, although existing precariously on the largesse of Royalist admirers, saw his path very clearly ; if John Dryden read these lines it must have been with emotion :

> Trust to good verses then,
> They only will aspire,
> When pyramids as men
> Are lost i' the funeral fire . . . .

Brave, moving words to a young man who already saw himself as a great poet ! And yet—was it an advantage to be estranged from large masses of your potential readers ? What did poetry have to do with politics ? Was it, perhaps, better to conceal your opinions and so gain your freedom to write ?

Such speculations came to puzzle Dryden, and events in the outer world underlined the puzzle. For as the elections to university scholarships drew near, even the cloistered calm of school life was shaken. Parliament was in the hands of the Presbyterians, but power lay with the New Model Army. The Presbyterians were jealous of that power, and besides they considered the Army too tolerant in religious matters. Event succeeded startling event ; Cromwell snatched the King from Parliament, and while John Dryden was publicly contending before the Master of Trinity College, Cambridge, in Latin, Greek and Hebrew, for a scholar's place, a hundred yards away in Whitehall, His Majesty :

> Nothing common did nor mean,
> Upon that memorable scene,
> But bowed his comely head,
> Down as upon a bed . . . .

The reverberations of the judicial killing of the King were heard all over England, and half the world. To thinking men of both sides, it gave pause, and a wave of nausea and a deep longing for peace swiftly followed. With it came a profound distrust of " enthusiasm " and dogmatic fanaticism. There seemed, however, no hope of earthly escape from the Saints and Anabaptists and Ranters, and men like Marvell turned to their gardens and the simplicity and innocence of children ; another poet, Henry Vaughan, suffered a serious illness which turned him towards the inner, spiritual life ; Izaak Walton began composing his book of rural life, The Compleat Angler ; the young philospher, Henry More, sought " the dark night of the soul " ; and many would have echoed Benlowes' cry in his Theophila's Love Sacrifice :

> Peace ! Home of pilgrims, first song at Christ's birth ;
> Peace, his last legacy on earth ;
> Peace, gen'ral preface to all good ; Peace,
> Saints' true mirth . . . . .

But the thinking men were few, and for the masses the death of the King was merely the starting point of widespread hysteria. The extreme Puritans wandered the streets, crying for blood ; there were horrible excesses when Cromwell put down insurrections at Tredah and Drogheda in Ireland ; there were more battles with the Scots, and the faintest glimmer of hope seemed to die with the flight of Prince Charles after the battle of Worcester. Public morality declined ; there was a vast increase in crimes of violence, and particularly sexual violence. The murder of bastard children, for instance, grew to such proportions that in 1655 the Lord Mayor of London " ordered a precept on the subject to be read in all the Churches of London on Sunday Feb. 11, *together with the Statute of Child Murder of 21, James I* ". It was in this period, too, that serious suggestions were made in Parliament that polygamy should be made lawful ; the Barebones Parliament of Puritan Christians enacted that only Civil Marriage should be valid—and that to most people meant the abolition of marriage.

It was at the beginning of this post-war period of disturbance and near-madness, that Dryden learned that he had been successful in his contending in the great hall of the school, and he was admitted to Trinity College, Cambridge on May 11, 1650. He was 19, comparatively old to be still at school—but Dr. Busby had the habit of holding back pupils of whom he had the greatest expectations. It was a wise habit, for a youth of 19 is old enough to have felt and understood the impact of events in his world and that, too, is valuable. Dryden had seen what the " dregs of a democracy " could achieve ; such worldly wisdom is invaluable to undergraduates.

On the other hand, he could not believe—scarcely anyone, indeed, could believe—that it would help, or that it was even possible, to go back to monarchy. Where then to go, what to do ? He felt lost in a world that had no place for poetry or much for scholarship, under the rule of men who had banned plays and turned music out of the churches. True that many of his Puritan acquaintance loved music and poetry ; but most of them were as unable as he to visualise a future where such things would again have an honourable place. The stronger Puritans, in fact, gave up poetry, and plunged into the arena of propaganda and power ; such was John Milton, author of the lovely *Comus*, and the plangent *Lycidas*. An epic ? What " vain desires " lay there—how mocking seemed " that darling Fame ".

Dryden was, then, quite worldly-wise when he went to Cambridge —but very ready for a lead, for a set of ideas to use as a guide, even temporarily. At first, Cambridge seemed to have little to offer. He was told when he arrived that in some colleges Latin and Greek stood one in little stead, and the student was examined only in such questions as " the state of the soul ; whether he was of the number of the elect ; what was the occasion of his conversion ; upon what day of the month and what hour of the day it happened ; how it was carried on and when completed . . . . and whether he was prepared for death ? ".

Trinity was not so bad, and the lead came, quite naturally, through Dryden's tutor, the Rev. John Templer. Templer, like many other clergymen of the time, had written a confutation of the theories of the "old beare", Thomas Hobbes. Like many others, Templer had quickly seen that, however Hobbes dissembled, his philosophy undermined the whole seventeenth-century nature of things. Beneath all his protesting about God and the church, there was a hard and atheistic materialism. Templer had " confuted " him ; but to confute someone, it is necessary to know his work inside out, and it was not so much the confutation but the Hobbesian ideas themselves that Dryden was interested in eliciting from his tutor. Yet it was neither materialism nor atheism which attracted him. It was rather Hobbes's political thought, his view that it is an obligation on all citizens to support the powers that be for the sake of civil quiet and even at the expense of conscience, his hatred and distrust of the masses, and his tendency, as Bishop Burnet put it, to think " the worst of men and parties ". The latter tendency is shared profoundly by the writers of the Restoration, and not less by Dryden himself ; the events of the previous twenty years thoroughly justify the attitude, which indeed can be salutary in certain states of society. Hobbes's political absolutism came just as pat to many minds in the years immediately before the Protectorate ; and others besides Dryden read *Leviathan* with sympathy.

But Dryden never wholeheartedly embraced Hobbesian opinion, though he would make some use of it in his heroic plays. For the deep-rooted desire for peace which made him sympathetic to Hobbes also led him away from any form of dogmatism : it was so obviously dogma run mad that had caused the civil war—and Hobbes was nothing if not dogmatic. Dryden hated that " positive assertion of his Opinion " as " if he had the rod over the reader " that he found in Hobbes as in Lucretius. And over the years, he will draw gradually away from Hobbes until he reaches his very opposite, the Pyrrhonistic-Fideism, " I do not know, therefore I will believe ", of *The Hind and the Panther*. The scepticism of Dryden, as he himself realised, was natural to him and all-pervasive.

There was, however, still another side to Hobbes : his ideas about poetry. The old man had been in France with Waller and Denham and Cowley and the others ; inevitably problems of aesthetics were mooted in his writing, and here again his basic premises did not differ greatly from the new ideas simmering in the minds of the exiled poets. His materialism was paralleled by their growing dislike for the airy and inflated fancies of the late metaphysical poets ; his view of imagination as " decaying " sense-impressions fitted their desire to bring poetry down to earth ; his development of the term " wit " from its early seventeenth-century meaning of ingenuity, quickness and subtlety of thought to something like propriety and decorum was applauded by them. Fancy is not to be trusted alone for it infrequently falls in with " probability ", and its total effect is to hinder intellectual progress. It must always and everywhere be controlled by " judgment "; otherwise poetry becomes a deception upon the public instead of serving some useful function in interpreting everyday " reality ".

In the heroic romance, *Gondibert*, published in 1650 by his friend Sir William Davenant, Hobbes found these precepts put into admirable practice. The poem was comparatively free from conceits—or at least from the deteriorated conceit then common, its tone was prosaic, though the theme was heroic ; there was even a tendency in it towards the closed couplet and the medial pause, which were to mark much of the poetry of the next hundred years. As Edmund Waller was quick to see, in *Gondibert* poetry was brought down to earth ; it was full of the new " realism " :

> . . . . No bold tales of gods or monsters swell,
> But human passions, such as with us dwell.
> Man is thy theme ; his virtue or his rage,
> Drawn to the life in each elaborate page.

Gondibert, with its author's preface and its attendant *Answer to Davenant* by Hobbes, was probably the first full statement of the new ideas that Dryden came across, though his sensitivity to atmosphere was such that he had most likely noticed change in the air earlier. He did not react at once—he seldom did even as a mature man ; but the ideas of Hobbes and Davenant bore fruit, for the description of wit in the preface to *Annus Mirabilis* sixteen years later is very similar to that given in various parts of the Hobbesian corpus.

There is little sign of change in this direction in Dryden's only extant work as an undergraduate. Yet the 26-line introduction to a volume of poems by a fellow scholar, John Hoddesdon, does mark advance. Ideas are less tortuous, the thought runs clearer, and the lines smoother ; there is no sign of the sickly broodiness of the Hastings poem in :

> Good thief who darest, Prometheus-like, aspire,
> And fill thy poems with a celestial fire,
> Enlivened by these sparks divine, their rays
> Add a bright lustre to thy crown of bays . . . . .

But the conceits are there, too—as they will be still, thirty years later, in the ode to Mrs. Anne Killigrew.

The carapace that Dryden grew around himself in Westminster was strengthened at Cambridge ; but while preserving his sensibility and his personality intact, it also set him apart from his fellows and bred pride, the pride that " struck out new sparkles of her own ".

It was pride and the possession of a lashing tongue that now at Cambridge " sawcily traduced a nobleman " ; it was a young man being taught caution who was as a result put out of Commons for a fortnight and forbidden to leave college for " disobedience to the vice-master, and his contumacy in taking his punishment inflicted by him ".

iii

Then quite suddenly Cambridge is behind him, and he is back in Titchmarsh, standing beside an open grave. Hobbes and *Gondibert* and the Rev. John Templer are tiny specks seen from the wrong end of a telescope ; his B.A. and his chatting with long Tom Shadwell and the Puritan Samuel Pepys, and even his punishment for disobedience have shrunk into insignificance.   His speculation and doubts seem to be temporarily ended, for he has hope and ambition and determination ; his path, though narrow, seems clear.   The country is more peaceful at last and a degree of toleration has returned ; the Lord Protector has taken over government, and though the Army and Parliament are still at loggerheads, some sort of order and justice have been restored. Already many of the Royalist writers have returned from their exile and are to be met with in London ; poetry and plays are being discussed again ;   there is exciting talk of " science " and meetings of " virtuosi " at Gresham House.   It is time, the fresh-faced, plump young man at the graveside feels, to go to town and meet these men of the future ; and as he looks down on to his father's coffin, he realises with a start that this is possible since half the rents from the Blakesley estate are now his.   But will they be enough ?

His eye travels round the mourners as the minister reads the service, and falls upon Sir Gilbert Pickering.   Much as he despises him, his craftiness and power have to be admitted ; he is now the £1,000 a year Lord Chamberlain of the Protector's Council, and a very important person.   He will have a word with him later ; a small sinecure under him would round out the rents nicely and enable him to cut more of a figure.   His spirits rise incontinently . . . " Dust to dust ", and his mother is weeping.   He has a sudden pang of sorrow for his father. And then his eye catches that of his pretty cousin, Honor ; he smiles but only because he is young and fresh and the whole world seems ready to open before him.   He turns from the grave and makes towards Sir Gilbert.   The carapace will be stronger yet, but it is already firmly in place.

He will go back to Cambridge for a month or two ; he will write once or twice to Honor (for he has discovered that she has, indeed, become an attractive young woman) ; he will enjoy a few more months of reading at Trinity, " to which foundation I gratefully acknowledge a great part of my education ".

But Honor will soon be forgotten, though she will never forget him, even though her sister has spotted the truth about " Mr. Conceit ". Soon, too, at least in public,

> Oxford to him a dearer name shall be
> Than his own mother university . . . .

His M.A. will come from other sources and in far different circumstances. For now, as his college acquaintance, Dr. Robert Crichton, later wrote : " His head was too roving and active, or what else you'll call it, to confine himself to a college life, and so he left it and went to London into gayer company, and set up for a poet, which he was as well qualified for as any man ".

CHAPTER TWO

The Making of an Augustan

BUT THE London into which the fresh-faced young man with wavy brown hair and the mole on his right cheek descended in the winter of 1656 was a disappointment. Gay society indeed ! he must have thought somewhat bitterly as he lay upon his hard bed in the cold, top back room, with a round window no bigger than a pocket looking-glass, of his cousin's fine house in Whitehall, the seat of the Lord-Protector's government.

The very minor post his cousin had obtained for him condemned him to long hours in the vast room beneath the Council Chamber, endlessly copying out (in his painstaking, sloping hand) an incredible number of orders, letters and memoranda from Mr. Secretary Thurloe —for the management of affairs was now " quick, sudden and with expedition ", as it had not been since Elizabeth's time ; not a few memoranda came, too, from Sir Gilbert Pickering himself, grown into a fussy Lord Chamberlain to Cromwell, intent on points of punctilio and minor details of protocol.

Dryden's fellow clerks, indeed, enjoyed a society of sorts—drinking over at Marsh's, rough, bawdy conversation, schoolboy pranks, sport with the ladies of Fleet Alley. Dryden had no stomach for their company, though he was not above a sly visit now and again to Fleet Alley ; nor did the other clerks find him amusing. He did not pretend to be good company ; he felt himself to be of a morose and even sullen nature, and he was shy. To his fellow clerks it even seemed that his aloofness, the slightly superior air, was due to his having kinsmen in high places—his slightly mad uncle Sir John Dryden also had a job in the government.

His eye has a sleepy look ; he is somewhat countrified in his ways, not bothering to change his drugget suit for something finer, nor able to take part in witty repartee. They call him " the squire ", and it seems to fit him well, especially since, in fact, he is a squire and once a month meets the Oundle carrier at Smithfield to receive a letter from his mother and his share of the Blakesley rents.

The clerks amuse each other by stories of Dryden's rural simpleness in the big city ; there was, for instance, that tale of his lack of *savoir faire* in the coffee house—a tale that a clerk junior even to Dryden retailed a quarter of a century later : " When he first came to town, being a raw young fellow of seven and twenty, as he called himself when he told the story, he frequenting but one coffee house, the woman (it seems finding him out) put coffee upon him for chocolate, and made him pay threepence a dish for it for two years together ; till at length, by what providence I know not, he discovered the cheat ". The clerk was Tom Shadwell, who had followed Dryden from Cambridge, gone to the Middle Temple, then into the great room beneath the Council Chamber—and who, all his life, was to haunt the fringes of Dryden's career.

It was not only the clerks who found Dryden slow and uninteresting : Sir Gilbert also took him for a rather lumpish, phlegmatic person whom, however, he suspected of sneering at him behind his back—with his Cambridge notions, his nose perpetually in a book (and what books !), his inability to chat confidentially with those who might help him, his apparent lack of desire to cultivate those of his superiors, such as the Latin Secretaries, John Milton, and Andrew Marvell, who might be supposed to attract him, for they wrote verses, did they not ?

No, in Sir Gilbert's view, Dryden was not a good person to invite to the parties now becoming increasingly common in the upper circles of the Republican government, and nowhere more so than in the great rooms of Sir Gilbert's house where his wife, Lady Pickering, sister of Sir Edward Montagu, the Joint-Commander of the English battle fleet, entertained the cream of Cromwellian high society. A pity perhaps, for Lady Pickering had a pretty taste in fine clothes and looking glasses and silver bedsteads *and* in books ; Dryden might have helped her in the accumulation of such objects, and—it was this that he needed —have found among the smart set in her lavishly furnished drawing-room some sort of congenial *ambience*.

Instead, Lady Pickering went to her brother's household for assist-

ance in her artistic purchases ; there she found a young man of about
Dryden's age who like Dryden was a Cambridge graduate, though
only the son of a tailor from Salisbury Court—a short, bright-eyed
young man, assiduous in carrying out her behests, a clever young man
called Samuel Pepys.

So Dryden lay in his little room, listening to the sounds of revelry
below—and reading. When he read, by the light of a dim wick, he
gradually forgot his loneliness, his nagging ambition to write, and his
recognition of the fact that at twenty-eight he had nothing to his credit
but a few " school-magazine " efforts. Cowley had made a hit with
his poems when he was only fifteen ; Edmund Waller had come out
" forty thousand strong " before he was eighteen. But the fact
remained that in his head was still " only a confused mass of thoughts,
tumbling over one another in the dark " ; the impetus to bring them
out was yet lacking.

Dryden already knew that it was an impetus and an audience that
he required ; he knew that his was not the aspiring nor the meditative
mind, for whom an audience did not matter. All the mysterious side
of life and being—that was channelled off into his study of astrology,
a private whim. Not for him the mystical rapture of his elder contemporary, Henry Vaughan, content to gaze alone in Brecknockshire
upon eternity " like a great Ring of pure and endless night ", nor the
quiet meditations in fields of orient and immortal wheat of Thomas
Traherne, who so little regarded an audience that his immortal reveries
first enchanted readers over 200 years after his death.

Dryden was well aware that the society in which he found himself
was little concerned with poetry of any sort, and least of all with new
poetry ; that part of it indeed believed that poetry did the work of the
devil, and had banned plays and closed the theatres (he himself had
never seen a play, though he had read a great many).

It was a society he could not pretend to care for, nor believe in.
As he took his lonely walks, past Charing Cross and the great houses in
the Strand, and turned into narrow, cobbled Fleet Street where the
old overhanging Elizabethan houses obscured the daylight and the
passing cart churned up heaps of refuse and ordure, he was faced at
every turn by madmen—Anabaptists rolling their eyes and foaming at
the mouth in religious ecstasy, Quakers warning of the wrath to come,

hysterical preachers ranting of the wickedness of the people, Fifth Gospel men raving about the Second Coming. Dissenters—the very name spoke of disorder and barbarism, and Dryden had seen enough of both. Yet it was upon these that Commonwealth society was based.

Worse still was the mob, the apprentices, the good-for-nothings, ever ready to riot through the town in a spirit compounded of dangerous mischief, blood lust and desperation. It little mattered to them what the issue—Royalism, republicanism, religion ; always they were straining at the leash, ready to plunge all into anarchy.

Dryden despised but at the same time feared the mob ; and he knew that the government, through its *agents provocateurs,* was quite prepared to use it to further its ends. Dryden had seen the mob at its annual game of burning the Pope in effigy—the Pope's suffering being made more realistic by the inclusion of live cats in his sacking stomach. It was not a pretty sight as the rejoicings, under the influence of drink and the weird flames shooting into the night, turned into a crude and violent Saturnalia.

He had also seen, from his vantage point in Whitehall, that a great deal of the religious fanaticism, strictness and morality was merely a mask for self-seeking, and money-making opportunism. Past the soldiers in coats of buff and red, steel-breasted and capped, bearing pike and musket who guarded the seat of Government, came a stream of sanctimonious hypocrites with their far from hypocritical pleas for sinecures or monopolies, their whispered denunciations of unfrocked priests in secret rooms celebrating Communion according to the Anglican form, their offers of women and wine and loot for the rulers of England. These men would refer to the regicides as " doing the great work of the Lord " ; when they offered some means of gain it would be " seeking experiences " ; and as they talked of choice young virgins it would be a question of " using the creature ". To Dryden they had the appearance of foxes, dressed in the sober robes of the preacher :

A fox full-fraught with seeming sanctity,
That feared an oath, but, like the devil, would lie ;
Who looked like Lent and had the holy leer,
And durst not sin before he said his prayer—
This pious cheat . . . .

C

Were the reformed priests any better than the idle, irreligious ones his father and his cousin had been so mad against ; were the rulers of his youth more corrupt and evil than the new rulers ? One face or another, all hid only corruption and self-seeking. As an old man, looking back over his life, he allowed himself to say—he was usually more circumspect : " No government has ever been, or ever can be, wherein timeservers and blockheads will not be uppermost. The persons are only chang'd, but the same jugglings in state, the same hypocrisy in religion, the same self-interest and mismanagement, will remain for ever. Blood and money will be lavished in all ages, only for the preferment of new faces with old consciences ".

In his reading, at least, Dryden found confirmation of his cynicism and his fear of mob disorders. There was Hobbes, who had returned from France in 1652, soon after the publication of his *Leviathan* ; that work had been displeasing not merely to the Republicans, but also to the Anglicans. That alone recommended it to Dryden, as did Hobbes's cool remarks about fanatics.

More interestingly still, Hobbes also deprecated excess in poetry, believing it to be too full of " windy blisters ", and " the ambitious obscurity of expressing more than is perfectly conceived ".

Dryden found this theme in all the poets whom he already regarded as his masters. Cowley, for instance, condemned poetry that dealt with mad fancies, " Gods, devils, nymphs, witches and giants race ", he thought that such things tended to take men's minds away from reality into realms where imagination ran riot, and became bad for poetry and dangerous to the state.

" Man and manners " were to be the subject, said Cowley ; Hobbes went further with : " The subject of a poem is the manners of men ". The best poetry, Davenant wrote, is that which " gives us a familiar and easy view of ourselves ".

An equally great contrast with the distasteful ranting and disorder Dryden felt all round him was the sweetness and clarity he found in Waller's poetry, and the peaceful reasonableness of Denham's *Cooper's Hill*. *Cooper's Hill* he took to be " the exact standard of good writing ". Cowley was another matter ; his was an agile mind, loving to describe things and at the same time enjoying conceits—the conceits that Dryden loved, too, but which ultimately he regarded as being the wrong thing for the poetry of his own time. But Cowley, too, was a mild poet, largely eschewing bombast and more and more trying to avoid erratic and obscure imagery.

Yet even as Dryden read and admired these older contemporaries, he was aware, darkly and diffidently perhaps, that a gulf lay between him and them. He knew that he would never have gone to prison, as Cowley for instance had done, for a political cause. He was of a different generation and had been brought up a Puritan, a youth unacquainted with joys. He had never known the "good days"; and it was the memory of such days seen through a golden haze at the other side of years of bloodshed, exile and turmoil, that was the driving force upon the Romantic hearts of such poets as Cowley, and which in these years sent him back to London as a spy for the Royalists abroad.

Dryden was much too cynical for such dreams. To him it seemed that spying and fighting and being an M.P. should be left to spies and soldiers and politicians. Poetry was much more important, and poetry required the quiet room where joy would come in the loving beating of ideas into poetic shape, in the moulding of the *materia poetica* into the harmony of measure, the bubble of images, the dance of words.

Poetry is a high profession and a full-time occupation. So Dryden believes. Small wonder, then, that he is unhappy under the Protectorate, for he is really the first Augustan.

ii

It was a chance meeting in the street, as Dryden idly strolled along glancing into a bookshop or at the curious goods for sale in the "virtuosi" shops, that suddenly let a ray of light into his series of dull days. Near where the Strand passes into Fleet Street, Dryden round about 1657 ran into a young man from his own part of Northamptonshire, who had been up at Cambridge in his time. His name was Francis Gifford; unlike Dryden he had taken his M.A., but also unlike Dryden he had no job.

Instead, he told Dryden over a glass in "The Rainbow," he was eking out a small allowance by translating for the bookseller and publisher, Henry Herringman, whose shop and house were at the sign of the Blue Anchor in the lower walk of the New Exchange on the south side of the Strand. The money was not good, and the work was hard.

What had he translated ? He was just finishing a long romance by Honoré D'Urfé, *Astré*,—and, said Gifford who knew few people in London but remembered that Dryden had got into print while he was still at the university, would Dryden like to write a small preface to each volume, telling the reader something of the novel's fame in France—that, for instance, the late Cardinal Richelieu had recommended it ?

Dryden could see no objection ; it did not commit or compromise him in any way ; it would make a little extra money. What was required was of course no more than a blurb, but even so it would be a pleasant change to write something which for once would see the light of day. So he and Gifford strolled over to the Blue Anchor, Mr. Herringman proved amenable, and the bargain was sealed over the customary glass of ale.

In due course, Dryden's three blurbs appeared over the initials " J. D. " ; they were full enough of polite French expressions to please Mr. Herringman who, though only a rough and uneducated man, knew his snobbish ladies of the Protectorate very well. Mr. Herringman asked the sober and serious looking young gentleman to drop in at his shop anytime and when there was suitable work he should have it. So during the next four or five years Dryden turned out a number of " Advertisements to the Reader ", prefixes and was soon giving a hand, too, with the reading of manuscripts and the correction of the work as it came from the printer.

It was during his visits to Herringman's shop that, at first imperceptibly, Dryden's mode of life and thought began to change. It could not be avoided, for the Blue Anchor in the last year or so of the régime of Cromwell became the recognised meeting place for writers.

This was a mixed blessing for Mr. Herringman because the talk inevitably turned to politics and then Mr. Herringman would rush in and warn the gentlemen to have a care of his credit. But when the famous old philosopher, Hobbes, began to drop in there was no stopping talk on any subject whatever, for the " old bear " was one of the wittiest men of his generation, and his talk, cynical, and subversive, ranged from heaven to hell, from poetry to the latest experiments of the " virtuosi " at Gresham College : nothing escaped his acute mind and his barbed tongue.

He laughed at the Platonism of Ralph Cudworth and Henry More, and (though he was careful never to write such things) his talk tended to suggest that the idea of God himself was no more mysterious than that of, say, the imagination—which after all was merely " sense decaying, or weakened, by the absence of the object ".

But no one could help liking the old man ; he was such a " character ", he had lived so long and through so many extraordinary changes, and had yet preserved his equilibrium, his own stout and cynical view of the world ; he was a philosopher, too, in the common sense that he did not really care what happened to him and, therefore, said the first thing that came into his head, dangerous or not.

It was this that endeared him to the silent young man in the corner, pretending to turn over the pages of a folio ; it was the attraction of opposites, or perhaps the thrill of a non-athlete watching a professional performer upon a high trapeze.

With him would often come Edmund Waller, down on a visit from his house at Hall Barn near Beaconsfield ; Waller was no longer the rich young man famed for his eloquence in the pre-Civil War parliaments, but he was still good company, full of jollity, a man who used his gifts of flattery to make the company think better of themselves. His talk showed a delightful lack of pride, and he would tell quite openly how, when his plot was discovered, he had pleaded remorse, forsworn his Royalist principles and thrown himself upon the Parliamentarians' mercy.

Of course he hadn't forsworn his principles, he would confide, but —quoi faire ? It would be silly not to make use of the fact that he was related to Cromwell, he would say : a live poet was after all worth all the dead heroes, didn't they agree ? Not only that : although most of the Republicans were horrible bores, Cromwell himself—Waller assured them—was interested in the things of the mind, particularly in ancient history. When any of his enthusiastic friends came to advise or consult him, Waller had overheard him discoursing in the cant of the times (" fighting the good fight " and so on). But when he returned he would say : " Cousin Waller, I must talk to these men in their own way ". Then, said Waller, he would resume in the common style of conversation.

Which, the Sage of Malmesbury would wickedly interrupt, is no doubt why you wrote those encomiastic verses on " King " Oliver. Not in the least, Waller would reply. What I say of Oliver is what I believe—that he is a genius ; but I do not praise the way he rose to power, nor the Republican system, nor those who surround him and support him.

Cowley, who is sometimes present, peering eagerly into the new books, chatting in his rapid way about everything under the sun, agrees. Sir Robert Howard, son of the Royalist Earl of Berkshire, of course doesn't, and says so in no uncertain terms. Oliver cultured ? Bah, he has probably never *heard* of Statius (it is Statius whom at present Sir Robert is engaged in translating), a stupid ignoramus, surrounded by dolts and blockheads. How any one with sense, etc. etc. . . . The company laughs ; " Sir Positive " is known for his views, but there is no harm in him, and, indeed, some of his ideas, particularly on poetry, are shrewd enough.

It is, however, Walter Charleton, Doctor of Medicine, whose book on *The Immortality of the Soul* lies upon Herringman's shelves, who turns suddenly to the young man in the corner and asks for *his* opinion. Dryden is taken aback, but after a little while delivers himself some- what sententiously of the remark that it is the duty of all men to support that government which is in power. A very good answer, Sir, says Hobbes, with a twinkle in his eye—for one who owes his bread to the Government !

It is thus that Dryden's life begins to change ; he looks forward to hearing the gossip on everything under the sun—but particularly poetry and experimental science—in Herringman's shop. Although his taciturnity is still his predominating trait in society, the wits of the Blue Anchor—tolerant and educated men—begin to appreciate his thoughtful mind, his capacity for quick assimilation, and his sympathe- tic responsiveness to a variety of ideas, some of them mutually contradictory.

From Dryden's point of view, it means a gain in confidence, a first- hand knowledge of the way some of the brightest intellects of his time talk and think, a breakaway from his Puritan background.

So it is that, upon the death of Cromwell on September 3, 1658, Dryden is bold enough to believe he can emulate Waller in writing a poem on the late Lord Protector. If Waller, a Royalist, can write such a poem, then why not he ? Furthermore, an irritatingly bright young man, Thomas Sprat, son of a Devonshire parson and recently down from Oxford where he has been a protégé of Dr. Wilkins, the scientist, has also declared his intention of writing a poem about Cromwell ; Sprat, too, has joined the circle at the Blue Anchor—and emulation is a strong spur to a young man.

Sitting in his room over Sir Gilbert's house, Dryden now forgets his boredom and distaste for his surroundings ; in a flurry of excitement he begins to write. He has chosen the stanza used by Davenant in *Gondibert*—but one he knows equally well from Spenser's *Colin Clout* and its use by Donne.   The style, he realises, is stiff and formal—but so is the occasion. It is the occasion, the opportunity to celebrate a national event and the knowledge that, at least within his own small circle, his poem will be appreciated, compared and criticised, that is the real spur to him—not particularly his personal feelings about Cromwell.

Yet, as he begins to consider Cromwell's career and achievement, he is dimly aware that Waller had been right : however history considers the Civil War and its outcome, there can be no doubt that Cromwell himself was a great man, and in spite of all a great Englishman. It is the great Englishman he will hymn, and he will cautiously avoid the question of politics.

So as he sets down :

> And now 'tis time ; for their officious haste,
> Who would before have borne him to the sky . . . .

his mind warms to his task, the pen cannot scratch away fast enough, and a vision of one man's glory pushes him on :

> His grandeur he deriv'd from heaven alone ;
> For he was great ere fortune made him so ;
> And wars, like mists that rise against the sun,
> Made him greater seem, not greater grow . . . .

> He made us freemen of the continent,
> Whom Nature did like captives treat before . . . .

> By his command we boldly cross'd the line,
> And bravely fought where southern stars arise . . . .

Recalling the storm and flood that preceded the Protector's death, he gave his poem the true touch of journalism :

> But first the ocean, as a tribute, sent
> That giant prince of all her watery herd ;
> And th'isle, when her protecting genius went,
> Upon his obsequies loud sighs conferr'd.

> No civil broils have since his death arose,
> But faction now by habit does obey ;
> And wars have that respect for his repose,
> As winds for halcyons, when they breed at sea.

> His ashes in a peaceful urn shall rest ;
> His name a great example stands to show
> How strangely high endeavours may be blest,
> Where piety and valour jointly go.

The poem appeared in 1659, separately at first, and then with those of Waller and Sprat (Sprat had gone mad with flattery not only of Cromwell but also of those who supported him).

But scarcely had he seen it through the press than his penultimate heroic stanza was falsified, and now again began civil broils such as Dryden remembered only from his early boyhood and his latter years at Westminster, but which were familiar enough to his friends, Waller and Hobbes. And—Cowley had vanished from the Blue Anchor and was said to have sailed with a mission to his Royal Master . . . .

Soon London and all England had other things to do and to see than to read poetry. For, as naturally as the sap rises, men began to tire of the corrupt way of life and government that was all that remained after the genius of the Protector had gone. Moreover, the young men felt themselves lacking in, and hostile to, the religious ecstasy of their parents. Roger North, whose father was a Puritan, recalled that his feelings at this time were that " the experiment of reformation had proved a deformation of all that was good, and religion so furious as was before held out found to be mere hypocrisy to serve as an engine of power and tyranny, and all the pretensions of public advantage found to be nothing but private wealth ".

Samuel Pepys and many others found themselves drawn irresistibly to those obscure corners of London—cellars and upper rooms—where ministers of the banished church defied the law and read the old Prayer Book. There was Mr. Gunning at Cary House by Exeter 'Change and Robert Mossum at the little chapel of St. Peter's by Paul's Wharf. Such visits were still dangerous, but many young men were willing to take the risk.

So it was that a few weeks after the first appearance of Dryden's *Heroic Stanzas*, an unpaid army, at the dictation of the military chiefs in Wallingford House, dissolved Richard Cromwell's Parliament and prevailed on Richard to " dispose himself as his private occasions should require ". A month later it restored the Rump, the fifty survivors of what had been nineteen years earlier a national parliament of over 500, but of which all but this remnant had been expelled.

These men now made short work of those who had supported Cromwell's strong, authoritarian government ; for they were the died-in-the-wool republicans whom Cromwell had kept in check. Among those expelled was Oliver's Lord Chamberlain, Sir Gilbert Pickering, and his wife, who had to flee London leaving all her carefully assembled *objets d'art* and books to the soldiery and the fanatics.

And Dryden ? Homeless, his tiny post insecure, indeed untenable, he was of course left behind by Sir Gilbert to shift for himself. So now, with " fear and despair universal " (as Pepys observed), Dryden sought aid from his friend, Herringman, and from a room above his shop, observed with horror and detestation the events of the next few months.

Early in December, his worst fears came true : the London mob, realising its opportunity, swept through the City and presented a petition to the aldermen assembled in Common Council at Guildhall demanding the restoration of the City's ancient liberties. The aldermen, in fact, agreed with their demands, and no doubt according to the old and vicious custom had stirred up their apprentices to take such violent action.

But the Government's Committee of Public Safety replied by packing the town with troops. Pepys wrote to his cousin, Sir Edward Montagu, who had now retired to the country, that : " The soldiers as they marcht were hooted at all along the streets and where any stragled from the whole body, the boys flung stones, tiles, turnups, etc., at, with all the affronts they could give them ; some they disarmed, and kickt, others abused the horse with stones and rubbish they flung at them ; . . . . many souldiers were hurt with stones, and one I see was very neere having his braines knockt out with a brickbat flung from the top of a house at him ".

All over England—at Portsmouth, Plymouth and Colchester—townsmen rose against the soldiers demanding a free parliament. Apprentices were killed. In London, pikesmen piled grenades in St. Paul's . . .

But there was hope just over the horizon. In Scotland, General Monk had a powerful army ; it arrived in London on February 6th, 1660, and that night everyone was aware that the great cloud over England was about to be lifted. The church bells pealed out, bonfires were lit, and outside Herringman's shop the butchers sacrificed " rumps ", basted them and swallowed them down with great draughts of ale. The taverns were full of merry pamphlets about the Rump ; there was some disorder as the apprentices broke the windows of such as Praise-God Barebones ; but generally there was singing and joy in the taverns, and Pepys wrote in a diary he had recently begun : " The city from one end to the other, with a glory about it, so high was the light of the bonfires . . . . and the bells rang everywhere ".

The rejoicings were but an *apéritif* to greater rejoicings. For it was clear that the return of the exiled son of the Martyr King would not be long delayed. Parliament dissolved itself, and the first free election in England for twenty years was to take place ; Sir Edward Montagu was secretly preparing a fleet for a not distant rendezvous ; men everywhere were openly toasting the King over the water, and the King's supporters rushed over to Flanders. A painter walked into the Exchange, and set a ladder against the statue of Charles I, up which he slowly mounted and solemnly painted out the inscription : " Exit tyrannus, Regum ultimus ".

At this time, a curious observer might have watched a small cart piled with books and a few odds and ends of clothing crossing Lincoln's Inn Fields and discharging its cargo at " the sixth door from Turnstile, Holborn Row ". The property was that of Mr. Dryden, who was moving in to share lodgings with Sir Robert Howard—the most positive Royalist of all Mr. Dryden's acquaintance.

iii

It would be easy to be unfair to Dryden over the Howard affair. Years later Shadwell, trying to think up all the slander he could about Dryden, *was* unfair to him on precisely this question when he wrote :

> Then by the assistance of a noble knight,
> Th'hadst plenty, ease, and liberty to write.
> First like a gentleman he made thee live ;
> And on his bounty thou didst amply thrive.

It was true ; but there are several relevant points to be made. Dryden was now thirty, and as a Poet Laureate of the eighteenth century, Laurence Eusden, observed :

> Great Dryden did not early great appear,
> Faintly distinguished in his thirtieth year.

Time was passing quickly, and Dryden had realised that if he was ever to be in a position to produce the work he felt himself capable of, now was the time to set about it. He knew that the Court would dominate the literary scene in the new decade, and dominate it in the very practical sense that it would hold the purse strings. For a poet such as Dryden hoped to be, an Augustan holding up the mirror to a cultured society, the nearer he got to the court the better.

In those early months of 1660 he was, in any case, dependent on his small rents and what he might earn by his pen : ease and liberty to write were a necessity. He knew, too, that unless he had some person welcome at Court to put in a word for him he would stand little chance against all those who would soon be claiming place, honours and largesse in return for loyalty. Dryden, after all, had been an employee of the Cromwell government through his kinsman, the Lord Chamberlain.

The truth is that Dryden knew his own nature very well ; he was aware that he needed, not luxurious, but congenial surroundings in which to produce good work, and that the only way to a literary career, that was more than a hand-to-mouth Grub Street existence, lay in patronage.   The alternative was to be an amateur ; that would mean a government post, the law or high academic or clerical preferment, for his income was insufficient for his needs as a " gentleman ".   There were times in later life when in a bitter moment he complained that his talents fitted him for such a post and he felt that he would have been better rewarded had he forgone poetry ; he would certainly at some moments have given up the life of the professional poet if the academic preferment he sought had come his way.

But he chose not to be an amateur ; he chose instead to lodge with Sir Robert Howard.   In so choosing he took the decisive step towards the great poetry of *Absalom and Achitophel*, *All for Love* and the rest ; he turned his back on the thin volume of translations, the little epic— the sort of slight poetry which Sir Robert Howard brought out a month before the Restoration, and for which Dryden (unhappily for his reputation) supplied complimentary verses. For, although patronage was the common way of authors in the later seventeenth century, it was also a standing butt for the attacks of other writers, themselves equally dependent on patronage and no less fulsome in their flattery than those they attacked.

In their small way, the verses to Howard are typical of Dryden's new outlook.   He will lavish praise on Howard, according to the fashion of such things, but when it comes to Howard's poetry he is careful not to go " an inch beyond my conscience " (as he later said in another connection).

Dryden finds in Howard's poems " a native sweetness " (where most of his contemporaries, placed in such a position, would have found greatness comparable with that of Virgil or Ovid).   Then he goes on to use Howard's poems as tags to criticise the recrudescence of a debased form of metaphysical verse which marked the first year of the Restoration.   For, as Sir Walter Scott said, when the muse awoke after her 20-year sleep, like the sleeping beauty of the fairy tale she was dressed in the same antiquated and absurd vestments in which she went to sleep.   But not Howard's muse :

> . . . No metaphor swell'd high
> With dangerous boldness lifts her to the sky ;
> Those mounting fancies, when they fall again,
> Shew sand and dirt at bottom do remain.

It was probably Wild he was thinking of, whose poem, *Iter Boreale*, in the harsher and more tortuous manner of Cleveland, had a mad moment of popularity in this extraordinary year—particularly, Dryden remembered a few years later, in the City. "They have bought more editions of his works than would serve to lay under all their pies at the lord mayor's Christmas. When his famous poem first came out in the year 1660, I have seen them reading it in the midst of change times ; nay, so vehement they were at it, that they lost their bargain by the candles' ends . . ."

Howard was also praised for his "easier" odes ; but the main praise is reserved for Howards' percipience and loyalty in the dark days, "when nothing flourish'd but fanatic bays " :

> But what we most admire, your verse no less
> The prophet than the poet doth confess.
> Ere our weak eyes discern'd the doubtful streak
> Of light, you saw great Charles his morning break.

This sort of tact (the more tactful since there is a glancing reference, and a hinted excuse, in " our weak eyes ", to his own doubtful past) was a speciality of Dryden.

iv

Scarcely were Howard's poems on the bookstalls than " great Charles's " morning really broke at last, and there began the Stuart honeymoon that lasted seven years (until the Dutch sat in the Medway and Clarendon was exiled). No one who was young in the year of the Restoration could afterwards look back on it without a nostalgic feeling.

"How shall I ", Dryden asked, " speak of that triumphant day " :

> When you renew'd th'expiring pomp of May ! . . .

> And now Time's whiter series is begun,
> Which in soft centuries shall smoothly run . . .

And then with a final burst :

> O happy age !   O times like those alone
> By fate reserv'd for great Augustus' throne !

To a young man brought up during the civil wars and the succeeding régimes, the Restoration must have come with an almost physical impact, like being struck across the face with a sweet-smelling bunch of flowers.   The very streets seemed lighter and livelier ;   in place of the black habits and long faces of the Puritans were the gay and elaborate dresses of fine silk and satins with elegant trimmings of cambric, worn with an air by men and women — perfumed creatures, the men in high perukes, the women with fine coiffures.   Gaily painted coaches crunched along the muddy ways, making the old buildings appear shabby and out of date.   There were balls and banquets and revelry by night.

In Whitehall courtiers laughed gaily and boldly, eyeing the fine ladies who passed to and fro, and chipping the serving maids.   Love became a thing in which to rejoice, and to be pursued as though it would last for ever ;   a matter for happiness and song, easy warblings to the lute and viol, glances of " young loveliking ".   Dryden observed this with surprise and such interest that he thought it worthy of note in his coronation panegyric to " His Sacred Majesty " :

> Your cavalcade the fair spectators view
> From their high standings, yet look up to you.
> From your brave train each singles out a prey,
> And longs to date a conquest from your day.

There was witty talk in the coffee houses, full of swaggering figures ; there was the rattle of the dice and the flip of cards ;   there was tennis ; and the game of ninepins came into fashion.

Instead of the maddened cries of enthusiasts warning of the Second Coming, there were riotous parties when the young bucks stormed through the alehouses and taverns.   One day three young courtiers got drunk at the " Cock " in Bow Street and entertained passers-by with indecent dances on the balcony ;   one of them, Sir Charles Sedley, went too far, stripped naked and harangued his audience in profane language so that a crowd tried to burst down the door, stoned the performers and broke the windows.   (Both Sedley and

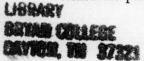

one of his companions, young Charles Sackville, Lord Buckhurst and later Earl of Dorset, were men who were to play an important part in the life of Dryden).

Now, too, the drone of the versified psalms of Sternhold and Hopkins, popular among Puritans since Elizabethan times (" Poor slaves in metre, dull and addle-pated ", as Dryden recalled them years later), gave way before the light airs for violin and voices and cornets which the King preferred. Out of the taverns and from their obscure retirement strode musicians like Lanière who now became Master of the King's Music. His Majesty, being fond of music, formed a band of 24 violins (on the model of the band of the French monarch) and reopened the Chapels Royal. Corants and jigs were heard everywhere ; the brilliant young composer, Pelham Humfrey, was sent to study the best models in Italy and France ; gentlemen again took up the amateur singing, playing and even composing that had occupied their fathers. Sir Roger L'Estrange, later a leading Royalist pamphleteer, could spend his hours of leisure playing " with tolerable perfection " on the bass viol and bearing his part in a consort at a moment's notice. Mr. John Evelyn, dining happily now with his peers and co-religionists, listened to " rare " music after dinner.

And at the centre of all this gay throng was the monarch himself, witty, highly intelligent, dark, handsome with sensual lips, interested in the arts and science, and easily accessible : he strolls in the park, chatting amiably to his smart, lively friends ; cynical and profligate, yet the real force behind the new life of England in these early years. With him is his brother, the Duke of York, equally profligate, but also an efficient administrator, a brave soldier and sailor whose deep-lying bigotry is not yet apparent.

It seemed to Dryden, as he sat down in Howard's lodgings in the summer of 1660 to write his poem on the Restoration, that life had suddenly and gloriously expanded ; he felt a strength and power running through his couplets ; and whatever he had learned from Waller of speed and sweetness, or from Denham of easy sententious-ness—

> 'T was not the hasty product of a day,
> But the well-ripen'd fruit of wise delay . . .

it is, in a strangely prophetic way, Dryden himself who stands forth in :

> Thus banish'd David spent abroad his time,
> When to be God's anointed was his crime.

There is, too, an energy and lifelikeness, typical of his later work, in the description of the crowds welcoming the King ; it is smooth and easy, carrying the reader on without a pause, yet as vivid as the best sort of descriptive journalism can be :

> Methinks I see those crowds on Dover's strand,
> Who, in their haste to welcome you to land,
> Chok'd up the beach with their still growing store,
> And made a wilder torrent on the shore ;
> While, spurr'd with eager thoughts of past delight,
> Those who had seen you court a second sight ;
> Preventing still your steps, and making haste
> To meet you often, wheresoe'er you passed.

But again he avoids any extravagant political statement, as he had done in the poem on Cromwell ; and a poem by Sprat on a similar theme is an interesting contrast. Dryden is already expressing, by omission, his true feelings of doubt and cynicism about political forms. What he could and did praise wholeheartedly was the fact of freedom and order restored :

> At home the hateful names of parties cease,
> And factious souls are wearied into peace.

It was an exact observation of the nation's deepest feeling : there is no need even to say, as Dr. Johnson said, that " if Dryden changed he changed with the nation ", for what he praised here, he had always praised.

The poem, *Astræa Redux* had a certain success, though Howard and others had objections on the grounds of accuracy to the line :

> An horrid stillness first invades the ear ...

As one wit parodied it :

> A horrid silence does invade my eye,
> While not one sound of voice from you I spy.

Still, it was good to be parodied ; it meant one was read. It encouraged Dryden and when, to the sound of music for sackbuts and cornets by that irritable composer and writer, Matthew Locke, Charles rode up Whitehall to the coronation, there was another poem by Dryden for the event.

In the following year Dryden, still pursuing greatness, addressed Edward Hyde, Earl of Clarendon, the statesman who guided Charles in these early years of his reign, in a poem for the New Year. This was at the suggestion of Sir William Davenant. Davenant had known Clarendon a long time, and knew that he " loved polite learning and history ". Had he not indeed contributed a poem of ten lines to Davenant's own play, *Tragedy of Albovine*, in the dim and distant days of 1629 ?

Davenant was now Poet Laureate, and Dryden and Howard met him often. Dryden liked him ; he noted his " quick and piercing imagination." It was Davenant who insisted always on Shakespeare's greatness, and from whom Dryden learned that liberal outlook to writers of the past which usually marks his own critical utterances. Soon he was to work with him more closely, for Davenant was also in charge of one of the two theatres that had been opened on the orders of the King.

But—not yet. In the very year of the Restoration Dryden, busily exploring all the avenues for his talent, had considered that a play " setting forth the rise of the late rebellion " might be well received. The Act of Indemnity prevented his overtly treating the theme, so he found what he considered a suitable story from the past—the career of the Duke of Guise. He wrote it, and then came the set-back. " As this was my first essay, so it met with the fortune of an unfinish'd piece ; that is to say, it was damn'd in private, by the advice of some friends to whom I shew'd it ; who freely told me it was an excellent subject, but not so artificially wrought as they could have wish'd ". He put the play away in a drawer where it lay unheeded for twenty years.

CHAPTER THREE

World of Ideas

IN TURNING away from the theatre—although only temporarily—
Dryden, always sensitive to criticism, followed the advice of his
friends ; it was the same friends who now led him to take a more
direct interest in the subject that increasingly occupied their own minds
—experimental philosophy or, as it came to be known, science.

Dryden, of course, had heard talk of the experiments of the
" virtuosi " when he was still at Cambridge ; there were meetings of
scientists at Gresham College, and the Philosophical Society was
founded in 1645, though much of its activity was abandoned during the
Civil War itself. Dryden, like John Eachard, had smiled at the young
undergraduate returning home for his vacation " with his atoms and
globuli ; and as full of defiance and disdain of all country parsons, let
them be never so learned and prudent, and as confident and magisterial, as if he had been prolocutor at the first council of Nice ". That
undergraduate had gone further and wondered why clergymen are
" all so sottish and stupid, as not to sell all their libraries, and send
presently away for a whole wagon full of new philosophy ".

Now Dryden began to take a more serious interest. Partly it was
because Cowley, whose darting mind and wide interests he admired,
wrote his *Proposition for the Advancement of Experimental Philosophy,*
and Dryden, at first somewhat tentatively, began to feel that there
was something here which suited his own mind. Cowley proposed
a college whose aims should be : " First, to weigh, examine, and
prove all things of nature delivered to us by former ages . . . Secondly
to recover the lost inventions, and, as it were, drown'd lands of the
ancients. Thirdly to improve all arts which we now have ; and lastly
to discover others which we yet have not ".

But it was Dr. Charleton, who had been early interested in the slow,
thoughtful young man, who talked most to him about science ; and

34

it was Dryden whom he asked for a poem to go in front of his book on Stonehenge. Later he gave a presentation copy of this book, *Chorea Gigantum*, to Dryden, in which he wrote in his own hand " To my learned and obliging friend Mr. John Dryden ".

The poem tells us something—but by no means all—of what Dryden thought of the new science. He believed, being a good Renaissance humanist, that science dissolved the " tyranny " of Aristotle and the mediaeval quibbling philosophy. Columbus, he thought, had given the lead ; he had shown by experiment that the other side of the world was not, as had always been held, a torrid but a temperate zone. Dryden, filled with that new sense of patriotism and of the greatness of England, went on to speak of Bacon, of the Elizabethan Dr. Gilbert's book about the magnet, and of Robert Boyle and his brother, Roger, later Earl of Orrery (whom Dryden met at about this time). Of Dr. Charleton he naturally speaks even more warmly.

A few weeks later Charleton introduced Dryden to the Royal Society and he became a Fellow in November, 1662. He attended meetings quite regularly ; after all was not His Majesty himself deeply interested ? The King, indeed, had installed for his own entertainment a laboratory in Whitehall itself ; sometimes he sent notes to the meetings of the Fellows—one, for instance, recommending in the truly broadminded way which was as natural to the King as to his scientists, that the admission of tradesmen (one of whom had read a paper to the society) was a good thing and " urged them to admit as many such men as possible ".

As Dryden listened to the papers and the discussions, he realised that poetry—the Augustan poetry he envisaged—must be aware of science, as of all manifestations of the contemporary spirit, to be truly representative. Each age, he thought, had its special genius, and science was certainly part of this new age. " Mere poets ", he afterwards wrote, " and mere musicians are as sottish as mere drunkards are, who live in a continual mist, without seeing or judging anything clearly. A man ", he came to the conclusion, " should be learned in several sciences, and should have a reasonable, philosophical, and in some measure a mathematical head, to be a complete and excellent poet . . . . ".

Again, if it was true that poetry was to mirror nature, then the poet must study science, for was it not evident that " in these last hundred years (when the study of philosophy has been the business of all the virtuosi in Christendom), that almost a new nature has been revealed to us ?—more errors of the school have been detected, more useful experiments in philosophy have been made, more noble secrets in optics, medicine, anatomy, astronomy discovered, than in all those credulous and doting ages from Aristotle to us ?"

How deep did this go with Dryden himself ?   Certainly in his next big poem he drew some of his images from the ideas he had heard discussed at the Society. " Trade ", he wrote, " which like blood should circularly flow " ; he pondered over the origin of comets and wondered :

> Whether they unctuous exhalations are
> Fir'd by the sun, or seeming so alone.

He always paid dutiful lip service to science and its aims, but it was in other and more subtle ways that those talks with Charleton and Cowley and the meetings of the savants at the Royal Society really influenced him.   There was, he began to realise, the undoubted fact that if you spent your days weighing and testing and analysing, your mind, too, began to be more rational and balanced ; you were not so susceptible to emotional fears and hatreds, nor to the fanaticism that had bred the Civil War.   Perhaps he remembered Jeremy Taylor's good advice to people that, instead of exercising their curiosity on their neighbours' business, they would do better to be considering such questions as why apples and wheat have seeds in different places.   In other words, instead of being filled with religious zeal you considered the nature of zeal.

This, of course, was not only good for other people ; it was the sort of life, Dryden thought, that he himself would prefer to lead, except that it would be poetry that he weighed and considered.   And then— astonishing thought !—was not his shyness, too, allied with the out- look of the scientists ?

He was shy, partly at any rate, because he was uncertain ; his mind saw all sides of disputes, and it was therefore difficult to come easily to a conclusion.   He was not even certain whether in certain problems there *was* a conclusion to be arrived at.   But this sort of " scepticism " was exactly the position of the scientists ; it was right to weigh and measure and investigate—but certain matters did not permit of investigation.   They had to be believed, or disbelieved, according to taste.

And yet Dryden had his unscientific reservations : astrological terms are to be found in his poem to Howard and even in the poem to Charleton ; in later life, in his refurbishing of Chaucer's Knights' Tale, he amplifies and dwells upon the astrological details.   It is the " chymic flame " of alchemy which he naturally thinks of in *Annus Mirabilis* as giving birth to a " city of more precious mould " after the fire of London.   There are in existence horoscopes he cast for his sons; he knew William Lilley, the best known astrologer of his time.   In his old age he accurately forecast the death of a servingman at a relative's house.

It might indeed be maintained—and it is partly true—that these things were merely the mental lumber carried about in the mind of a man who, for all his originality and faithfulness to the spirit of the time, was still a man of the Renaissance.   But while there is no evidence that Dryden ever experimented with the scientific apparatus of the " virtuosi ", he did experiment with astrology in a matter that concerned him very nearly—the health of his sons.

Astrology, indeed, represents what we might call the romantic, and suppressed side of Dryden's nature.   Sir Walter Scott long ago observed this when he wrote :

" As every work of imagination is tinged with the author's passions and prejudices, it must be deep and energetic in proportion to the character of these impressions.   Those superstitious sciences and pursuits, which would, by mystic rites, doctrines and inferences, connect us with the invisible world of spirits, or guide our daring researches to a knowledge of future events, are indeed usually found to cow, crush or utterly stupefy, understandings of a lower rank ; but if the mind of a man of acute powers, and of warm fancy, becomes slightly imbued with the visionary feelings excited by such studies, their obscure and undefined influence is ever found to aid the sublimity of his ideas, and to give that sombre and serious effect, which he can never produce, who does not himself feel the awe which it is his object to excite.   The influence of such a mystic creed is often felt where the cause is concealed; for the habits thus acquired are not confined to their own sphere of belief, but gradually extend themselves over every adjacent province . . . ."

The Royal Society, however, also concerned itself with other matters to which Dryden's attitude was less equivocal. Surprisingly enough, it proposed a reformation of literary style and an improving of the language itself. In this Dryden was more directly interested ; these were the tools of his trade. When the Royal Society voted to establish what would now be called a sub-committee " for improving the English language ", Dryden was elected one of its 22 members. It met some three or four times at Gray's Inn ; Cowley was there and the bumptious Dr. Sprat, the witty young Duke of Buckingham, Dryden's senior by two years, and, of course, the ubiquitous Waller.

One of the aims was to set up a British Academy on the lines of the French one ; this came to nothing, although Dryden still thought it a good idea fifteen years later. What he thought about it at this time he put thus, referring to a play he had written : " I have endeavoured to write English, as near as I could distinguish it from the tongue of pedants and that of affected travellers. Only I am sorry, that (speaking so noble a language as we do) we have not a more certain measure of it, as they have in France, where they have an Academy erected for that purpose, and endowed with large privileges by the present king ".

The Royal Society " exacted ", as Sprat put it in his history of the Society, from its members—Dryden among them—" a close, naked, natural way of speaking, positive expressions, clear senses, a native easiness, bringing all things as near the mathematical plainness as they can, and preferring the language of artisans, countrymen, and merchants, before that of wits and scholars ".

Excellent precepts—but none of the members ever wrote such good prose as Dryden.

ii

New ideas, tempting speculations, strange impressions—how they chased each other round Dryden's skull as he sat at the table next to his bed with thick serge hangings in Howard's lodgings in the early years of the new reign ! His narrow, inquisitive nose sniffed its way through books of theology, philosophy and metaphysics as well as poetry in search of—it was not yet quite clear what.

Something certainly of what he sought there was in Joseph Glanvill's

Vanity of Dogmatising—the very title was right ; again there was the
right note in John Vincent Canes's *Fiat Lux, or A general conduct to a
right understanding in the great combustions and broils about religion here in
England.* " There is no colour of reason or just title ", Canes wrote,
" may move us to quarrel and judge one another with so much heat
about religion . . . All things are so obscure that no man in prudence
can so far presume of his own knowledge as to set himself up as guide
in religion to his neighbour ".

True enough but, of course, John Owen was correct in seeing
that Canes was merely leading to a justification—a curious one,
too—of Roman Catholicism : " After a small progress ", Owen
said, " the snake begins to hiss in the grass, and in the close openly
to show itself, in an enticement unto an embracing of the Roman
Religion ".

The scepticism that led, by way of Charron and Sextus Empiricus,
to Rome could not be tolerated ; yet the scepticism remained, and so
did the philosophical inquisitiveness.

Nor did the scepticism remain a philosophical notion, a matter of
the skull, with Dryden ; scepticism in its lower manifestations was
forced upon him by his everyday life, his growing acquaintance among
the wits and intellects of the time.   Rather it would be fairer to call it
cynicism, never far below the surface in Dryden's early life : it could
all be summed up, he thought, as he turned over the first part of Butler's
Hudibras, in that verse :

> What makes all doctrines plain and clear ?
> *About two hundred pounds a year.*
> And that which was proved true before
> Prove false again ?   *Two hundred more.*

Hudibras as a poem he did not care much for ; its versification often
appalled him with its rough-and-readiness, and there was insufficient
subtlety about it—it gave " a boyish sort of pleasure " only.   Butler's
book was praised by the King and the whole Court read it upon
Charles's recommendation, laughing and chuckling at the right places.
But Butler himself (more cause for cynicism) got no reward—he
remained secretary to the Earl of Carbery.

But to Dryden in his early thirties there was something else be

yond the life of the mind, of society or even of writing : the private
life of the emotions and appetites.   He knew himself to be interesting
to the fair sex ; for the large brown eye, that appeared sleepy to a man,
seemed to be the veil for strong passion to a woman ; the impression
was strengthened by the full, yet sensitive and beautifully shaped lips.
There were those young women who blushed when he appeared ;
and others who gave even clearer tokens of their regard.   He had no
need now to visit Fleet Alley, nor to be dependent upon the buxom
girl who dressed him and combed his hair before he took the air in the
mornings.

That was one side of it ; the other was that he was now over thirty,
and still—he felt in his more depressed moments—completely unestab-
lished in the world, living a bachelor life, existing in society on the
skirts of his friends ; if he were to quarrel with Howard—and Sir
Robert could be very trying—he might well lose his access to the higher
circles of society.   He would not, indeed, starve, but he would lose a
most important advantage.   There was also the question of children,
the desire to perpetuate oneself, to enjoy again through them a sort of
innocent simplicity they alone can recreate, and to have a home.

It must have been in the autumn of 1663 and during one of his
visits to Berkshire House, near St. Martin-in-the-Fields, the London
home of the Earl of Berkshire, father of Sir Robert, that it crossed his
mind that most of his expectations and hopes of marriage would be
fulfilled were he to marry his friend's sister, Lady Elizabeth.   She was
an attractive, lively young woman, full of chatter, and without the
slightest touch of the blue-stocking.   A lover of French romances and
London life ; an incredibly bad writer and a worse speller—and little
else.

Her father, the Earl, was by no means rich, having a large family
and small acres down at Charlton in Wiltshire.   But it would be a good
marriage ; and certainly Lady Elizabeth would not let him remain
long in his morose moods.   It might be that she had been, well, somewhat flirtatious in her teens ; there were stories—but then there were
stories about all lively young women.

It was in the end Sir Robert who broached the subject remarking
that he had observed Dryden's interest, that it would be a good thing,
and that moreover he felt Dryden's chances were good.   " After all

she *is* 25—and is bound to wish to marry my friend ", was his remark with his usual egotism.

Would it have made any difference to Dryden had he known that five years earlier the wild and profligate Philip, Earl of Chesterfield, had tossed into his desk this letter :

"From the Lady Elizabeth Howard, daughter to the Earl of Barkshire.

"1658

My Lord,—I received yours, though not without great trouble, but I am not guilty of anything you lay to my charge, nor will I ever alter from the expressions I have formerly made, therefore I hope you will not be so unjust as to believe all that the world sayes of mee, but rather credit my protestation of never having named you to my friends, being allwayes carefull of that for my own sake as well as yours ; and therefore let it not be in the power of any, nor of your own inclinations, to make me less,

Your very humble Servant.

"If you will meet mee in the Old Exchange, about six o'clock, I will justify myself".

Did she ever tell Dryden of her affair with Chesterfield ? Perhaps —or is it only imagination that sees certain glancing references, certain points overemphasised, when Dryden, over 60 years old, dedicated his translation of the *Georgics* to Chesterfield, now himself past the climacteric, and mentions that he cannot imagine " (if your Lordship will give me leave to speak my thoughts) but you have had a more than ordinary vigour in your youth ; for too much of heat is requir'd at first, that there may not be too little left at last. A prodigal fire is only capable of large remains . . ." ? Is there not a certain irony, too, in : " Your Lordship is a man of honour, not only so unstain'd, but so unquestion'd, that you are the living standard of that heroic virtue ; so truly such, that if I would flatter you, I could not " ?

If so, there was only an old man's tolerant smile behind it.

Whatever the revelations of the future, the young Dryden's suit was well received. He was a gentleman and seemed to the Earl a very quiet, amiable young man of whom, so his son told him, great things were expected. So the Bishop of London's clerk, Henry Smith, junior, wrote : " Ultimo Novembris 1663, Which day appeared personally John Driden of St. Clement Danes in the County of Midd Esqr aged about 30 yeeres and a Batchelor and alledged that hee intendeth to marry with Dame Elizabeth Howard of St. Martin in the Fields in the county aforesaid aged about 25 yeeres with the consent of her Father Thomas Earle of Berke not knowing or believing any impediment to hinder the intended marriage of the truth of the promises he made faith and prayed Licence for them to bee married in the parish church of St. Swithins London ".

The couple spent their honeymoon in lodgings which Dryden had found and where they were to live for the next six years. There he learned, perhaps among other things not so much to his satisfaction, that his wife would soon receive £3,000 from the Excise ; this was part of a grant to her father on account of services he had rendered to the King during his exile, and which he was making over to her in lieu of dowry.

Whatever his satisfactions, or otherwise, in his marriage, two months later he was back to his old pursuits ; for the first time, he is thought worthy of observing and writing about by one of his contemporaries. On the night of Feb. 3, 1664, Pepys on the way to fetch his wife from the theatre stopped " at the great Coffee House " (in Covent Garden, i.e. Will's), " where I never was before ; where were Dryden, the poet I knew at Cambridge, and all the wits of the town. . . there, I perceive, is very witty and pleasant discourse ".

So Dryden is now placed in his best-known milieu for the first time ; but why should Pepys pick *him* out particularly as the first to be noticed in the great Coffee House, full of all the wits ? The reason is that, while we have been watching his intellectual life, his friends and his marriage, that " roving " mind has been a step ahead of us, cannily setting himself to furthering his fame and his fortune. His first play has been presented at the beginning of the year, and his second a few days after his wedding ; he is already at work with Howard on a third. Everyone knows—and that always includes Pepys—that the first play, though a failure, took the fancy of the king's mistress, Lady Castlemaine, and that it has been played privately at court on several occasions. Dryden has made his mark at last.

iii

It is no longer a " round O " but a square box that we are in, with a lushly ornamented ceiling ; it is a gay scene to come into from the sunshine outside at 3.30 in the afternoon, full of fashionable ladies in their cocked hats and red plumes, sitting in the stage boxes chattering to the beaux with their enormous perukes and fine cambrics. The light from the great sconces full of candles throws fantastic shadows across the pit where sit the wits, and the wives of the citizens and merchants, the dancing masters and the people of the middle sort.

In front of the drop curtain the orchestra begin to assemble ; a man moves in front of them lighting the footlights which now throw up the brilliant colours of the curtain. As the violins, the harpsicals and the theorbos strike up Mr. Locke's latest overture, the curtain slowly rises, the chattering stops, and the company gaze their fill on the frontis-piece, a noble arch with wreathed columns, round which roses are wound ; on either side is a figure with a trumpet and a palm ; in the middle of the arch several angels hold the King's arms ; the backcloth is a maze of brilliant colours ; and on to the stage steps the prologue, a beautiful and famous young lady dressed in the height of fashion who with a languishing and pseudo-innocent air recites a string of lines, each couplet of which contains a *double entendre*.

There is wild applause, for this is a famous actress. Then in dashes Nokes, for this is a comedy and he the greatest comic actor of the day. It is he who through the extraordinary surprises, mistakes, disguises and escapes which follow, and the varied use of sliding panels, closets, veils, masks, large cloaks and dark lanthorns, holds the play together.

His scope is remarkable. Now he is " sunk into such a mixture of piteous pusillanimity, and a consternation so ruefully ridiculous and inconsolable, that when he had shook you to a fatigue of laughter, it became a moot point whether you ought not to have pitied him. When he debated any matter by himself, he would shut up his mouth with a dumb studious pout, and roll his full eye into such a vacant amazement, such palpable ignorance of what to think of it, that his silent perplexity (which would sometimes hold him several minutes) gave your imagination as full content as the most absurd thing he could say upon it . . . ."

Such was the theatre into which Dryden stepped in the first years of the Restoration. It was a theatre voracious for plays, which, however, ran for very short periods, and its audience was capricious in the extreme : like the theatre of later days, it could now take up an author and laud him to the skies, now heartlessly forgetting its previous satisfaction smash him just as easily. It was a place of heartbreak, yet also a place of magic as the theatre always is for the writer emerging from his study and seeing his own creations made flesh-and-blood. It was hard work, but there was money in it, and the possibility of fame, for the King himself and all his courtiers had an unquenchable appetite for the play.

But heartbreak—yes, and it was difficult for even the wisest and most philosophical author to remain unmoved by the reception of his play. Dryden went one day with young Sprat to see Cowley's play, *Cutter of Coleman Street,* Cowley himself remaining at home. His play was hissed, and worse than that the courtiers present construed it as a satire on the king. Afterwards Dryden and Sprat went along to tell the author of his play's effect. " When they told Cowley how little favour had been shown him, he received the news of his ill-success, not with so much firmness as might have been expected from so great a man ".

Yet the lure was too strong for Dryden. It was not that he loved the theatre or had it " in his blood ". Indeed he did not care for comedy (at this time the great demand) and even tragedy, where he was to triumph, was not in his mind the highest literary form.

But comedy was the most popular form of writing at the time. So when Howard encouraged him to write, he wrote. Howard had a personal interest in the King's Company, one of the two theatres licensed by His Majesty ; he in fact owned a quarter interest in this company, then directed by Thomas Killigrew, the king's friend and almost court jester during the years of exile. The King's Theatre, unlike the Duke's, was still a makeshift one ; it was, in fact, Gibbons' Tennis Court. There the company remained until their new house in Brydges Street was ready ; and at the tennis court on February 5, 1663, Dryden's first play, called *The Wild Gallant*, had received its first performance.

It is noticeable throughout Dryden's literary career that, in turning his hand to a new type of writing, he usually leaned heavily upon someone else's work : he was, as we saw, psychologically a " moulder " preferring to express himself in materials and forms already to hand, but doing it so successfully that, looking back on his work from this distance of time, both material and form seem to have been his creation. The truth is, as Johnson said (though his remark referred only to prose), that he found brick and left marble, but the brick was still very much in evidence to his contemporaries.

So his first attempt at comedy, *The Wild Gallant*, was a refurbishing of a play by Ben Jonson's secretary and friend, Richard Brome. It is in prose and has the typical " humour " characters of Jonson's comedy, though without his flexibility. Dryden also inserts some of those wit-combats in which two characters show off their cleverness at repartee, as in Fletcher and Shirley, and according to the oldest traditions of comedy—" prize-fights of wit ", the Duke of Buckingham aptly called them.

The taste of the time, interested enough in French fashions in other matters, did not object to a mixture of styles such as Molière would not have countenanced, but it did demand swift-moving plays with plenty of action, plot and counter-plot, surprises and bustling intrigue. Dryden's " prize-fights of wit " held up the action enormously, nor are the " humorous " characters, Trice and Bibber and Lord Nonsuch, particularly well done.

The play was a failure. Pepys saw it and thought that " it was ill acted, and the play so poor a thing as ever I saw in my life ". Worse than that, the King was present, and according to the sharp eye of Pepys " did not seem pleased at all at the whole play ".

But one person—and a very important one—*was* amused ; this was the clever Barbara Villiers, Lady Castlemaine, the King's mistress. It was perhaps the pair of light-hearted lovers, Constance and Loveby, who took her fancy ; she might well have seen, beneath their flirtatious and somewhat immodest chatter, something of her own relations with his pleasant, witty Majesty.

It was Lady Castlemaine who saved Dryden from complete despair, for she persuaded Charles to have *The Wild Gallant* played at Court on several occasions. " It was ", said Dryden when he published the play some years later, " more than once the divertisement of his Majesty, by

his own command ". In return for this, Dryden wrote a poem to
Lady Castlemaine, speaking of her as the god that descended and
" preserv'd the play ", adding that it was her applause and favour that
infused " New life to my condemn'd and dying muse ".

But failure it was, and Dryden now sat down and considered why.
He also considered what had succeeded in the comic line elsewhere and
recently. His thoughts naturally came round to a play which had a
few weeks earlier been acted at the Duke's Theatre under his friend
Davenant and had had what was then the very long run of 13 days.
This was *The Adventures of Five Hours* by Sir Samuel Tuke based
closely on a Spanish original, *Los empenos de seis horas* by Antonio
Coello. Dryden had known of this play when he wrote the prologue
to *The Wild Gallant ;* in his canny way he had tried to bluff it out by
suggesting that *his* play had no need to pretend to anything new or to
borrow from abroad, for it was " English and the growth of your own
. . . English wit ", he had asserted, " will continue to triumph ".

A pity, perhaps, but " English wit " for the moment clearly preferred
other models ; and as he set about a new play, he endeavoured to
please that taste. *The Rival Ladies,* his next play, takes place in Spain,
the plot is as involved as any Spanish plot, and just as improbable.
Like Tuke's play, it is a tragi-comedy, and following the King's
expressed preference, the tragic scenes are in rhymed couplets, which
Dryden effusively defends in a preface. It is, strangely enough, the
comic scenes which are in blank verse.

The whole thing reads poorly today ; but Dryden must have been
satisfied that he had done right in following public taste, for it was a
mild success : Pepys thought it " a very innocent and most pretty
witty play ". It was perhaps helped by the fact that it was presented
in the new Theatre Royal in Brydges Street, and had the benefit of
lavish production : after all the poor " Gallant " had not even had
painted scenery.

Meanwhile, Dryden's friend, Sir Robert, had been preparing a new
sort of play altogether, a strange and rather fearsome drama, in which
the ideas of the French classical drama, the dramatic rules based by
French and Italian critics on a misunderstanding of Aristotle, and a
post-Marlovian blood-and-thunder, were all mixed up together to
form what soon came to be known as " heroic plays ".

Dryden afterwards said that the popularity of these plays was entirely due to " the countenance and approbation they have received at court ". But if Charles was expecting a grave and stately imitation of Corneille or Racine, he must have suffered a considerable shock when he attended the first performance of the first of such plays to be seen on the English stage, Sir Robert Howard's *Indian Queen*. The whole aim of Howard's play was to assist the imagination to run riot, with fanciful events twice as large as life and characters of an impossible nobility and an equally impossible wickedness, and to give as much scope as possible to the ambitious stage-managers of the new Theatre Royal, anxious to use as many of the remarkable " engines ", the aerial demons singing in the air, the god of dreams ascending through a trap, the rich and fantastic dresses and lush painted scenery as could conveniently be brought together in one play in one afternoon. Such has been the *beau idéal* of stage-managers from the time of the Tudor masques to the modern pantomime and *Oklahoma !* It was very different from that of the producers of *Le Cid* in 1636 or of *Andromaque* three years after *The Indian Queen*.

But Charles's first surprise must soon have given way to pleasure at this particularly British amalgam of the most discrete elements. Or perhaps it was his ladies who, though they had a snug feeling that they were listening to high-class poetry, could not help enjoying another component of these dramas—the romantic element of gallant knights and faithful ladies, pathetic queens and wicked barons, the vistas of strange lands and bizarre customs, the incantations and apparitions, the battles and blood in which, however, one could see no contemporary reference because of the trappings of high-flown verse, music and elaborate stage sets.

It was such stories, after all, that the ladies enjoyed in the quiet of their boudoirs—the chivalrous romances of D'Urfé, La Calprenède and the fabulous Mme de Scudéry. They were transferred and " realised " on the stage to the great delight of the ladies ; the tumult, the bustle and the sound and fury pleased the masculine mind, and so everyone was satisfied—or nearly everyone : the Duke of Buckingham sneered at the rodomontade and there were other more grave and stuffy censurers, including in some moods, Dryden himself.

But Howard's success was undeniable, and it spurred Dryden on to emulation. Moreover, the opportunity to write verse and rhymed verse and to hear Hart and Major Mohum recite it with a great mouth, to make the maximum effect of the " full resounding line ", was extremely attractive. This sort of poetry—which Dryden, like the early Shakespeare, loved—also went so well with music : the later critics in the satire *The Censure of the Rota* were more than half right when they said : " Mr. Dryden would never have had the courage to have ventured on a Conquest " (his later heroic play, *The Conquest of Granada*) " had he not writ with the sound of drum and trumpet ".

There were other attractions in the form. Dryden felt himself to be a poet ; the epic, or " heroic poem ", was universally considered to be the highest form of poetry, and as he himself says " the greatest work which the soul of man is capable to perform ", and after all, the romances upon which the heroic drama was based were in a sense heroic poems in prose. Thus Dryden could feel that when he was writing an heroic drama he was to some extent executing a modern epic, or as he said " an imitation in little of an heroic poem "; and as " the heroic poet is not tied to a bare representation of what is true, or even probable ", so the heroic dramatist can accept the most improbable circumstances and characters. Thinking about it later he went further and claimed the liberty of " drawing all things as far above the ordinary proportion of the stage as that is beyond the common words and actions of human life ", adding that, as in the epic, the subject ought to be " Love and Valour ".

The truth was that the heroic play was a sort of rag-bag for Dryden in which he deposited whatever was in his mind at the time of writing. So he puts into the mouths of his heroic characters diverse philosophical ideas, and thoughts about politics and the world at large, which were not always suitable to the character, but were always exactly representative of his own reading and thoughts at the time : it was his way of expressing his deepest speculations when no other means lay to hand.

What part Dryden played in the composition of his friend's play is not clear, but he certainly helped. His own heroic play, *The Indian Emperor*, was produced with the same flourish and lavish hand, at the Theatre Royal in the spring of 1665. It enjoyed an even greater success than *The Indian Queen*, to which it was meant to be a sequel, and it established Dryden's name in the public mind as a dramatist of the first rank.

It was *meant* to be a sequel to Howard's play, but there were difficulties.   As Dryden says, *The Indian Queen* " left little matter to build upon, there remaining but two of the considerable characters alive ". Howard had disposed of almost everyone by means of "the bowl and dagger ".   The exception was Montezuma and he, with the sons and daughters of those killed in the first play, take the stage in *The Indian Emperor*.   To avoid confusion Dryden, or Killigrew's producers, printed a short outline of the play which was handed to the audience as they arrived at the theatre.

The story of the play is what might be expected ; the poetry is another matter and quite terrific.   In it, for the first time, Dryden's bounding energy found an outlet where he could let rip without fear of being pulled up by considerations of either poetic decorum or personal questions, and for which, emboldened by his comparative success already, he felt himself ripe.   The pleasure of it lies only in its regularity of cadence and its emphasis upon the rhyme ; there is little diversity in it, such as he had produced in his earlier poetry, and such as was to be the delight of his later work, but there is a strong ground-rhythm, like a powerful machine turning over.   It was a thrilling sound such as had not been heard so stridently in English since *Tamburlaine*.   It must, as Mr. Van Doren has justly said, have sounded suddenly and loudly like a gong :

> I went, in order, sir, to your command,
> To view the utmost limits of the land ;
> To that sea-shore where no more world is found ;
> But foaming billows breaking on the ground ;
> Where, for a while, my eyes no object met,
> But distant skies that in the ocean set ;
> And low-hung clouds that dipt themselves in rain,
> To shake their fleeces on the earth again.
> At last, as far as I could cast my eyes,
> Upon the sea, somewhat methought did rise,
> Like blueish mists, which still appearing more,
> Took dreadful shapes, and moved towards the shore.

In a discussion between a fanatical Spanish priest and his two Indian victims, and Montezuma and the Indian high priest, Dryden gives us his views of deism—as well as his detestation of fanaticism. He gives, however, even his deistic views only in the form of a debate. He likes to see, and let his listeners hear, both sides of any philosophical argument ; he balances the scales evenly—except when writing against inhumanity :

Montezuma.	Where both agree, 'tis there most safe to stay ;
	For what's more vain than public light to shun,
	And set up tapers, while we see the sun ?
Christian Priest.	Though nature teaches whom we should adore,
	By heavenly beams we still discover more.
Mont.	Or this must be enough, or to mankind
	One equal way to bliss is not designed ;
	For though some more may know, and some know less,
	Yet all must know enough for happiness.
Chr. Pr.	If in this middle way you still pretend
	To stay, your journey never will have end.
Mont.	Howe'er, 'tis better in the midst to stay,
	Than wander farther in uncertain way . . . .
Chr. Pr.	Renounce that carnal reason, and believe.
Mont.	The light of nature should I thus betray,
	'Twere to wink hard, that I might see the day . . .
Pizarro.	Increase their pains, the cords are yet too slack.
Chr. Pr.	I must by force convert him ; to the rack.

Dryden, of course, was not a deist, but he was interested in the deeper meaning of life and belief ; the ideas of his time are, as it were, in solution in his mind in these early years.

In his later plays in this style, the energy with which Dryden clothes ideas often results in the verse becoming truly poetry, poetry of a severe and stoic cast, in which, however, the words have a gleam and a rich sheen.

CHAPTER FOUR

Success of a Poet

IT WAS THUS in the warm spring of the year 1665 that Dryden's life began to fan out before him ; he strode a little more importantly from his lodgings, and down the Strand. The great houses there were no longer quite so forbidding, for he now had friends who lived in them.

He began to be sought after by such wits and noblemen as Sir Charles Sedley, himself a dramatist and the author of a few charming songs ; Charles Sackville, Lord Buckhurst, became an intimate, though there was always an awareness in Dryden of their difference in rank.

With them, and Sir Robert Howard and others, Dryden passed those " genial nights " he so loved ; sometimes they met at the lodgings of one of the company, on other occasions at one of the better taverns. Here " the discourse is neither too serious nor too light, but always pleasant, and, for the most part, instructive ; the raillery neither too sharp upon the present, nor too censorious on the absent ; and the cups only such as will raise the conversation of the night, without disturbing the business of the morrow ". And then home to Lady Elizabeth in the moonlight with the moon throwing the gabled houses into strange, gothic relief, and Dryden feeling himself so large in comparison to their smallness as though they had been made for a race of pygmies ; the cobbled streets rough to the feet and rougher still on the jolting wheels of a passing coach with its curtains pulled close. Past the houses in Drury Lane with red crosses on their doors, where men, said to be French, had died of the plague. Happily to bed with a book by candlelight.

It was a great spring, fresh and sweet, to Dryden and to Englishmen, who then shared Dryden's feeling of being twice his normal size : hope sprang into the air from men's minds and sat singing in the throats of birds on the trees down by the river ; pride and consciousness of

being Englishmen in this great reign were everywhere, and the war that
had come again with the Dutch was welcomed (except by the Clerk of
the Acts at the Navy Office in the City who knew the ill-state of the
navy, and who, as Dryden passed from the theatre to Will's, confided
his fears to his immortal diary).

But the war was necessary ; as Captain Cocke, the great hemp-
merchant, succinctly, and with historical accuracy, bluntly put it : the
trade of the world was too small for both nations and one or the other
must go down.   More officially, the House of Commons, on a report
from the Committee of Trade, had come to the same conclusion,
resolving that " the wrongs and dishonours and injuries done to His
Majesty by the subjects of the United Provinces by invading of his
rights in India, Africa and elsewhere " were the cause of the decay of
the nation's trade.

At the end of the year Admiral Teddiman sailed into Portsmouth
with twenty captured merchantmen, and Pepys wrote : " The war is
begun : God give a good end to it ".   In April the fleet led by the
Duke of York sailed for the Dutch coast.   In the parish of St. Giles, in
the same week, two men died of the plague and eight of the spotted
fever ; men said the germ had come from Holland where the plague
had been rife the year before.

Then, with all the world watching, the Duke of York returned to
port—because of a shortage of beer in his fleet's victuals.   The Dutch
put to sea; Pepys redoubled his efforts, and on May 30th the Duke again
set forth with 109 warships, 28 fireships and 21,000 men, his officers-in-
command being his uncle, Prince Rupert, Lord Sandwich and Sir
William Coventry.

On June 1st—the hottest June for years—the rival navies sighted
each other off the Suffolk coast.   A haze of heat lay over London and
beneath it an uplifting of the spirit such as had not been felt since the
arrival of Charles upon Dover beach five years earlier.   News was
eagerly sought and exchanged ; the Londoner went about with his
nose in the air, like a pointer awaiting a scent.

Dryden arranged with some friends, among them Sedley and Howard,
to take a trip down the river on the next day but one, the Saturday.   It
turned out to be " that memorable day in the first summer of the late
war, when "—and even the phlegmatic Dryden could not help feeling

that history was being made—" our navy engaged the Dutch : a day wherein the two most mighty and best appointed fleets which any age had ever seen, disputed the command of the greater half of the globe, the commerce of nations, and the riches of the universe. While these vast floating bodies, on either side moved against each other in parallel lines, and our countrymen, under the happy conduct of his Royal Highness, went breaking, little and little, into the line of the enemies ; the noise of the cannon from both navies reach'd our ears about the city : so that all men, being alarm'd with it, and in a dreadful suspense of the event, which they knew was then deciding, every one went following the sound as his fancy led him ; and leaving the town almost empty, some took towards the park, some cross the river, others down it ; all seeking the noise in the depth of silence ".

Dryden and his party in a barge hired by Sedley shot the bridge, and " left behind them that great fall of waters which hindered them from hearing what they desired : after which, having disengag'd themselves from many vessels which rode at anchor in the Thames and almost blockt up the passage towards Greenwich, they order'd the watermen to let fall their oars more gently ; and then everyone favouring his own curiosity with a strict silence, it was not long ere they perceiv'd the air to break about them like the noise of distant thunder, or of swallows in a chimney : those little undulations of sound, though almost vanishing before they reach'd them, yet still seeming to retain somewhat of their first horror which they had betwixt the fleets ".

The party felt victory in the air, only Howard fearing in his bluff, humorous way that it would mean his reading and hearing a vast quantity of bad verse on the subject. And so they fell to talking of poetry and plays and whether French writers were better than English, and whether the ancients had the advantage over the moderns.

So the day passed ; and as the sun went down, they came slowly back upstream, past Tower Stairs, under London Bridge and past the mist-covered fields of the Paris Gardens on the left bank. Before they realised it, the barge was tied up at the foot of Somerset Stairs, below Somerset House, and stiff and thirsty, but sorry to part, they stepped ashore, then " stood awhile looking back on the water, upon which the moonbeams played, and made it appear like floating quicksilver : at last they went up through a crowd of French people who were merrily dancing in the open air, and nothing concern'd for the noise of guns which had alarm'd the town that afternoon ".

The party separated in the Piazza at the front of Somerset House ; Sedley and his noble companion went " to some pleasant appointment they had made " ; Howard and Dryden walked back to their lodgings. As they went they spoke of the Bills of Mortality which showed an appalling rise in the number of dead from the plague, and the fact that it had spread from St. Giles's to other parishes and even into the city. They passed along streets where an unnatural silence prevailed because authority had closed the houses where men had died from the plague, and also because neighbours were now beginning to avoid each other's company for fear of infection.

On the Thursday the great victory was confirmed : Pepys rushed over to the Cockpit and there found Monk, Duke of Albemarle, mad with happiness : when the Duke of York and his courtier-sailors returned to Whitehall there was great rejoicing. But on the previous Monday, the King, after conferring with the authorities and his physicians, had taken more stringent measures to stop the spreading of the plague. One—and it emphasises the King's concern—was an order forbidding " acting any more plays ". This put a temporary end to Dryden's main employment.

As the summer wore on, the plague became worse, whole areas being stricken and bodies lying unburied. Dreadful tales were told about the horrors of the pest-house. Soon the streets were full of coaches and waggons, piled with baggage and household goods, making for the country and comparative safety—but only *comparative* safety for no one was aware that the infection was carried by the fleas whose host was the black rat, and fleas travelled into the country, too.

When it appeared that there was no end to the plague, and Whitehall and 'Change were deserted, and not a boat was to be seen on the river, Dryden and his wife at last left town. Lady Elizabeth was already pregnant and very irritable, but at least they had somewhere to go, for Lady Elizabeth's father, the Earl of Berkshire, offered them sanctuary at his house at Charlton in Wiltshire.

ii

Country life suited Dryden : it enabled him to enjoy his favourite pastime of fishing, and in later years it also allowed him to get away from London where there were too many calls on his time. It was in the country, too, that many of his best things were written—a great number of his translations, *The Hind and the Panther*, and probably *Absalom and Achitophel*.

Of course, town life, talks with friends and other writers, nights at Will's stimulated him. In these early years, indeed, it was necessary for him to be in town to keep contact with taste, an eye open for opportunity and in order not to be forgotten. At this time, it was an irritation to have his budding dramatic career interrupted, but after all the same applied to all his rivals so the set-back was more apparent than real.

Moreover, to be withdrawn for a time from the literary fray was undoubtedly an advantage. He could, for instance, pull together all his scattered thoughts on poetry and plays which in the rush of writing and rehearsing he had overlooked ; it was valuable to be able to sit down and consider calmly the question of the drama, not just his own part in it. He could visualise more clearly exactly what he was doing himself against the background of his knowledge and of his wide reading of drama of the past. He could think and ponder at his ease his own nature, his real beliefs and position with regard to the questions of his day.

Thus came into being the celebrated *Essay of Dramatic Poesy*. He says himself that it " serv'd as an amusement " to him during his stay in the country, and that his thoughts about the theatre had " the same delight " as those of men on their absent mistresses. Dryden is modest about his own work and pretends to have remembered the Essay only when looking through his " loose papers " ; but in fact the Essay is an epoch-making document in English criticism, and, it may be added, in English prose, for it is done in the most delightful and human way.

It is, he tells us in a note, an attempt to vindicate English writers from those who always pretend the French are better—a curious snobbery which still persists ; he had no books to check his facts with, nor any friends from whom to seek advice. He says he may later extend his theme to poets who have also written in the epic or lyric style, but he never did.

Remembering his trip down river with his friends on the memorable day in June, he casts his essay in the form of a literary chat on the smooth waters of the Thames between himself, Neander, and his friends, Eugenius, Crites (by whom he meant Howard) and Lisideius (who stood for Sedley). This enables him, not merely to give a diversity of views on a variety of subjects without seeming scrappy-minded, but also to dispense with the closely-argued piece of criticism his readers might otherwise have expected. He opens his mind to us, and gives us his views on various literary topics, but without pretending to a finality of judgment.

Early in the Essay, after referring to the twisted metaphysical poetry of Cleveland and others, he speaks of the poets of his own time, praising Waller for being " even, sweet and flowing " ; Denham " so majestic, so correct " ; and Cowley " so elevated, so copious, so full of spirit ". Earlier English poets, with all their genius, underestimated and did not attempt the " sweetness " of English verse. This, since " the genius of every age is different ", is perhaps to be our special aim. Moreover, " every age has a kind of universal genius, which inclines those that live in it to some particular studies " ; this " correctness " is perhaps part of the spirit of the age, as is the revelation of " almost a new nature " by the scientists.

He considers more closely imagination in poetry. The word he used for imagination was " wit ", which in his time, and in his writings, bears a variety of meanings, none however completely unconnected. Wit itself he was to define a few months later, as far as it concerned poetry, as " no other than the faculty of imagination in the writer ". Imagination in the writer is " like a nimble spaniel (which) beats over and ranges through the field of memory, till it springs its quarry it hunted after ; or, without metaphor, which searches over all the memory for the species or ideas of those things which it designs to represent ".

But imagination " is most to be admir'd when a great thought comes drest in words so commonly receiv'd that it is understood by the meanest apprehensions, as the best meat is the most easily digested ". Unhappily this is not what happens in, for example, Cleveland, not one of whose verses we can read without " making a face at it, as if every word were a pill to swallow ".

That is not, of course, true of all the metaphysicals ; if we compare

Cleveland's satires with those of Donne, we find " that the one gives us deep thoughts in common language, though rough cadence ; the other gives us common thoughts in abstruse words ".

The same thing obtains in a heroic or historical poem, he said a little later. One does not want " the jerk or sting of an epigram, nor the seeming contradiction of a poor antithesis, (the delight of an illjudging audience in a play of rhyme,) nor the jingle of a poor paronomasia " (play upon words).

No, rather it is—and now Dryden, the critic, looks at the methods of Dryden the poet—" it is some lively and apt description, dress'd in such colours of speech that it sets before your eyes the absent object as perfectly and more delightfully than nature ". Yes, more delightfully than nature, for otherwise it is merely copying.

Now, what exactly happens in poetic composition ? Well, the first happiness of the poet's imagination is properly " invention, or finding of the thought ; the second is fancy, or the variation, deriving or moulding of that thought, as the judgment represents it proper to the subject ; the third is elocution, or the art of clothing and adorning that thought, so found and varied, in apt, significant and sounding words : the quickness of the imagination is seen in the invention, the fertility in the fancy, and the accuracy in the expression ".

Dryden now considers some of the poets of the English past. Jonson : everyone praises Jonson, and he too will admit he was the " greatest " man of the last age. In a way, Dryden thinks he himself is not unlike Jonson, for " You seldom find him making love in any of his scenes, or even trying to move the passions : his genius was too sullen or saturnine to do it gracefully . . . ."

But while admiring him for his correctness, the regularity of his plots, for being the " pattern of elaborate writings ", there is someone for whom his feelings are far beyond admiration. This is Shakespeare.

Dryden knew this was an unpopular notion ; but careful though he was never gratuitously to offend political or religious susceptibilities, he was always ready to rely on his own judgment, to back his own fancy, in literary matters. In fact, his famous description was responsible for that burgeoning of Shakespeare's reputation which began after the Restoration.

Yes, Shakespeare . . . . Dryden drew in his breath and bent his mind to exactly what it was in Shakespeare that held him. As he pondered, he realised that he was drawing from his mind a picture that had slowly formed over the years, only half-consciously, of a universal genius. " To begin then with Shakespeare ; he was the man who of all modern, and perhaps ancient poets, had the largest and most comprehensive soul. All the images of nature were still present to him, and he drew them not laboriously, but luckily ; when he describes anything, you more than see it "—after all that is *our* poor aim—" you feel it, too. Those who accuse him to have wanted learning, give him the greater commendation : he was naturally learn'd ; he needed not the spectacles of books to read nature ; he look'd inwards and found her there ". This is Dryden, the sensitive recording instrument before something so much bigger than himself and aware of its being bigger, yet so cleansed of *amour propre* by the contemplation that the very qualities he himself has in superabundance—learning and vast knowledge of books—are declared unnecessary and unimportant in producing the greatest poetry. Of course, Shakespeare had faults : " He is many times flat, insipid ; his comic wit degenerating into clenches, his serious swelling into bombast. But he is always great when some great occasion is presented to him ".

Coming nearer to his own time, he speaks of what the French can teach us in the way of writing good plays : for instance, they don't use divine machines or sudden conversions to get themselves out of plotting difficulties in the fifth act ; and they stick closer to the rules. But lately they have taken a leaf out of our book and, against those rules, have mixed tragedy with comedy. In fact, says Dryden, thinking of *The Rival Ladies,* most of their new plays are, like some of ours, " deriv'd from the Spanish novels ".

But though we may learn from them and they from us, it must be remembered that the French theatre and the French mind differ vastly from their British counterparts. They do not mind, for instance, if an actor gives a set harangue, measured like our parsons measure their sermons, by the hour-glass. Well, that suits them, but not us. " We, who are a more sullen people, come to be diverted at our plays ; so they who are of a more airy and gay temper come thither to make themselves more serious "—which is also why we prefer comedy, and they tragedy.

As for their superiority—that is nonsense ; for whatever has happened to us, we have a natural genius to carry us through : " Be it spoken to the honour of the English, our nation can never want in any age such who are able to dispute the empire of wit with any people in the universe. And though the fury of a civil war, and power, for twenty years together, abandon'd to a barbarous race of men, enemies of all good learning, had buried the muses under the ruins of monarchy; yet with the restoration of happiness we see reviv'd poesie lifting up its head, and already shaking off the rubbish which lay so heavy upon it ".

Having dealt thus with one class of people, Dryden now turns to the Ancient *versus* Modern controversy which supplied coffee houses with subjects enough to last a hundred years (which, in fact, it did). The point about it, surely, is that no true comparison can be made: the great Ancients were great because of, and in the context of, their time. So, too, were Jonson, Fletcher and Shakespeare. " They are honour'd and almost ador'd by us, as they deserve ; neither do I know any so presumptuous of themselves as to contend with them. Yet give me leave to say this much, without injury to their ashes, that not only we shall never equal them, but they could never equal themselves, were they to rise and write again. We acknowledge them our fathers in wit, but they have ruined their estates themselves before they came to their children's hands. There is scarce a humour, a character, or any kind of plot, which they have not used. All comes sullied or wasted to us : and were they to entertain this age, they could not now make so plenteous treatments out of such decay'd fortunes ".

That was a point worth making, for too long a regarding of the Ancients, or even the recently dead great, could induce paralysis. And that surely is the aim of criticism—in the words of his motto from Horace : " Fungar vice cotis, acutum—Reddere quae ferrum valet ; exors ipsa secondi ".

With the argument that rhyme is more dignified than blank verse, though the latter may certainly be used especially in comedy, the debate as far as Dryden was concerned comes to an end. Unfortunately, Dryden was mistaken ; when the Essay was published some eighteen months later, certain aspects of it were to start quite another sort of debate, and that within his own family circle.

Indeed, family matters generally were becoming rather trying by

the summer of 1666. Not long after Lady Elizabeth had given birth
to a son—to Dryden's great joy—there were squabbles with the Earl,
his father-in-law, over money. Dryden was not earning anything at
this time ; often there was delay in receiving his rents ; and the
impecunious Earl became rather pointed in his remarks about the
cost of his hospitality. So Dryden and his wife pressed the Exchequer
for payment of the sums made over as dowry by the Earl. They
wrote to Sir Robert Long, the auditor of the Exchequer, putting their
case before him—with some effect, for before the end of the year they
were receiving regular sums from the Exchequer.

iii

During his stay at Charlton Dryden paid several short visits to
London. What he saw and heard on his visits did not please him ;
although the plague had abated somewhat, the war that appeared to
have been so thoroughly won in June was still dragging on, the Dutch
having received encouragement from the return of their hero De
Ruyter.

Londoners, as a result of their disappointment of victory combined
with the effect of the plague, had become moody and perhaps dangerous ; there was much talk among them of all these things being the
visitation of God upon London for the wickedness and dissoluteness of
the rulers of the country, and this was encouraged by the remnants of
the sects, always ready to cry "Woe, Woe" and to see a *dies
irae*.

When a *dies irae* in fact came—though Dryden was not there to see
it—in the form of the great fire which spread from the City and destroyed the old houses as far west as Temple Bar, the signs became ever
clearer that God was displeased with the English. The Opposition in
politics, compounded of tradesmen, middle-class Puritans, and men
whose estates were becoming larger at the expense of the squirearchy
along with certain of the old families, took advantage of this. Pamphlets, positively seditious in tone, made their appearance, avoiding the
strict censorship first imposed in 1663, under such titles as *Mirabilis
Annus, the Year of Prodigies*. It had been discovered from Revelation
xiii. 18, that 1666 was in fact the *annus mirabilis* and also the year of
reckoning, the passage being: " Let him that hath understanding count

the number of the beast ; for it is the number of a man ; and his number is six hundred threescore and six ".

Back in Charlton again, Dryden, to distract his mind from family squabbles and from what he had seen in London, occupied himself with writing a new play, *Secret Love or the Maiden Queen*, which was afterwards put on with great success. This he read to Howard who made various useful suggestions.

But now his mind, which had been mulling over the affairs of the country and remembering, too, a meeting with Sir Roger L'Estrange, chief licenser of the press and controller of the news-letters, " Intelligencer " and " The News ", turned to something more serious and greater in scope. This was the *Annus Mirabilis*, which was Dryden's attempt to " justify the ways of God to man ", or, more specifically, to show that God was not visiting judgments on his people, but merely submitting them to trials—which they had faced bravely and come through triumphantly under the inspired leadership of their King. Thus he countered the superstitious terrors, and put a spoke in the Opposition's wheel. To make his aim still clearer, he addressed his poem, not as was usual to a person, but to the " metropolis of Great Britain ". It is you, in your strength and courage, he tells the people, who have made this a Year of Wonders. Now there is reason to think that the trials are over " as is the wish of all true Englishmen " ; and Dryden signs himself " the greatest of your admirers ".

For Dryden himself the writing of this poem had much more than a mere propagandist interest. He tells the reader something about it in his prefatory letter to Howard. It is, he says, a heroic subject—and in a way his expiation for not serving his king and country in the late war (thinking perhaps of Sackville and other friends at sea).

But though the subject is heroic, his poem is not an epic but an historical poem, and so not as elevated in style as an epic would naturally have to be. He has chosen to write it in quatrains " or stanzas of four in alternate rhyme, because I have ever judged them more noble, and of greater dignity, both for the sound and number, than any other verse in use among us ". For a further discussion, he recommends the reader to the preface to *Gondibert*, in which poem the stanza had been used for similar purposes.

It seems a curious choice, but at that time few alternatives suggested

themselves to him.   The Spenserian stanza was quite out of fashion as
was the eight-line stanza used by the Elizabethan translators of Ariosto
and Tasso ;   the Chaucerian stanza had barely survived Elizabethan
times.   The couplet—well, the couplet was a possible choice, but
Dryden felt himself not yet ready to essay a long historical poem in
that medium.   Blank verse he did not even consider as a proper
medium for narrative.   (The publication of *Paradise Lost* changed his
views, but that epic was then only just in the hands of the printers).

One other thing Dryden tells us he is doing in *Annus Mirabilis* : he is
trying out something new—the use of idiomatic naval terms in his
description of the battle with the Dutch, which, he says, he has never
before seen.   (Lucan, though an exception, was in another language,
and his terms were no help.)   Dryden has bothered to enquire about
the correct terms, though where he is in the country without " the
converse of any seamen ", he has been unable to confirm them.   He did
not try this again; and it may be added that when he was an old man, he
explained (in his Dedication of the *Aeneid*) why : " I will only say that
Virgil has avoided those proprieties, because he writ not to mariners,
soldiers, astronomers, gard'ners, peasants etc., but to all in general ".

The prefatory letter takes us so far into his confidence but it does not
go the whole way.   It does not speak of his excitement and sense of
tension as he sat down to produce a 1,200-line poem upon such a subject
of public import and interest—his biggest task yet in the purely poetic
sphere.   It was his great test and he was well aware that it could make
him famous, or get him ridiculed.

So nervous was he, indeed, that before beginning he had his blood
let ;   then he cast a horoscope, and not till the propitious day did he
settle himself in the heavy-panelled, Jacobean library of Charlton
House.   Then, with his confidence restored and at the back of his mind
the thought that this was the day he had dreamed of a quarter of a
century before on the bosky banks of the quiet-flowing Nene, a
heightened mood of pride in his country came over him ;   and he
found himself turning over in his mind, and moulding, phrases of
high dignity and power :

> The mighty ghosts of our great Harries rose,
> And armèd Edwards look'd, with anxious eyes,
> To see this fleet among unequal foes . . . .

The whole poem, indeed, is imbued with a spirit of noble patriotism, culminating in the final vision of a London, mistress of the world, rising from the ashes, and setting forth into an era of universal peace :

> Thus to the eastern wealth through storms we go,
> But now, the Cape once doubled, fear no more ;
> A constant trade-wind will securely blow,
> And gently lay us on the spicy shore.

Movement and action again stimulate him to extraordinary vividness of phrase, for example, in the description of the arrival of Prince Rupert with naval reinforcements :

> His presence soon blows up the kindling fight,
> And his loud guns speak thick like angry men.

Or the hub-bub of the ships refitting :

> So here, some pick out bullets from the sides,
> Some drive old oakum through each seam and rift;
> Their left hand does the caulking-iron guide,
> The rattling mallet with the right they lift . . .
>
> To try new shrouds one mounts into the wind,
> And one, below, their ease or stiffness notes.

Later when the Dutch boats have been captured :

> Our greedy seamen rummage every hold,
> Smile on the booty of each wealthier chest . .

Or after the battle to the sleeping seamen :

> In fiery dreams the Dutch they still destroy,
> And slumbering smile at the imagined flame.

But perhaps the most brilliant and lively of such passages is that describing the fire of London, how it began—

> Then in some close-pent room it crept along
> And smouldering as it went in silence fed :
> Till th'infant monster, with devouring strong,
> Walk'd boldly upright with exalted head.

And now it comes into the open—

> And now, no longer letted of his prey,
> He leaps up at it with inrag'd desire ;
> O'erlooks the neighbours with a wide survey,
> And nods at every house his threatening fire.

> Far off the cracks of falling houses ring . . . .

His inspiration was not at such constant heat throughout ; there are *longueurs* in the description of the naval manoeuvres, and sometimes his verse gives out with a bathetic plop.   The poem is not integrated ; and although the tone, or " elevation ", was fairly kept, there are irregularities even there.   Often they are due to Dryden's half-conscious memories of other men's poems—Cowley and the early Milton and, interestingly enough, his boyish idol Sylvester's translation of Dubartas (in the metaphor of the elephant).

There are lines of curious prophecy cast, it seems, by accident into a poem which has no satirical object at all—lines which show the natural way his mind took when, perhaps it was tired, or the baby was crying. Such a line, for instance, is that describing the King reviewing the ravages of the fire.   Charles, he says : " Outweeps an hermit, and outprays a saint ".   Or, less indecorously, but equally in satirical vein, the brilliant couplet on the Dutch generals :

> Designing, subtile, diligent, and close,
> They knew to manage war with wise delay.

One thing more appears—it is part of his character—and that is a tendency to blasphemy ; we shall notice it again in *Absalom and Achitophel*, along with a strange sensuality of image.   In the first edition of *Annus Mirabilis* appears the stanza :

> For now brave Rupert's Navy did appear,
> Whose waving streamers from afar he knows :
> As in his fate something divine there were,
> Who dead and buried the third day arose.

The last two lines were altered in the second and all subsequent editions.

Annus Mirabilis was licensed for the press on November 22, 1666,

and was published early in the next year. It was a great success :
Pepys, the barometer of educated, but not scholarly or aristocratic
taste, said of it : " I am very well pleased this night with reading a
poem I brought home with me last night from Westminster Hall, of
Dryden's, upon the present war ; a very good poem ".

Many others were equally pleased, Herringman, the poet's old
friend, who published it, for instance, and—His Majesty King Charles
II. Two months later the King heard Dryden's name again, in equally
pleasant circumstances, at the performance of the play written at
Charlton, *Secret Love or the Maiden Queen*. This tragi-comedy, based
mainly on themes from a romance by Mme de Scudéry, was, its author
claimed, a compound of the French and the English dramatic styles—
" a mingled chime of Jonson's humour with Corneille's rhyme ".

The King was delighted with it and always referred to it as *his* play :
Nell Gwyn, newly commenced actress, played the part of Florimel
so well that Pepys said that he could never hope to see the like of such
acting again.

Dryden with his wife and child had returned to London in time for
the opening night. A few days later Waller, one of the King's
censors of plays, sent Dryden word that the King wished to see him.

Dryden, in the midst of his excitement at the summons, could not
help feeling the irony of the fact that the message should come through
Waller, with whom he had had some coolness. (It was political
rather than personal coolness. Dryden had praised Clarendon in a
poem and his daughter, the Duchess of York, in another; Waller had
been prevented by Clarendon from obtaining the post of Provost of
Eton in 1665 and had thrown in his lot with Buckingham, Clarendon's
bitter enemy.)

But Dryden, in a new coat and breeches, did not allow such speculations to worry him unduly. As he rumbled in his hired carriage
towards Whitehall, with new shining buildings already rising in the
landscape to the east, the " squire " thought rather of his earlier, obscure
days as a clerk in the great room under the Council Chamber in the
same Whitehall to which he was now summoned by the King himself,
and smiled to himself; his hard work was at last about to bear fruit, and
what did rumours of an empty treasury, starving civil servants,
corruption in high places, and the danger of a foreign invasion mean

F

when one was turning into the gates of the palace, the bodyguards saluting, courtiers in their fine clothes drifting across the courtyard ?

How, stepping from his coach with Waller and Buckingham affably greeting him, could he imagine that he was too late, that the Stuart honeymoon and the Stuart largesse was nearing its end ? How imagine, in the long, rich room with the tall, handsome figure moving towards him, smiling and murmuring his Royal pleasure at meeting the author of *Annus Mirabilis*, that this would lead eventually to disappointment ?

How believe, as the King talked brilliantly of Corneille and his hopes, more his *certainty*, that Dryden would emulate him, and then turned to inquire into Dryden's personal circumstances, his wife, his father-in-law, his fortune—how believe that in a few months, as charmingly as ever, His Majesty would ask him for a loan of £500 ?

This was indeed the beginning of a period of financial and worldly success ; but it also marked a deepening of his cynicism, and the opening of his eyes to the venality of power.

CHAPTER FIVE

A Swollen Head

THE NEXT FEW years of Dryden's life sped by like a dream, and with the brilliance, the inconsequence and the kaleidoscopic changes of a fast-moving film. Now the camera picks out the line of the Thames, and out to sea the dim outline of the Dutch fleet sailing slowly towards the Medway, whilst nearer at hand there are scenes of sailors refusing to man the English ships until they receive the months of back-pay owed to them. Then we are in the middle of London, where gaily-dressed crowds push through the sunlit streets in search of amusement, of excitement, of ever faster and more feverish pleasures. The town has gone pleasure mad ; fine courtiers like Lord Buckhurst and Sir Charles Sedley " run up and down almost naked through the streets and at last fighting and being beat by the watch are clapped up all night " ; the apprentices in the City are out of hand, and even their usually sober masters are infected by the frenzied spirit so that they flood the theatres demanding only the lightest of farces or the grotesque unrealities of the heroic play. The dreadful nightmare of the plague and fire is giving way to the need to relax, to forget, to snatch at pleasure where it may be found. Gone is the mood of high patriotism which filled Londoners in the hot summer of 1665 ; instead there has come disillusion—the war has dragged on so long, and has so often been nearly won—and cynicism, the cynicism of a nation which had expected so much of a restored monarch, and has now come to the conclusion that all he is concerned with is getting money from them to spend on amusement and pleasure. Well, they too will have their pleasures, and he and the country can go hang. After all, they do not understand that there is no organised means for the King to raise taxation and to fill the treasury ; they are aware only that their wages are months and years in arrears. They do not know that, in order to raise money, the King has to go to the money-lenders in the City who charge him 10 or 12 per cent interest, and thus the treasury gets further and further into difficulties ; they see only the fine clothes, the racing, and the light ladies ; they hear only the stories of luxury and licence.

So the camera flicks from crowd scene to crowd scene, where no face is distinguishable, and at last settles on a room. It is a fine, big room in a great house in the Strand ; it is brilliantly lit from numerous sconces on the walls, which throw up the oil paintings in strange effects. Servants rush to-and-fro with great dishes of meat as plate follows plate on the long table ; glasses are filled and emptied and filled again, and the company round the table are in merry mood.

For a moment the flickering lights prevent our seeing the faces ; then one is picked out for he is giving orders to a butler. This is the Duke of Newcastle, the host, a man well aware of his consequence in the great world. Next him (the camera moves slowly along) is the ravaged face of Wentworth Dillon, Earl of Roscommon, gambler, duellist and Latin scholar ; he is talking learnedly with his soldierly-looking neighbour, the twenty-two year old John Sheffield, Earl of Mulgrave, about the classical parallels of Buckhurst's fine poem " To all you ladies now on land." Another wild-looking young man is far gone already in drink, and is muttering about casting horoscopes and how he has foreseen his own death, and how the King wants no end to the Dutch war because of his deep indebtedness to the French king ; then this " young man of a very unsettled head or of a roving shattered brain "—so men refer to Thomas, Lord Clifford—starts up and begins to fling insults across the table at the most striking of all the company— a handsome youth whose head and eyes bespeak a brilliant intellect, but whose mouth is already set in a mixture of indulgence, meanness and ill-faith. This is John Wilmot, Earl of Rochester, who burst like a comet into the circles of the Court when he was only seventeen, and became at once the favourite of the King. His learning and wit are equalled only by the extremities of his debauchery and drunkenness ; he has led even the King into scrapes, and refers to him to his face as the monarch " who never said a foolish thing, and never did a wise one ". He is frequently banished from Court and as frequently recalled, for the King discerns in him something he finds in no one else : a meta-physical gleam, a touch of genius, an almost supernatural brilliance of intellect. And how he can write poetry ! His *Satire against Mankind* is beyond the achievement of any of his contemporaries—even beyond the plump, red-faced man he is talking to now, the new poet who has had such success recently, and now enjoys the favour of His Majesty.

This is John Dryden, but a different John Dryden from any we have met so far. For one thing, he has drunk far more than his habit, and has lost his shyness even among the great company he is dining with. Already he has picked up the easy manners and loose talk of his new friends ; he is as cynical as the worst of them, and quite ready to laugh at the things he holds dearest—poetry and the great writers of the past. " My *Essay of Dramatic Poesy* ? Faugh, Sir, 'twas written for frowsy scholars at Cambridge. Shakespeare ? I'gad, Davenant and I will show you a better Shakespeare . . ." Rochester leads him on ; it amuses him to see this fat little man, who can, indeed, write good poetry and probably better yet, making a fool of himself. They discuss the adaptation of *The Tempest* that Dryden and Davenant are working on, and Dryden tells him that they are " improving " the play by giving Miranda a sister and writing in the character of a boy, Hippolito, who has never seen a woman. Dryden bends forward and, vinously delighted to be hobnobbing with the famous Rochester, takes him by the arm and mutters : " The playhouse, my boy . . . . They will laugh at anything so long as it's smutty, and pay you well for panderin' to 'em, i'gad !" He asks Rochester to look at his *Sir Martin Mar-all ;* nothing in it but farce and smut and they lap it up like alley-dogs. Thirty performances in Lincoln's Inn Fields ; four at the Court itself. The company got more profit from it than any other comedy they ever put on.

The noisy room sways around him, and the lights in the sconces are dying ; some of the company are already asleep, their heads on the table ; Dryden can see only the wavering shadows of the servants moving softly to-and-fro, and somewhere a long way off a keen pair of blue eyes still boring into his own—but it is only imagination that there is also a sneering mouth. " I tell you," Dryden mumbles, " that Killigrew of the King's Company has offered me a twelfth share in the profits to write three plays a year for 'em—and I can do it as easily, as easily as—". A drowsiness begins to overtake him, and the last thing he remembers, before his servant helps him away, is the baleful, malignant look in Rochester's eye . . . .

Then it is morning and he awakes in his new house on the north side of Long Acre ; below he hears the sound of a baby crying, for his second son John has recently been born. His party of the night before has left him shaky and bemused ; but, as he slowly regains consciousness he tells himself determinedly that that is the only way to fame and fortune, and it is " fame that darling fame " and fortune that are now the spur. What matter that he knows that what he is writing is of little value ? The theatre is the thing, and afterwards, when his fortune is made, is time enough for other things.

Dryden spends a great deal of time in the theatre in Brydges Street these days. There is much to learn, and stage-craft is in itself interesting. This morning, for example—now that he is a sharer in the company—he must go and see about the painting of an Elysian scene required for a new production. The usual painter, Isaac Fuller, is ill, but Dryden is determined to get him to bestir himself, for he is a most capable man. He meets the company's joiner, Wright, and with him goes to Fuller's lodgings. This little incident, in fact, led to legal proceedings—which is why it is remembered—and Fuller later deposed that " Mr. Dryden and Mr. Wright (a joiner belonging to the company) . . . did come unto this defendant then lying sick at his own house and did propose unto him the painting of the said scene of Elysium . . . and to encourage this defendant to undertake the painting thereof the said Dryden and Wright or one of them told this defendant he should be well satisfied for the same ".

There were, of course, moments when Dryden stopped suddenly amid the bustle and the noise and the invitations from his great friends, and wondered—what he was doing, what was happening to him, where it would all end ; moments when he knew that this was not his real life or his real work. Such a moment came, for instance, when he was writing the prologue to the vandalised *Tempest*, and he slipped in the couplet :

> But Shakespeare's magic could not copied be ;
> Within that circle none darest walk but he.

It was the moment of truth, but it did not come very often, and when it came he would have another drink, for, as he said to his friends, " there's no deceit in a brimmer." At other times he would counter his depression by remembering that he was now a man of considerable consequence in whom such moments were a sign of weakness ; he must be strong and haughty and assured as the rest. He held himself the more importantly and was quick to put his inferiors in their places ; he chose more carefully where he should flatter, and less carefully what he should say in his flattery. And when things became too oppressive, his mind and spirit unresponsive to his new way of life, there was always Anne Reeves to rid him of the vapours. Anne was a beautiful young actress who had appeared in many of his own plays, and had a *sympathie* for the large-eyed, smartly dressed, and most successful dramatist. They had been lovers for some time—after all, it was necessary in the circles in which he now moved to have a mistress or two ; Lady Elizabeth did not seem to mind very much, even if she really knew of the affair, and in any case she was fully occupied with her two small sons, soon to be increased to three by the birth of Erasmus Henry in May, 1669. It was possible to talk with Anne about the theatre, and to bask in her admiration : he took more care with his dress now, and achieved in his outward appearance a sort of precise hauteur, far different from his " squire " look of early days in London, or even from the calm, complacency of a few years before. It was all very satisfactory, and Dryden remained faithful to Anne until, some seven years later, she retired into a nunnery.

And all this life *was* rewarding—or so Dryden thought on the morning of April 13th, 1668, when he received a royal warrant to become Poet Laureate, Davenant having died some six days earlier. It was a moment of great triumph for the man of 37 whose career had been so slow in developing ; it confirmed him in his belief that he was a new man whose past had been slow, too academic, too serious altogether, but who was now all set for royal favour and royal riches.

Seventeen days later, Dryden quietly renewed the loan he had made to His Majesty of £500. A few days after that, His Majesty responded by ordering his Archbishop at Lambeth to present John Dryden with the degree of Master of Arts.

The patent for his appointment as Poet Laureate was not granted for another two years, but then as a mark of especial royal favour he was granted a salary of £200 for the post—and that had never been done before. Witty Charles could not, however, leave it at that ;

there were other things in life, too, which Dryden would appreciate, and so he had his clerk add to the patent the words : " Further, know ye, that we, of our especial grace, certain knowledge, and mere motion, have given and granted, and by these presents, for us, our heirs and successors, do give and grant unto the said John Dryden and his assigns, one butt or pipe of the best canary wine, to have, hold, receive, perceive, and take the said butt of canary wine unto the said John Dryden and his assigns during our pleasure, out of our stores of wines yearly and from time to time remaining at or in our cellars within or belonging to our palace of Whitehall . . . ."

To all this was added another post, that of Historiographer Royal, which had not been filled since the death of John Howell four years before.   (Sprat who had thought himself the person for the post was furious, and did not forget his disappointment).   It seemed as though His Majesty could not do enough for the man whose plays had taken his fancy ; but His Majesty was clever and highly observant, and it may have been that it was not the plays of Dryden but his *Annus Mirabilis* which really interested him.   For *Annus Mirabilis* was not merely a fine poem ; it was also, from the point of view of the King, an excellent and effective piece of propaganda . . . .

To Dryden, it was simply a confirmation of his already high opinion of himself, the mark of his assay upon his writing (crushing all doubts), and his next play, *An Evening's Love or the Mock Astrologer* was more flippant, more smutty, more fashionable than ever.   Even the prologue was smart and daring :

> When first our poet set himself to write,
> Like a young bridegroom on his wedding-night
> He laid about him, and did so bestir him,
> His Muse could never lie in quiet for him . . . .

At home, as he read and re-read the patent that told him that he had now joined the distinguished line that descended from Chaucer, Gower, Leland and Ben Jonson, his cup was full and his pride soared into the seventh heaven.

ii

For the first time in his life, Dryden now disposed of a considerable income.   His plays had been very successful, and he shared in the profits ; there was further profit when they were published, from their sale and from the dedications. He had, after 1670, his salary as Poet Laureate, and his wife was still receiving money from the Exchequer. He found, in fact, that he had something like £600-£700 a year—the equivalent of £3,000 to-day. He spent more on clothes, on servants, on food—and on entertaining his great friends. He was, he felt, a gentleman, not merely in name, but in fact, and his days of eating humble pie were over.

He was no longer quite so subservient to those who had helped him in his early days in London ; he was no longer willing to tolerate their eccentricities. He reserved his attentions now for higher beings— Newcastle, for instance, to whom he had dedicated *An Evening's Love*.

Among those who had helped him, and whom he was now no longer ready to be humble to, was his brother-in-law, Sir Robert Howard. The trouble there really started, it is true, with Howard himself who had been very cross to find that in the *Essay of Dramatic Poesy* he (under the name of Crites) had been made to express certain views which were neither popular nor exactly representative of his own ideas, though these were variable and more often than not dictated by the spleen and contrariness for which he was well known. In the preface to his play *The Great Favourite or the Duke of Lerma*, Howard sharply rejected Dryden's arguments in favour of rhyming plays (which, of course, Howard himself had practised). Moreover, the preface was condescending—the tone is that of a man of quality, " conscious ", as Scott remarked, " of stooping beneath his dignity, and neglecting his graver avocations, by engaging in a literary dispute ".

To this Dryden in his *Defence of an Essay of Dramatic Poesy* replied with equal acerbity, and did not confine himself to literary matters. He sarcastically mentions Howard as being master of more than twenty legions of arts and sciences—an allusion to Howard's affectation of universal knowledge which Shadwell had made fun of in the character of Sir Positive At-all in his comedy, *The Sullen Lovers*. Dryden also ridiculed some slips in Latin and English grammar and referred to a foolish speech Howard had made in the House of Commons. The sentences Dryden uses are sharper and more flippant than his usual style ; their tone is that of the racy prologues and epilogues he was now writing for his plays.

The controversy was not confined to Howard and Dryden. Howard's brother Edward joined in, as did other " wits " delighted at this public spectacle of a family quarrel. One pamphlet on Howard's side is worthy of note, for it is by R.F. who has been identified as Robert Flecknoe, an Irish poet later to receive his apotheosis at Dryden's hands.

Dryden's *Defence* is interesting not only in its haughty flippancy but also for its open admission of his time-serving attitude to the public : " I confess my chief endeavours are to delight the age in which I live. If the humour of this be for low comedy, small accidents and raillery, I will force my genius to obey it ". He goes on to mention once more that his genius is not really for comedy, that his argument in the *Essay* was " sceptical ", that the end of all poetry is to delight, that his final appeal in his imaginative works is " to every man's imagination ".

Dryden's *hubris* was now at full tide. The *Defence* was subjoined to his heroic play *The Conquest of Granada* (which we shall consider in a moment) ; in the epilogue to that play he deals flippantly and irreverently with the dramatic poets of the past, comparing their plays to their disadvantage with the plays of his own time, and in particular his own plays. He refers to Jonson's " mechanic humour ", adding :

> Fame then was cheap, and the first comer sped,
> And they have kept it since by being dead.

In the *Defence* he had dealt equally harshly with Jonson, had pointed out Shakespeare's faults and had suggested that the modern version (by the Duke of Buckingham) of Fletcher's famous *Chances* was much better than the original.

His jealous contemporaries were swift to observe the *hubris* in it all, and happily took advantage of Dryden's thus exposing himself. They began to write pamphlets against him, and one of these came from someone we have already noticed as being Dryden's shadow ; this was Thomas Shadwell. He too, had been having his successes, mainly in the sphere of comedy for which he had considerable aptitude, but he was envious of Dryden's greater success. As he grudgingly admitted, his resentment scarcely hidden :

> You in the people's ears began to chime,
> And please the town with your successful rhyme.

Jonson was Shadwell's great hero and he observed in his preface to *The Sullen Lovers* that Dryden had been " so insolent to say that Ben Jonson wrote his best plays without wit, imagining that all the wit plays consisted in bringing two persons upon the stage to break jest and to bob one another ".   He also attacked Dryden for the bawdiness of his comedies, though Shadwell could be bawdy with the best when it suited him.   In recent comedies he says : " The two chief persons are most commonly a swearing, drinking, whoring ruffian for a lover, and impudent, ill-bred tomrig for a mistress . . . . their chief subject is bawdy and profaneness, which they call brisk writing . . ."

Dryden ignored it—for the present ; indeed he shortly afterwards worked with Shadwell.   But he did not forget ; he merely made a cool, mental note of Shadwell's character—his love of vulgar pleasures, his reeling home drunk from the tavern night after night, his corpulence, and his addiction to opium.

What Dryden in his buoyant mood did not observe was that other, more acute eyes were watching *him*.   He still did not really notice that Rochester's flattery concealed the baleful stare of the aristocrat, already summing him up as a plump upstart, a " Poet Squab ", trying to be a " tearing blade ", and succeeding through his bawdiness.   Nor was he aware that his personal characteristics were being noted by the envious Butler, the bumptious Sprat, cross that he had failed to get the post of Historiographer Royal, and the debauched Duke of Buckingham.   Nor did he imagine that a dirty, but amusing, remark he made during a visit to Windsor would reach the ears of Shadwell, and be repeated in print.

Dryden, in any case, was immersed in the production of a new play, *Tyrannic Love or the Royal Martyr* which, he boasts in the preface, was composed in seven weeks.   The play, another " heroic " drama, is bombastic and scarcely capable of holding modern interest from the point of view of character.   The speeches of the Emperor Maximin, the villain of the piece, cannot be taken seriously.   He sits down on the body of his assassin whom he has still strength to stab, with the words :

> And after thee I go,
> Revenging still, and following ev'n to th'other world my blow ;
> And shoving back this earth on which I sit,
> I'll mount—and scatter all the Gods I hit.

Dryden confessed eleven years later (in the Epistle Dedicatory to *The Spanish Friar*) : " I remember some verses of my own Maximin and Almanzor which cry vengeance upon me for their extravagance . . . All I can say for those passages, which are, I hope, not many, is that I knew they were bad enough to please, even when I writ them . . . . "

But there is good poetry in the play and for such a passage as this, Dryden did not apologise :

> Thus with short plummets heav'ns deep will we sound,
> That vast abyss where human wit is drown'd !
> In our small skiff we must not launch too far ;
> We here but coasters, not discov'rers are.
> Faith's necessary rules are plain and few.

Just as he had done in *The Indian Emperor*, he tries out in *débat* from ideas from his recent reading. The beautiful part of St. Catherine contains cogent arguments on the rational and ethical superiority of Christianity with which she converts the heathen philosopher, Apollonius. The rationalistic aspects of religion—almost the principles of natural religion—are much in Dryden's mind, so that he allows St. Catherine to convert her heathen without a single mention of Christ or the Sacraments :

> But where our reason with our faith does go,
> We're both above enlightened, and below.

Tyrannic Love was another great success. Moreover, the King had become vastly interested in the woman who had played the part of Valeria—Mrs. Nelly Gwyn. One result of this was the despatching of her then " protector ", Sackville, Dryden's friend, on what Dryden himself referred to as " a sleeveless errand " to France.

Dryden was anxious to repeat both successes and to write a new play with Mrs. Gwyn in it. Unfortunately there was some slight delay owing to Mrs. Gwyn's being confined. But after she had presented the King with a son, later the Duke of St. Albans, she appeared in one of the most resounding successes of Dryden's whole career—*The Conquest of Granada* (Part I).

It, and its heroic sequel, are indeed extraordinary plays whose very extravagances seem to have a glow and life of their own. Today they are best read, as Professor Nichol Smith says, not as dramas but as poems that carry on an argument, interspersed with observations on various subjects, for the characters are entirely representations of single virtues and vices.

In 1670 in the theatre it was different. There was all the pomp and splendour of elaborate scenery and extraordinary machinery ; the stage was full of bustle and noise, and so the outrageous rodomontade seemed appropriate and indeed stirring.

The story is set in the kingdom of Granada under its last monarch, Boabdelin ; the country is riven by faction, and, in the second part particularly, there are amongst the plots and counterplots, a number of observations on the nature of government in which what we may regard as typically-Drydenish comments on " the many-headed beast " the people, the commonwealth where the people are their own tyrants and the danger of foreign conquest while civil war takes place. Yet these sentiments were typical of the heroic drama ; they can be paralleled in Davenant and in the plays of Orrery.

But what is certain is that here we already see in full play Dryden's gift for reasoning and statement in smooth and vigorous verse—such things as :

> O lottery of fate ! where still the wise
> Draw blanks of fortune ; and the fools the prize ! . . . .
>
> Reason was giv'n to curb our headstrong will,
> Reason but shows a weak physician's skill :
> Gives nothing while the ranging fit does last,
> But stays to cure it when the worst is past.

Equally certain is it that these two plays are studded with lines of true poetry :

> A blush remains in a forgiven face,
> It wears the silent tokens of disgrace.

As Saintsbury remarked, the audience that cheered this was " not wholly vile " :

> Fair though you are
> As summer mornings and your eyes more bright
> Than stars that twinkle on a winter's night ;
> Though you have eloquence to warm and move

> Cold age and fasting hermits into love ;
> Though Almahide with scorn rewards my care
> Yet than to change 'tis nobler to despair.
> My love's my soul and that from fate is free,
> 'Tis that unchanged and deathless part of me.

Dryden may, though I doubt it, have drawn " the reason and political ornaments " in these two plays from Hobbes, as the authors of *The Censure of the Rota* claimed, but such lines as these on the fate of empire are his own :

> Then down the precipice of time it goes,
> And sinks in minutes which in ages rose.

One hundred and ten years later it was these lines that rose unbidden to the mind of Mrs. Thrale as she contemplated the parlous state of the British nation.

Tyrannic Love had been dedicated to James, Duke of Monmouth, the handsome but unfortunate illegitimate son of Charles. *The Conquest of Granada* was addressed to Monmouth's uncle, James, Duke of York. Though rivals later for the throne, both these Royal personages agreed in expressing their pleasure in Dryden's work. " Mr. Conceit's " view of his importance reached new heights.

And yet, sobering doubt would come sidling back into his mind ; was he really so great a man or poet as his worldly success suggested ? One day on his way to the theatre he had picked up from a book-stall a poem that had recently " fallen dead from the presses ", had dipped into it and found it so powerful that he stayed awake all night to read it. The book was *Paradise Lost*; it was written in an unfashion-able style and on an unfashionable subject, but Dryden, no matter how conceited or worldly he became, nor however lightly he might dismiss in some moods the poets of other ages, knew poetry when he saw it. It was Dryden a few years later who made the reputation of this obscure poem which he alone of his critical contemporaries recognised as " undoubtedly one of the greatest, most sublime poems which either this age or nation has produced ".

" This man," he soberly thought as he read on into that great poem of good and evil, " cuts us all out and the ancients, too ". He had not yet observed " the flats among his elevations ". But it was partly

Milton's influence that began slowly to turn Dryden away—imperceptibly at first—from the specious triumphs of the stage and from the pride that he felt in himself and which was bodied forth, enormous and terrible, in Milton's fallen angel.

Dryden's honest recognition of great poetry wherever he found it was the Achilles' heel of his pride—and his saving grace.

CHAPTER SIX

Making Enemies

BUT LIFE rushed on and was delightful, and *Paradise Lost* was relegated, after the first flush of excitement, to the back of Dryden's mind, though it was never forgotten. There were so many things to do, plays to write, actors and actresses and noble lords and other writers to talk to, wine to be drunk and gay nights down the river.

In particular, soon after he had read Milton's poem, there came an invitation from His Majesty himself to stay with him and his party at Windsor. It was a flattering honour and Dryden went down there more than ever cock-a-hoop, but more than ever convinced, too, that it was no more than his due.

At first, the visit went very well indeed. The King asked Dryden to show him his sketches for a new play he was writing, to be called *Marriage à la Mode*. Both His Majesty and the rest of the company, which included the Duke of Buckingham, now the chief minister, Sir George Etherege, the dramatist, and Dr. Sprat, Buckingham's chaplain, were much amused by the dialogue, and insisted on playing over for the gratified dramatist some of the scenes he had completed. Rochester was there, too, and positively exaggerated in the compliments he paid Dryden in the presence of the King ; according to him, there never was such a fine play as *Marriage à la Mode*, nor ever such a brilliant wit as the Poet Laureate.

But before long Dryden began to detect a note of derision in the brilliant chatter, an undercurrent of antagonism towards himself. It began when Buckingham, who had been a wit in his rash and wanton youth, spoke of a squib he had sketched out in 1664 making fun of Davenant's plays and those of Edward Howard (brother of Sir Robert and author of an extravagant rhyming play, *United Kingdoms*). After the Duke had amused the company by his story of how he had led a party of young men into the theatre during a performance of the play,

" hissing and laughing immoderately at the strange conduct thereof" he looked straight at Dryden and said that he had a mind to bring his squib up to date.   Sprat coughed and smiled knowingly, and said that his Lord, in fact, had already rewritten some of the scenes and that the play would be presented very soon—to the discomfiture of some *great* ones, he added.

The moment passed, and Dryden put it out of his mind until shortly after his return to London he discovered that his suspicions of some antagonistic undercurrent were completely justified.   A play called *The Rehearsal*—its authors unknown—was put on, and the central character, Mr. Bayes, the laureate, was none other than himself !

Of course, he told himself at first, it *was* rather flattering to be so distinguished and at the hands of the greatest man in England.   But . . . a slight sense of injustice persisted, though he was careful to conceal it. It was not so much that Lacy, the actor who took the part of Mr. Bayes, wore exactly the clothes he affected, imitated superbly his tricks of speech and his halting manner of reading and his partiality for the expression " i'gad."   But were the jokes about his mistress really necessary, and was it kind to have repeated some of his boastful remarks in his cups and, worse than all, was it decent to have made use of *Marriage à la Mode* which had not yet been staged ?   The man greedy for applause, inordinately vain, a flatterer of all flatterers . . . it came too close home.   It induced in him another twinge of doubt ; supposing the authors were right in seeing all these unpleasant facets of his character, what then did his " greatness " mean ?   Was this the aspect of himself that he wanted to go down in history—it was by no means " the darling fame " he had thought of.

The Rehearsal, however, was very successful, and the audiences loved it.   This at least was something, for it was put on by the King's Company in which Dryden had shares.   In any case, it was a *sort* of fame ; it showed that he was become important enough to have a whole play devoted to him, and there was concealed behind it, as he knew, a great deal of envy and jealousy, emanating from Dr. Sprat.

It was not long before Dryden recovered his equilibrium, and plunged again into his former life, but already the seeds of doubt had been sown in his mind.   For the moment he had no time to let them

G

develop. Soon after *The Rehearsal*, catastrophe overtook the players when the King's Theatre was burned down and the company had to retire discomforted to a makeshift place in Lincoln's Inn Fields. They reopened there in February, 1672, with a prologue by Dryden in which he apologised for entertaining the audience in a " shed ". But, he promised :

> . . . as our new-built city rises higher,
> So from old theatres may new aspire,
> Since fate contrives magnificence by fire.

In the " shed " two or three months later was shown *Marriage à la Mode*. The play is Dryden's best comedy. The plot is more or less original, and instead of a pair of witty lovers he has a quartet. Rhodophil and Doralice are a fashionable couple who, though still retaining some mutual affection, are convinced that they must, to remain in the fashion, be unfaithful to each other. Rhodophil, therefore, turns his attentions to Melantha who is intended, though he does not know it, to marry his friend Palamede. Palamede, fashionably distressed by the idea of matrimony, devotes himself to Doralice.

Doralice and Melantha are most interesting studies ; Melantha is not quite a Millamant, but she is in the same tradition. The dialogue is witty, the repartee—which Dryden thought to be " the greatest grace of comedy "—is skilful and amusing. Unfortunately, there was a serious sub-plot—the play is a tragi-comedy—and long afterwards Cibber cut this part out and amalgamated the comic scenes with those of the *Maiden Queen*, calling the result *The Comical Lovers*.

The play was a great success, and the downcast players had reason to be grateful to Dryden. His next two plays—he was working at top-speed in 1672-3—were not so successful ; indeed they were very inferior productions. *The Assignation or Love in a Nunnery*, a comedy, is in fact carelessly written and dull. Moreover, there were those who saw in it an oblique criticism of the Duke of York who had recently announced that he was of the Roman faith. In the epilogue the author denies this, saying that they have been " cozene'd " who expected :

> That to please the malice of the town
> Our poet should in some close cell have shown
> Some sister, playing at content alone.

Amboyna, which followed, is even duller ; it is a revival of the story of the Amboyna massacre, furbished up into a play with the intention of stirring up popular feeling against the Dutch. But in fact it raised not anger but a laugh, as a versifier shows in this verse printed the same year in *Covent Garden Drollery :*

> But when fierce critics get them in their clutch,
> They're crueller than the tyrannic Dutch ;
> And with more art do dislocate each scene
> Than in Amboyna they the limbs of men.

Two successive failures gave Dryden pause, and there were other causes for being displeased. A rival, a brilliant young man in his early twenties had appeared to challenge Dryden's pre-eminence on the stage. This was Elkanah Settle, the boy wonder who while still at Oxford had written an heroic play, *Cambyses*, first acted by the Duke's Company when its author was only 18. He had followed this with another heroic play, *The Empress of Morocco*, first acted in 1669 by the ladies and gentlemen of the Court at Rochester's instigation and then transferred for a phenomenally successful run at the Duke's Theatre in July, 1673. The prologue for the performance at Court in 1669 had been written by John Sheffield, Earl of Mulgrave ; for the public performance Rochester himself wrote a prologue. Further than that, when the play was printed it was decorated with six " sculptures " or cuts, an unprecedented piece of magnificence.

Apart from the threat to his —and his company's —pocket from such energetic rivalry, it seemed that Rochester was in process of transferring his patronage. Could it really mean that Rochester had forsaken him ? For quite recently in return for the adulatory preface addressed to Rochester by Dryden when *Marriage à la Mode* was printed, Rochester had paid him lavishly and had also written him— from the country where he was once again exiled from Court—a most flattering letter.

At the time, Dryden had not thought it necessary to answer, but now pleading his laziness as excuse for delay, he wrote a cheerful, friendly, yet respectful epistle, clearly intended to be a sort of reconnaissance. " You are ", says Dryden, " above any incense I can give you ". He then retails the story of the discomfiture of Buckingham when Schomberg had refused to take joint command with him of the army on Blackheath, then being prepared for the Dutch war. Upon this, Buckingham had resigned his commission.

Dryden also sent Rochester a prologue and epilogue he had recently written for a visit to Oxford by the players of the King's Company— pieces most flattering to the University :

> So, poetry which is in Oxford made
> An art, in London only is a trade

—and very lively in descriptions of recent performances in London by foreign companies :

> A French troop first swept all things in its way ;
> But those hot Monsieurs were too quick to stay :
> Yet, to our coast, in that short time, we find
> They left their itch of novelty behind.
> Th'Italian merry-andrews took their place,
> And quite debauch'd the stage with lewd grimace . . .
> For love you heard how amorous asses bray'd,
> And cats in gutters gave their serenade . . . .

He sends them, he tells Rochester cynically and confidingly, to show him " how easy 'tis to pass anything upon an university, and how gross flattery the learned will endure ".

Tentatively, he ends : " I dare almost promise to entertain you with a thousand bagatelles every week, and not to be serious in any part of my letter, but that wherein I take leave to call myself your Lordship's

Most obedient servant
John Dryden ".

But there was no answer and this strengthened Dryden's suspicions. Moreover Settle not content with his success, nor with the fact that when *The Empress of Morocco* was first printed he was allowed to add after his name the words " Servant to His Majesty " (which more correctly belonged to Dryden), refers slightingly in his dedication to the Earl of Norwich to the failure of *The Assignation*, and to Dryden as " a fawning scribbler ".

This Dryden, already nonplussed by Rochester's vacillation, unwisely allowed to anger him ; he gave vent to his anger in a pamphlet, in collaboration with Shadwell and a younger dramatist, " Starch " Johnnie Crowne (so called on account of the unalterable stiffness of his cravats). The pamphlet is called *Remarks upon the Empress of Morocco*. It is lively but unsubtle, describing Settle as " an animal of a most deplored understanding, without reading and conversation : his being is in twilight of sense, and some glimmering of thought, which he can never fashion either into wit or English ". Settle replied and, as Sir Walter Scott aptly says, Dryden gained no more by his dispute than " a well-dressed man who should condescend to wrestle with a chimney-sweeper ".

To Rochester, the dispute signified nothing, for already his tortuous and cynical mind was again occupied. He now dropped Settle, and took up Crowne. Through Rochester, Crowne, a mediocre poet, was asked to write a masque for the ladies and gentlemen of Court to act for their private amusement, and this too was an insult to Dryden, for that was part of his function as Poet Laureate. The masque, *Calisto*, was successful and ran thirty nights ; so Crowne, too, had his Rochester-inspired moment of success.

Having made it, Rochester, in his fantasy, hastened to break it. Crowne was dropped, and Rochester used his influence to build up another very young dramatist of quite a different stamp. This was Thomas Otway, a sentimental and romantic person, whose own life was perhaps more tragic than even his best play, *Venice Preserv'd*. Otway had come up from Oxford, and got a part in a play, but was so nervous that he was hissed from the stage. In the meantime he fell violently in love with the actress Mrs. Barry (whom Rochester had trained for the stage), but his love was not returned ; it was this that caused him a few years later to join the army, and it was this strong and repressed affection, perhaps, which gives still to *Venice Preserv'd* and to *The Orphan* their peculiarly lachrymose and sentimental tone. He died, of a broken heart and starvation, at the age of 33.

That was after Rochester had dropped him, too. But at the moment, by his practised methods of " puffing ", Rochester ensured the success of Otway's play, *Don Carlos*. The somewhat feckless Otway was innocently grateful, referring in the preface to " the unspeakable obligations I received from the Earl of R., who, far above what I am ever able to deserve from him, seemed almost to make it his business to establish it in the good opinion of the King and his Royal Highness ; from both of which I have since received confirmations of their good-liking of it ".   In the same preface, probably at the behest of Rochester, he spoke slightingly of Dryden, saying that the Poet Laureate had said : " I'gad, he knew not a line in it he would be author of ".

Long after Otway was dead, Dryden paid tribute to his power to move the passions ; but he did not care for him as a man ; even when shortly afterwards they were both working together in the Tory interest, he found it difficult to become friendly with the unhappy young man.

But Otway, too, paid the penalty of Rochester's patronage.   Scarcely had he offered his lush tribute than Rochester lampooned him un-mercifully in the *Session of the Poets* :

> Tom Otway came next, Tom Shadwell's dear zany,
> And swears for heroics he writes best of any ;
> ' Don Carlos ' his pockets so amply had filled,
> That his mange was quite cured, and his lice were all killed.
> But Apollo had seen his face on the stage,
> And prudently did not think fit to engage
> The scum of a playhouse for the prop of an age.

To Dryden, this final twist of Rochester's humour confirmed his suspicion that his former patron was temperamentally unstable, if not a little mad, and that hopes of his generosity were more than outweighed by the dangers inherent in his favours.

ii

But now in the middle years of the decade, and still almost imper-ceptibly, a change was coming over Dryden. It was not that his *hubris* was less pronounced, nor that he gave up the pursuit of worldly success ; his flattery was as extravagant as ever, and his desire for praise as great.   But the " moments of truth " became more frequent, and to forget them more difficult ; increasingly he felt the desire to remain in his room at home with his books ; he dined out rather less frequently ; an itch took him to write something for himself rather than for the theatrical public, something of which he might be proud.

The idea of an epic passed vaguely through his mind ; often he returned to *Paradise Lost*.

By a sort of chance—but was it not rather a half-conscious desire ? —during these days he found it necessary to visit the author of *Paradise Lost*. Dryden had been called on to provide a play for a Court performance at the marriage of the King's brother, James, Duke of York, to Mary of Modena ; he had been unable to think of a subject, and his thoughts had seemed to be *guided* towards *Paradise Lost*, as though unable to escape. He could not pretend even to himself that such material appeared on the face of it as suitable for dramatic treatment, but—he simply could not think of anything else.

So one sunny afternoon the Poet Laureate, a letter of introduction in his pocket from Edmund Waller, walked north from the Strand towards the home of the blind poet in Bunhill Fields. The old Republican greeted him civilly, and they chatted for some time of poetry, old and new, Milton telling him that " Spenser was his original ". Dryden observed the old man closely and curiously, trying to see behind the gentle façade the man who had thundered for Cromwell and then against him, pursuing always an inward vision of the right and the wrong ; trying to see, too, the lighthearted author of *L'Allegro,* the lover of three women, the mighty poet of *Samson Agonistes* and the two *Paradises*. One thing he noted with surprise— a little thing but very revealing : this was the old poet's exaggerated pronunciation of the letter " R ". This, in his opinion—he told Aubrey about it later—was the sure sign of a satirical wit. But—was Milton a satirist *manqué ?* There were indeed satirical strokes in *Paradise Lost* in the portrayal of the debate in Hell of the fallen angels. It was difficult to get to the bottom of the matter, but it gave Dryden food for thought.

Now it was necessary to mention the reason—or was it the excuse ? —for his visit. Dryden explained that he had a great admiration for *Paradise Lost*—the old man was visibly pleased — and hoped for permission to dramatise it and render its blank verse into rhyme. At this the dim eyes turned to the tiny window which he could only faintly discern, the lips had a slightly cynical line as he thought to himself of the words he had written so many years before—" the invention of a barbarous age to set off wretched matter and lame metre ", that was how he had referred to rhyme. What did it matter now? He was old and tired and wise, so he said: " Well, Mr. Dryden, it seems you have a mind to tag my points, and you have my leave to tag 'em, but some of 'em are so awkward and old-fashioned that I think you had as good leave 'em as you found 'em ".

And so Dryden left him, with the calm changeless smile of the old, neglected poet indelibly on his memory. He did tag the lines but the play, The State of Innocence, was never even performed ; it was not that there were not good lines in it, but that, in the end, it was felt that the fall of man was hardly the right subject for wedding celebrations. Eventually Dryden published it, and even there ill-luck followed, for the critics seized upon it, and tore to pieces such lines as :

> Seraph and cherub, careless of their charge,
> And wanton, in full ease now live at large ;
> Unguarded leave the passes of the sky,
> And all dissolved in hallelujahs lie.

As one critic rudely but amusingly remarked : " I have heard of anchovies dissolved in sauce ; but never of an angel dissolved in hallelujahs." There were other critics who saw too much of the coquette in Eve (even in the state of innocence), and this really hurt Dryden, for it forced him to the realisation that by too much playing with the pitch of the Restoration stage he had become defiled.

The State of Innocence was altogether an unhappy venture for his peace of mind, for in addition to these things, he had as a pure act of kindness allowed a young man called Nat Lee, a failed actor and now author of ranting plays, to write prefatory verses to him to be printed in front of The State of Innocence : these verses, referring to his having refined the ore of Milton, grated on him severely. He knew he hadn't and that he couldn't.

Yet the idea of writing something worth while remained, and an epic was what he had in mind. He began to make notes for a possible epic on the theme of Edward the Black Prince subduing Spain (he had considered and rejected the subject of King Arthur) ; but he discovered that, as the idea gripped him, he was neglecting his other work—the work by which he lived. Was it perhaps possible—he said it at first with bated breath—that the King in whose favour he felt he stood so high—would he perhaps give him money enough to exist for a few months without working at the theatre so that he could write his epic ? After all, it would " chiefly be for the honour of my native country ".

But he feared himself to mention it to His Majesty, for fear of being thought immodest and presumptuous—in this after all his deepest feelings and hopes were concerned ; it was no light matter of a new play. He did, however, summon up enough courage to mention it to his friend, Dorset, telling him that he had already written several " beautiful episodes, which I have interwoven with the principal design, together with the chiefest English persons ; wherein after Virgil and Spenser, I would have taken occasion to represent my living friends and patrons of the noblest families, and also shadow'd the events of future ages, in the succession of our imperial line ".

Dorset did mention it to the King and also to the Duke of York, both of whom encouraged the idea, but they did not seem to understand—or probably they did not wish to understand—that Dryden needed from them rather more than encouragement. Perhaps they hinted that some day such help might be possible, for Dryden hoped for some time that they would assist him, referring to " the unsettledness of my condition ". But nothing happened, and Dryden's hopes waned ; in the preface to *Aureng-Zebe,* he now publicly asks Dorset to " stir up that remembrance in His Majesty ", for " As I am no successor to Homer in his wit, so neither do I desire to be in his poverty, I can make no rhapsodies, nor go on begging at the Grecian doors, while I sing the praises of their ancestors ". But as though knowing now that the result of his appeal was a foregone conclusion he adds : " For my own part, I am satisfied to have offered the design ; and it may be to the advantage of my reputation to have it refused me ".

But now, as though to make up for his disappointment, Dryden plunges again into the study of pure poetry with an obstinate determination. Another chance meeting took place which focused his attention on certain technical aspects of verse which he had previously and unaccountably overlooked—and still more days are spent at home in Long Acre rather than in the theatre or the tavern.

The chance meeting was with Sir George Mackenzie, a voluminous writer, not only on legal and historical matters which were his

province—he later became Lord Chancellor of Scotland—but also of
heroic romances and a poem called *Celia's Country House*. He was a
man of somewhat pompous manner and not without snobbishness.
Seeing the Poet Laureate one afternoon in Will's, he approached him
civilly enough, telling him that he had certain ideas on poetry which
he wished to convey to him. He was a man of consequence, and
Dryden, though prepared for boredom, could not be rude to him, so
Sir George started, and went on and on and on. There seemed to be
no stopping him, and Dryden was barely awake in his chair when
something Sir George said in his orotund voice struck him sharply.

" Have you, Sir," Sir George was saying, his fingers tapping Dryden
lightly on the knee, " have you considered the question of ' *turns* ' in
poetry ? Do you not think, Sir, ever to imitate such ' *turns* ' as they
are employed in the verse of Mr. Waller and Sir John Denham ?"

Dryden hadn't, indeed, considered " turns ", though he knew what
they were ; they were plays upon words and expressions by the
repetition of a phrase in adjacent lines but in a different sense. An
example, he thought, was from Ovid's *Metamorphoses* :

> Heu ! quantum scelus est, in viscera, viscera condi !
> Congestoque avidum pinguescere corpore corpus ;
> Alteriusque animantem animantis vivere leto.

When Dryden managed to escape the verbose Sir George—a
"noble wit of Scotland " he afterwards gratefully called him—he
went home and began to search the poets for other examples. In
Milton he could find none (though, as Scott points out, they exist), nor
in " the darling of his youth ", Cowley. But he found them in
Spenser, in Virgil, in Tasso ; and the French modern poets, he afterwards wrote, judged " turns " to be " the first beauties : delicat et bien
tourné are the highest commendations which they bestow on somewhat which they think a masterpiece ".

From Dryden's point of view the study of " turns " was no mere
idle pursuit. It was all part of the movement towards making poetry
smooth, correct and polished. This aim was encouraged greatly by
the example of the French critics whom Dryden now read with
avidity. When he wrote his *Essay of Dramatic Poesy* he had been well
up in Sarrasin, Le Mesnardière, Chapelain and Corneille ; now he was

eagerly reading Rapin, Le Bossu and Boileau, whose *Art Poétique* and translation of Longinus came out in France in 1674. He also made the acquaintance of Montaigne's essays and his *Apology for Raymond Sébond*, then at the height of their popularity in England.

But the effect of his poetic studies and the new ideas from France scarcely affect his work until after *Aureng-Zebe*, which marks a turning point.

iii

Aureng-Zebe is another rhymed, heroic play, the last one he wrote. It was written when his thoughts had already turned elsewhere, and only in the hope that it would repeat the financial success of his other heroic plays. But he took great care over it, and it contains some of his finest poetry in this manner. There is, indeed, still plenty of insensitive rant in it, as in Nourmahal's speech after she has taken poison :

> I burn, I more than burn ; I am all fire.
> See how my mouth and nostrils flame expire !
> I'll not come near myself—
> Now I'm a burning lake, it rolls and flows

and so on. There is still a villain, consumed with the power-lust, who, when asked by Nourmahal not to spare *Aureng-Zebe*, replies : " I'll do it to show my arbitrary power ".

Yet compared with the *Conquest of Granada*, the play is almost domestic in tone ; the characters are more carefully and lifelikely drawn ; Dryden altered the historical background of the story and modelled his plot on the *Mithridate* of Racine. As Dr. Johnson put it : " The personages are imperial, but the dialogue is often domestic, and therefore susceptible of sentiments accommodated to familiar incidents ".

Aureng-Zebe is full of famous passages where a grave tone of moralising takes the place of the familiar bombast, and which often fuses into poetry. Such are the famous lines :

> How vain is virtue which directs our ways,
> Through certain danger to uncertain praise !
> Barren and airey name ! thee Fortune flies,

With thy lean train, the pious and the wise.
Heaven takes thee at thy word without regard
And lets thee poorly be thy own reward.
The world is made for the bold impious man,
Who stops at nothing, seizes all he can.
Justice to merit does weak aid afford,
She trusts her balance and neglects her sword.
Virtue is nice to take what's not her own ;
And while she long consults, the prize is gone.

Dryden can now vary the rhythm at will—largely by the disposition of the stress ; his management of the couplet is already beyond anything his predecessors conceived. It is interesting to note a tendency to enjambment—interesting because as George Saintsbury justly observed, " when this tendency gets the upper hand, a recurrence to blank verse is, in English dramatic writing, tolerably certain ". Indeed in the prologue to the play Dryden confirms that he is growing weary of rhyme :

Not that it's worse than what before he writ,
But he has now another taste of wit ;
And to confess a truth, thought out of time,
Grows weary of his long-loved mistress, rhyme.
Passion's too fierce to be in fetters bound,
And nature flies him like enchanted ground :
What verse can do, he has performed in this,
Which he presumes the most correct of his ;
But spite of all his pride, a secret shame
Invades his breast at Shakespeare's sacred name :
And when he hears his god-like Romans rage,
He, in a just despair, would quit the stage ;
And to an age less polished, more unskilled,
Does, with disdain, the foremost honours yield.

In the preface, he goes further (for reasons which we have already seen) saying that not merely is he tired of rhyme in plays, he is tired of plays altogether : " I desire to be no longer the Sisyphus of the stage ; to roll up a stone with endless labour, which, to follow the proverb, gathers no moss, and which is perpetually falling down again. I never thought myself very fit for an employment, where many of my

predecessors have excelled me in all kinds ; and some of my contemporaries, even in my own partial judgment, have outdone me in
comedy . . . ."

Changeableness was indeed one of Dryden's most marked—and in a
way most likeable—characteristics. He does not mind contradicting
himself, or admitting that he has changed his mind—and changing
again if he feels like it, as we may gather from the fact that two
years after his farewell to the stage he produced his greatest
play.

Flexibility of thought he had raised to a principle ; it arose naturally
from his detestation of dogma and fanaticism ; now at this stage in his
career his own views leaned increasingly on the statement of them that
he had found in Montaigne. In the same dedication to *Aureng-Zebe*,
he writes—and it is so typical of his mature spirit—of the criticism
made by some ladies of the unnaturalness of the conduct of Indamora
and Melesinda in the last act :

" Those Indian wives are loving fools, and may do well to keep themselves in their own country, or, at least to keep company with the
Arrias and Portias of old Rome : some of our ladies know better
things. But, it may be, I am partial to my own writings ; yet I have
laboured as much as any man, to divest myself of the self-opinion of an
author ; and am too well-satisfied of my own weakness, to be pleased
with anything I have written. But, on the other side, my reason tells
me, that, in probability, what I have seriously and long considered
may be as likely to be just and natural, as what an ordinary judge (if
there be any such among those ladies) will think fit, in a transient
presentation, to be placed in the room of that which they condemn.
The most judicious writer is sometimes mistaken, after all his care ;
but the hasty critic, who judges on a view, is full as liable to be deceived
. . . Yet, after all, I will not be too positive. Homo sum, humani a me
nihil alienum puto. As I am a man, I must be changeable : and
sometimes the gravest of us all are so, even upon ridiculous accidents.
Our minds are perpetually wrought on by the temperament of our
bodies, which makes me suspect, they are nearer allied, than either our
philosophers or school-divines will allow them to be. I have observed,
says Montaigne, that when the body is out of order, its companion is
seldom at his ease. An ill dream or a cloudy day, has power to change

this wretched creature, who is so proud of a reasonable soul, and make him think what he thought not yesterday ".

Montaigne's spirit, indeed, fitted Dryden's mature mind like a glove. But Montaigne was not his only reading. In the two years after the staging of *Aureng-Zebe*, he again plunged into an orgy of reading, not only the French critical authors, but English divines such as Hooker, and such works of a sceptical, fideist nature as *Religio Medici* (which in a note to his translation of Persius he was able later to paraphrase from memory). He re-read the ancient English poets ; he pottered a bit with the preparation of an English prosodia, " containing all the mechanical rules of versification ". And more and more he found his thoughts dwelling on a final farewell to the sordidness—or so he now felt it to be—of his career as dramatist and his recurrent need to write lush panegyric ; what he had written in one of his prologues to be spoken in Oxford was more than mere flattery of his learned audience :

> Oft has our poet wished, this happy seat
> Might prove his fading Muse's last retreat :
> I wonder'd at his wish, but now I find
> He here sought quiet, and content of mind ;
> Which noiseful towns and courts can never know . . . .

A year or two later he put the matter even more bluntly in a prologue for his friend, Nat Lee's, play *Caesar Borgia* :

> Th'unhappy man, who once has trail'd a pen,
> Lives not to please himself but other men ;
> Is always drudging, wastes his life and blood,
> Yet only eats and drinks what you think good . . . .

From this time forward Dryden pined to escape. Very late in life looking back he regretfully observed that " the same parts and application which have made me a poet might have rais'd me to any honours of the gown ". He wished to be a schoolmaster or a parson—indeed there were rumours that he was to be Provost of Eton. Again years later, in 1687, a news-letter stated : " A mandate is said to be gone down to Oxford for Mr. Dryden to go out Doctor of Divinity, and also that he will be made President of Magdalen College ". But he did not escape by such means.

Temporary escapes, of course, there were. He did leave London for some months in the summer and early winter of 1677, and his visits to the country became more frequent and prolonged.

Yet he could not—and in some moods did not wish to cut himself off entirely from his life in London. Some "sparkles" of his pride persisted in spite of his growing self-knowledge and his increasing devotion to poetry for its own sake. He still enjoyed his fame—being pointed out as Dryden the Poet Laureate, and having his opinions taken seriously, even solemnly, by younger writers. Even more flattering were the attentions paid him by his social superiors, the noble Lords and courtiers with whom he dined and wined.

So when Mulgrave asked him to read and "correct" a long poem he had written called *An Essay upon Satire* he could not refuse—the flattering imputation was too much for him. But life is fuller of irony than fiction, and it was the part he played in the writing of this poem that was to lead to the event which marked the final extinction of his *hubris*.

Mulgrave's poem dealt satirically with various well-known people of the time with whom he was at loggerheads ; he was always dabbling in politics, and was engaged, for instance, in trying to make bad blood between the Duke of York and his nephew, the young Duke of Monmouth. He was also cross with the King himself, and among many others with the Earl of Rochester. Rochester, indeed, he had challenged to a duel, but Rochester refused to fight. This was due to some curious twist in his mental composition, not to cowardice, for his bravery in the war against the Dutch was well known.

But by now Dryden also had a bone to pick with Rochester. The doubts he had had for some time about Rochester's attitude to him had been confirmed by a poem called *Allusion to Horace, the tenth satire of the first book*, which though circulated anonymously was known to be by the splenetic Earl. In this poem, Rochester had written :

> Dryden in vain tried this nice way of wit ;
> For he, to be a tearing blade, thought fit
> To give the ladies a dry bawdy bob,
> And thus he got the name of poet Squab . . .
> But does not Dryden find even Jonson dull ?
> Beaumont and Fletcher uncorrect, and full

> Of lewd lines, as he calls them ? Shakespeare's style
> Stiff and affected ? To his own the while
> Allowing all the justice that his pride
> So arrogantly had to these denied ?
> And may I not have leave impartially
> To search and censure Dryden's works, and try
> If these gross faults his choice pen doth commit,
> Proceed from want of judgment, or of wit ?
> Or if his lumpish fancy does refuse
> Spirit and grace to his loose slattern muse ?

Rochester was a close if malignant observer.   What caused Dryden to cringe was that he recognised the truth of the picture Rochester drew of him—but it was a picture of himself at the beginning of the decade.   He had already altered, but he had not so completely freed himself from pride as to be able to laugh at the picture of his arrogance.

It would have been beyond human nature if he had not seized the opportunity to alter some of Mulgrave's lines so that they became as biting and malignant and far more effective than those of Rochester. The couplets he inserted in Mulgrave's poem are as powerful as any he wrote in *Absalom and Achitophel* :

> Mean in each action, lewd in every limb,
> Manners themselves are mischievous in him.

Soon after making his contribution to Mulgrave's poem, Dryden was off again to the country, with a comfortable seat in the North-ampton coach, and glad to see the last dingy hovel of Smithfield fade into the distance, and the green fields and fresh air welcoming him. But news had got round of Mulgrave's poem—though none had yet seen it—and of Dryden's hand in it; indeed many believed the Poet Laureate to be the sole author.   Rochester certainly did, and as Dryden's coach trundled slowly northwards he was writing to a friend : " You write me word that I'm out of favour with a certain poet, whom I have admired for the disproportion of him and his attributes.   He is a rarity which I cannot but be fond of, as one would be of a hog that could fiddle, or a singing owl.   If he falls on me at the blunt, which is his very good weapon in wit, I will forgive him if you please ; and leave the repartee to Black Will with a cudgel ".

But retribution was to fall on Dryden not from Rochester but from quite a different source ; and it was to fall on him for these lines in Mulgrave's poem—lines which ironically enough Mulgrave himself had written :

> Nor shall the royal mistresses be named,
> Too ugly, or too easy to be blamed ;
> With whom each rhyming fool keeps such a pother,
> They are as common that way as the other ;
> Yet sauntering Charles between his beastly brace
> Meets with dissembling still in either place,
> Affected humour or a painted face.
> In loyal libels we have often told him,
> How one has jilted him, the other sold him :
> How that affects to laugh, how this to weep ;
> But who can rail so long as he can sleep ?
> Was ever prince by two at once misled,
> False, foolish, old, ill-natured and ill-bred ?

CHAPTER SEVEN

New Directions

IT WAS high summer when Dryden arrived in his native district, and
his first task was to put the affairs of his estate at Blakesley in order.
He did this without raising the rents, thus earning the regard of his
tenants. Although there was a general rise of prices during the latter
part of the century, the rents remained the same throughout Dryden's
ownership. The chief tenant, a man called Harriot, always said that
Dryden was " the easiest and the kindest landlord in the world " ; he
became, indeed, a kindly tradition in the Harriot family, so that the
grandson of Dryden's tenant recalled his grandfather's sentiments and
repeated them for the benefit of the inquiring Mr. Malone in the
eighteenth century.

Dryden was staying at the house of his cousin, Sir Thomas Elmes, at
Lilford near Oundle ; once again he was able to enjoy long mornings
fishing, the uneventful decorum of country-house life, the pleasures of
a quiet library facing smooth lawns. And—his wife was not with
him ; she had a noisy family of lusty boys to look after ; it was a
relief (for a time) to get away from their boisterousness, too.

Dryden turned now with renewed vigour and interest—it was as if
the colour of life had been renewed in him—to writing. He had
brought with him from London a book given him by the author, a
young barrister called Thomas Rymer ; this was *The Tragedies of the
Last Age (considered and examined by the practice of the ancients and by the
common sense of all ages)*. Dryden read it with great enthusiasm,
although it was in some sense a refutation of his own early *Essay of
Dramatic Poesy*. He described it generously in a letter from Lilford as
" the best piece of criticism in the English tongue, perhaps in any other
of the moderns . . . . If I am not altogether of his opinion, I am so in
most of what he says ". (The letter was to his old friend Dorset,
and so also contains some interesting data about a Miss Tresham,

known as the " flower of Northamptonshire ".)   Later in life Dryden
had a literary quarrel with Rymer, but in the end forgave him.

As Dryden read Rymer's book, he began to make notes on the end-
sheets ; the notes have been preserved through the efforts of Jacob
Tonson, soon to become Dryden's regular publisher, but the book
itself was destroyed in a fire at Sir John Hawkins's house in the
eighteenth century.   The notes were largely incorporated by Dryden
in the essay on tragedy he prefixed to his play *Troilus and
Cressida*.

What he found so interesting in this work was that Rymer knew
intimately the ancient Greek plays of which Dryden was somewhat
ignorant, and he learned that the view of tragedy slowly forming
in his mind under the influence of his reading of the new French
critics and of his own changing outlook had the support of Aeschylus,
Sophocles and Euripides.   Rymer, of course, being somewhat of
a pedant, went too far : in exalting the Greek dramatists as models
to be imitated by all following playwrights, he condemned the
tragedies of Shakespeare and most of the Elizabethans as crude and
brutish.   He had certain fixed rules by which he measured all tragedies;
he was concerned entirely with plot, and not at all with character-
drawing or style.

But he argued logically and his learning was great and wide.
Dryden, sunning himself in Elmes's quiet arbour, wrote on the flyleaf :
" My judgment on this piece is this, that it is extremely learned, but
that the author of it is better read in the Greek than in the English
poets ; that all writers ought to study this critique, as the best account
I have ever seen of the ancients ; that the model of tragedy he has here
given us is excellent, and extreme (sic) correct ; but that it is not the
only model of all tragedy, because it is too much circumscrib'd in
plot, characters, etc ; and lastly, that we may be taught here justly to
admire and imitate the ancients, without giving them the preference,
with this author, in prejudice to our own country ".

Rymer—and the sun and fresh air—made Dryden think of original
work ; not an epic—there were more pressing needs—but of a play
that should somehow express his new mood and sum up the thoughts
of the last two or three years.

A play it had to be for other, practical reasons.   This was one of the shadows that kept crossing his mind at Lilford ; he had after all made a contract with the King's Company to write three plays a year for them, and he hadn't done so. Indeed he had not written a single play since *Aureng-Zebe* two years before in 1675.

His excuse was that the company had not really kept its side of the contract. He was still receiving a certain amount of money from them, but his " share and a quarter " had diminished greatly from its original £300-£400 a year. This was partly due to the excessive cost of rebuilding the theatre—for which no one could be blamed— but partly also to the growing dissension, greed and bad management of the company itself.

In 1675, for instance, some of the actors had given written notice that since they were getting so little profit " they were minded to give over and desist from acting ". They went on strike and refused to return until the King himself ordered them back in February, 1676.

Previously Dryden had complained of this sad state of affairs, and because they recognised the justice of his complaints the company had not pressed him to fulfil his contract. However, a contract was a contract, and Dryden now began to write—he had planned it some months before—what was to be his last play for the King's Company (which some years later was amalgamated with the Duke's Company), and his greatest tragedy. *All for Love* was first presented in December, 1677, soon after Dryden returned to London ; its success was very great, and Dryden as well as having his normal gain as a sharer was allowed also the takings of the " third day ", usually given only to outside dramatists.

All for Love, Dryden tells us, was the only play he wrote for himself ; as such it is fair evidence of his mind in its serious and poetic mood. As usual, however, he did not take an original subject ; he chose the story of Antony and Cleopatra which had not only been used by Shakespeare, but also in dramatic form by Samuel Daniel, Thomas May and Dryden's friend, Sir Charles Sedley. Their example, Dryden says, gave him confidence—and, in a limited sense, he always needed that—" to try himself the bow of Ulysses amongst the crowd of suitors ".

But having said that, it must be stated at once that the play is pure Dryden ; he indeed claimed that " in my style I have professed to imitate the divine Shakespeare ", disencumbering himself from rhyme because he felt that here (though not necessarily as a principle) it was not fitting to his subject.

Dryden's play, totally unlike Shakespeare's, can yet stand comparison with *Antony and Cleopatra.* It obeys the principle of the unities, and the poet claimed that " the unities of time, place and action are more exactly observed than perhaps the English theatre requires ". The compactness that results is necessary to the spirit of Dryden's play, which is a sober, even sombre, study—and study is an important word here, for it correctly suggests Dryden's attitude to the situation between Antony and Cleopatra—of Love, Friendship and Honour.

In his treatment of these themes he gives evidence of great psychological insight, expressed in poetry of freshness and gravity, and his stagecraft is masterly ; the play remains eminently actable (in some ways much more actable than Shakespeare's).

Dryden realises that the themes are those of high tragedy ; but the impression left behind by it is not that of the greatest Greek tragedy, but rather that of a more nervous Seneca. He deploys a new, unique blank-verse style of great variety, owing nothing to Shakespeare and very little to Milton. It is fluent yet never flabby, easy and variable, a perfect example of the middle-style, slightly above the ordinary language of the theatre of his time but never obviously archaic nor merely sententious.

Critics have pointed to the beauty of many of the lines taken out of their context, for example :

> While within your arms I lay,
> The world fell mould'ring from my hands each hour.

or,

> . . . . my whole life
> Has been a golden dream of love and friendship.

But what has not always been remarked is the dramatic appropriateness of these poetic lines as they occur ; to their innate freshness, there is added the dramatic surprise—that the speaker should have seen suddenly and exactly *thus* at that moment in the play. It is Antony, too, and not merely his auditors, who sees with sudden shock in the last act that indeed his life *has* been a golden dream of love and friendship—but that all along there has been another hidden aspect of it which now overtakes him like a Nemesis.

Deft and admirable as the closing scenes of the tragedy are, dramatically fine as are the early scenes between Antony and Ventidius (which Dryden himself thought the best), it is really the fourth act that shows the triumph of the master craftsman's art.   Here the interest is not merely sustained—and the fourth act is notoriously dangerous to dramatists—but in the comings and goings of Dolabella, Antony's old friend (whom nature has cast " in so soft a mould "), of Cleopatra and of Alexas and Ventidius, one gets an impression of the dark and obscure coils lying behind all human action, and of man's impotence before Fate.   Fate in a subtle sense is the underlying theme of the play, and it is eventually Alexas, the subtle eunuch adviser of Cleopatra, who expresses this not only for himself but for the play and for us :

> I've saved myself, and her.   But, Oh ! the Romans !
> Fate comes too fast upon my wit,
> Hunts me too hard, and meets me at each double.

And so we are led into the dark splendour of Antony's :

> We two have kept its homage in suspense,
> And bent the globe on whose each side we trod,
> Till it was dented inwards : Let him walk
> Alone upon't ; I'm weary of my part.
> My torch is out ; and the world stands before me
> Like a black desert at the approach of night . . . .

ii

Refreshed by his days in the country, and cheered by the success of his play, Dryden now plunged with renewed energy into town life, and the pursuit of fortune.   But political matters began to intrude. When he printed *All for Love* in March, 1678, he dedicated it to Thomas, Earl of Danby, the bluff, unscrupulous Yorkshireman who had succeeded Shaftesbury as the King's chief adviser in 1673, and whose aims were to promote the Protestant interest at home and abroad, to keep on friendly terms with the Dutch and break with the

French and, above all, to suffer " no diminution nor embezzlement of the revenue either in England or Ireland ". But unfortunately Charles seldom took his advice from a single source, and in any case a break with France was no part of his real desires.

Danby, in fact, was at the end of his power when Dryden dedicated *All for Love* to him, and was shortly to pay the penalty for his master's equivocation by a term in the Tower ; but he was in a sense the founder of the Court party, and thus the Tory party, and it was not mere flattery when Dryden wrote to him : " Moderation is doubtless an establishment of greatness ; but there is a steadiness of temper which is likewise requisite in a minister of state : so equal a mixture of both virtues that he may stand like an isthmus betwixt the two encroaching seas of arbitrary power and lawless anarchy . . . Both my nature, as I am an Englishman, and my reason, as I am a man, have bred in me a loathing to that specious name of a republic : that mock-appearance of a liberty where all who have not part in the government are slaves. . . The nature of our government above all others is exactly suited both to the situation of our country and the temper of the natives : an island being more proper for commerce and defence than for extending its dominions on the continent ".

Whether this was Danby's view or not, it was certainly Dryden's. Nor was his reference to a Republic merely recalling the days of the interregnum ; once more the situation looked like getting out of hand, and it seemed that Charles might yet die in exile rather than in Whitehall. For this was the year of the Popish Plot " revealed " by the two clergymen, Titus Oates and Israel Tonge. Though the plot was a fake, it forced the Duke of York into exile, destroyed the Cavalier Parliament and raised the Earl of Shaftesbury as Opposition leader to the pinnacle of his power. In February next year, 1679, took place what has been called a " panic " election, fought for the first time on party lines ; it resulted in a defeat for the Court. In May the parliament thus elected voted for the Exclusion Bill, laying down that if the King were to die without lawful issue he was to be succeeded by the next Protestant heir ; then the King dissolved Parliament.

George Savile, Marquess of Halifax, known to history as " the great trimmer ", came to power accompanied by the egregious Sunderland and for a short time by Arthur Capel, Earl of Essex. The Opposition began to build up a new Protestant hero and rival to the Duke of York —the handsome illegitimate son of the King, James Scott, Duke of Monmouth. So popular did he become that the King, though he loved him, was compelled for the sake of his brother's succession to deprive him of his posts, including that of commander-in-chief.

Trouble was evidently brewing, but it so far concerned Dryden only as a spectator, if a worried one. For again he had his own more personal worries. There was the question of money. Dryden decided that he must make an attempt to set his finances on a new level of stability and he plunged again into writing for the theatre. First came a comedy called *Limberham*, designed, Dryden said, to be a satire on " the crying sin of keeping ". It was, however, a failure. Then came a joint play with his friend, Nat Lee ; this was *Oedipus*, and it proved more successful, though it had been difficult to write since Lee was already suffering from the attacks of insanity which finally removed him from dramatic activity. To this succeeded Dryden's adaptation of *Troilus and Cressida*, the play which it was at that time felt Shakespeare had left in a state of " strange imperfection " ; but the adaptation was not an outstanding production.

It was probably over money that Dryden about this time quarrelled with his old benefactor and publisher, Henry Herringman. When next year *Troilus and Cressida* was printed and published, it was by a young, and quite unknown publisher, Jacob Tonson. Dryden's only reference to Herringman after this is a contemptuous line in *MacFlecknoe* and in a poem he revised for Sir William Soame.

A much more serious quarrel, however, occurred with the members of the King's Company who, as we have seen, were on the downgrade, and Dryden gave his plays after *All for Love* to the rival Duke's Company. The company had already lost most of its best writers and it was determined to hang on to the remaining two, Dryden and Lee. So Charles Killigrew, who had succeeded his father as manager, and three of the old actors, Mohum, Burt and Charles Hart, petitioned either the Lord Chamberlain or the King, saying that, as well as breaking his contract, Dryden had also broken a promise to give them first refusal of all his plays after *All for Love*. In fact immediately after his promise he had given *Oedipus* to the Duke's Company " contrary to his said agreement, his promise, and all gratitude to the great prejudice, and almost undoing of the company, they (i.e. Lee and Dryden) being the only poets remaining to us ".

The company sought recompense such as the Duke's Company had demanded of them in a faintly parallel case concerning a play of Johnny Crowne. But apparently they were unsuccessful.

All these matters were annoying pin-pricks, but one thing at least in these months caused him satisfaction. He had made a new friend. This was John Oldham, the son of a nonconformist minister, who had been at St. Edmund's Hall, Oxford, and had come to London with a bare competency to seek fame if not fortune. Oldham had a great regard for Dryden's poems, and in his own juvenile work had imitated verses from Dryden's poem on the death of Lord Hastings and from *Annus Mirabilis* : Lord Hastings had died of smallpox, and Oldham, too, was celebrating the death of a friend from the same disease— ironically he was himself cut off in his prime by the same cause.

But much more important from Dryden's point of view (as from Oldham's) was the fact that Oldham had determined to devote himself to perfecting satirical verse, and was searching for a style and manner. Dryden had had for long a desire, an impetus, towards satire ; it was a desire into which many elements of his mind and spirit went—his deep knowledge and delight in the Latin poetry of Juvenal and Horace, his seventeenth-century interest in the appearance and character of men, not as they should be, but as they are (the impulse behind the great popularity of the " Character "), and the air of a polemical time—a time, too, when no holds were barred, and there was no law of libel.

Behind it all, one can see now, was the impulse to power ; power was indeed implicit in the satire since, as Dryden realised, a satirist could make or more usually break a man's character and reputation for ever. In Dryden himself, the satiric impulse was the obverse of the fawner and flatterer of the dedications. It was, too, an impulse that grew in strength as his pride decreased. Yet the old man who wrote to the *Gentleman's Magazine* in 1745 was only partly correct when he said : " Posterity is absolutely mistaken as to that great man (Dryden) ; tho' forced to be a satirist, he was the mildest creature breathing ... He was in company the modestest man that ever conversed ". Dryden was not *forced* to be a satirist ; but, on the other hand, it is likely on psychological grounds that a true satirist would be the most modest-seeming of men, and a new and truer modesty was slowly replacing the boldness and pride of the poet in these years.

To Dryden the artist in words the mere impulse to satire no matter from what deep sources it sprang was, however, not sufficient. Others had written satire in English, but not, Dryden considered, well ; their art had not been as developed as their desire to satirise was strong. They were too rough in their techniques, using the club rather than the rapier : Hall, Marston, Cleveland—they had thought it enough to write simply from their strong feelings and opinions, and as a result had usually sunk into diffuseness or into colloquial abuse, a verse equivalent of frothing at the mouth.

His friend Oldham's verse, on the other hand, was solid and stately, though often over-angry ; nor were his lines sufficiently polished. Writing his wonderful elegy on his friend, four years later, Dryden kindly excuses this, saying (though he knew and showed it to be untrue) that satire did not require a mastery of " numbers " for " wit will shine Through the harsh cadence of a rugged line ". Yet Dryden felt that he and Oldham were in a sense cast in the same poetic mould, and they discussed their problems mutually.

There was, however, one big difference between them. Oldham was driven to satire by the strength of his convictions, and his *Satires upon the Jesuits*, though gaining much of their success from their publication shortly after the Popish Plot, represented accurately Oldham's own strongly-held anti-Catholic views. Dryden, on the other hand, believed, and openly stated as we have seen, that it was better for a man to be able to admit being in the wrong, to keep an open mind, and to be " changeable ".

Yet in the end Dryden turned this to advantage. Combined with the large, but normally well-hidden opinion of himself that we divine behind the great satires, it enabled him to take that tone which at once pleases the reader and quite submerges the subject of the satire under a gale of laughter, or in the Olympian grandeur, a little tarnished, of *Absalom*. Of course, what he said he roughly believed ; but the motivating force was not belief but artistry.

iii

In 1678, under the stimulus of his friendship with Oldham, Dryden began to seek a suitable subject to try out a kind of verse which as yet was only a nebulous vision in his mind. He was disinclined for a generalised subject such as Oldham had in his satires on Roman Catholics, or the " boyish " sort of thing Butler had done in *Hudibras*; Dryden's mind, left to itself, preferred the topical, the personal, the contemporary; there was, as Mr. Jack has well said, a " realistic bias " to his mind—a bias characteristic of much of the best Augustan poetry. His eye picked out details of everyday life as a magpie seizes bright objects.

The poem he contemplated was to be written for his own amusement —and that of his immediate friends—so that he felt himself free in his choice of subject; and that freedom led him to that big, boozy, crude contemporary of his whose career had been like the shadow of his own, Tom Shadwell. Shadwell, said to base his mode of life on that of the great Ben Jonson, had had, as we have seen, his successes as a comic writer; he and Dryden had never been great friends, though they had worked together on the pamphlet against Settle. But recently Shadwell had made many slighting references to Dryden : there had been some hits in the preface and prologue to his comedy, *The Virtuoso*, a satire on the Royal Society first produced in 1676; the prologue to his *Sullen Lovers* had had a fling at heroic plays, of which Dryden had been the greatest practitioner; and finally in February, 1678, Shadwell in a dedication of his *History of Timon of Athens* to the Duke of Buckingham had pointedly recalled *The Rehearsal*.

Well, there was his subject, and his justification; but Dryden was not angry with Shadwell—it was much more that, from the artistic point of view, he provided exactly the subject he needed. As Butler had done, Dryden would show this comic character in an imaginary course of incidents, but the treatment would be the mock-heroic not the burlesque of *Hudibras*.

Shadwell was to be shown as the monarch of the kingdom of dullness, and the poem, *MacFlecknoe*, begins by describing the demise of the former occupant of the throne, Richard Flecknoe, who, as we noticed, may have had a hand in the earliest attacks on Dryden, but

who was renowned for his bad poetry—Marvell had lampooned him
while Dryden was still at school.   Flecknoe, said to have been an
Irish priest, died in 1678, the year Dryden wrote his poem.

But details of the real Flecknoe, even the real Shadwell, scarcely
matter for Dryden's poem stands on its own feet, living in the immense
gusto of its humorous contempt and the pleasure of its magnificently
varied verse.   It is based on a joke—a literary joke, that Shadwell was
a fit subject to be described in heroic style—and it lives in literary
history for the single and excellent reason that it is funny.   As Mr.
Jack says : " A small man is not in himself a ridiculous object : he
becomes ridiculous when he is dressed up in a suit of armour designed
for a hero ".   That is the basis of the poem.

There is, indeed, direct satire in it as well, for example in the latter
part of Flecknoe's second speech—

> Nor let thy mountain belly make pretence
> Of likeness ; thine's a tympany of sense.
> A tun of man in thy large bulk is writ,
> But sure thou'rt but a kilderkin of wit.

In the magnificent and immortal opening—" All human things are
subject to decay "—and in such lines that bubble with laughter, as
Flecknoe's speech to his successor, Shadwell, Dryden is clearly enjoying himself enormously :

> Let father Flecknoe fire thy mind with praise
> And uncle Ogleby thy envy raise.

Flecknoe ends his speech :

> He said : but his last words were scarcely heard ;
> For Bruce and Longvil had a trap prepared,
> And down they sent the yet declaiming bard.
> Sinking he left his drugget robe behind,
> Borne upwards by a subterranean wind.
> The mantle fell to the young prophet's part,
> With double portion of his father's art.

It was, for Dryden in 1678, a magnificent *tour de force ;* but it was
the beginning for him also of a new style of writing, a new command
of the couplet, which appears in his verse, not merely in the famous

satires, *Absalom* and *The Medal*, but also in *The Hind and the Panther* and even towards the end of his life in his *Fables*. It was an enchanting thing Dryden had invented in the verse of *MacFlecknoe* ; and in various forms it dominated English poetry—its characteristic cadence, its subtle attack—until at least the middle of the eighteenth century.

MacFlecknoe was not printed until 1682 (and even then without Dryden's name) when it appeared as part of a political warfare, the publisher inserting the words after MacFlecknoe " Or, a satire upon the true-blue Protestant poet T.S. " But, of course, it circulated widely before then, and was read with delight by half the Court, including no doubt the King himself. Shadwell himself heard of it, but did not reply to it in print until the year of publication when he produced *The Medal of John Bayes*. Then, too, he wrote his rather pathetic letter to Sir Charles Sedley : " But sure he goes a little too far in calling me the dullest, and has no more reason for that than for giving me the Irish name of Mack, when he knows I never saw Ireland till I was three and twenty years old, and was there but four months . . . (he) says in another pamphlet that to his knowledge I understand neither Greek nor Latin, though in Bury School in Suffolk and Caius College in Cambridge, the places of my youthful education, I had not that reputation, and let me tell him he knows the contrary ".

No doubt Dryden did ; but Shadwell was complaining in reality, and perhaps justly, against having a particular sort of immortality forced upon him, and against immortality there can be no redress.

In the summer of the next year, 1679, Dryden again left town, and did not come back until the autumn. His work in the country that summer was not so vastly productive, but he did write his " Remarks on the grounds of criticism in tragedy " which he gave to the printer on his return and which was attached to his *Troilus and Cressida*.

In this he was summing up, after digesting, what he had read in Rymer, in Boileau, Rapin and Bossu, and also what he had discovered for himself in writing *All for Love*. He now supports the simple, classical sort of plot, pointing out the errors of tragi-comedy, and con-demning extravagance of language and the use of " wit " in dramatic speeches : he points to his own Montezuma as being faulty in this respect. In the prologue to the play he puts these words into the mouth of Shakespeare's ghost ; though he had in the past criticised

Shakespeare—and why not ?—the words are those of a man who, in trying to adapt Shakespeare, had discovered the very strength and unalterable sinews of the master.   Shakespeare speaks :

> Now, where are the successors to my name ?
> What bring they to fill out a poet's fame ?
> Weak, short-lived issues of a feeble age ;
> Scarce living to be christened on the stage !
> For humour farce, for love they rhyme dispense,
> That tolls the knell for their departed sense.

★   ★   ★   ★

In November, 1679, Mulgrave's *Essay on Satire* was being handed round in Court and tavern society generally, but without its author's name.   Again Dryden's name was mooted and accepted by many. Some found support for the conjecture in the rumour that Dryden was at odds with the Court because his pension had fallen into arrears (and that was true enough).   What was also true was that Mulgrave had fallen into further disfavour at Court, possibly in part because he had cast ambitious eyes on the Lady Anne (later Queen), daughter of the Duke of York : next year he was sent to relieve Tangier and it was said that he had been given a leaky ship in the hope that he would perish.   His reasons for now making public his satire on Charles and his mistresses were clear enough ; but it was doubts of his capacity for writing such a poem that inclined the majority to believe that Dryden was the real author.

A week before Christmas, 1679, Dryden left Will's Coffee House late in the evening to return to his house in Long Acre.   As he passed through Rose Street, which was dark and deserted, three men jumped out of hiding and began to beat him with staves.   He defended himself as well as he could and called out for help.

Doors opened and lights showed and the attackers fled into the obscurity of the alleys nearby.   A reward was offered in the papers for their apprehension, but they were never brought to justice. Dryden was not, it appears, very severely hurt—save in his pride : it was the final blow to his *hubris*.

Luttrell, a contemporary, noted in his *Brief Historical Relation of State Affairs,* that the attack was thought to have been carried out by thugs

under the orders of the Duchess of Portsmouth, one of the King's
mistresses referred to in Mulgrave's satire. Some thought it was
Rochester's doing ; but the famous letter about " Black Will with a
cudgel " was written, as we have seen, some years before. A letter by
Rochester in November, 1679, while again asserting that Dryden
was the author of the satire, contained no threats. Dryden at least
does not appear to have suspected Rochester ; he referred to him in
his writing later, but without any such imputation.

It may be added that the satire was not published until after the
revolution in 1688. Then it was referred to as being by Dryden ; but
it is correctly ascribed in 1705, and, revised by Alexander Pope, it
appears in the sumptuous, posthumous edition of Mulgrave's works in
1723.

Mulgrave himself was by no means disposed to allow Dryden to be
thought the author. When the attack took place he was in Tangier,
but on his return he wrote these unequivocal lines in his *Essay on Poetry*,
published in 1682 :

> The Laureate here may justly claim our praise,
> Crown'd by MacFlecknoe with immortal bays ;
> Tho' prais'd and punish'd for another's rhymes,
> His own deserve as great applause sometimes.

Dryden's enemies, of course, never forgot " Rose Alley ", nor
allowed him to ; that age was accustomed to the sight of violent
attacks on public figures, and for the most part found in it only
material for laughter and jibe.

But soon the Rose Alley affair was pushed to the back of the
public mind by the threatening political situation. Shaftesbury,
backed by his Green Ribbon club in the City, had tried to indict the
Duke of York as a " popish recusant " ; behind him were many of the
old Republicans of Commonwealth days. At the end of 1680, the
Commons whose Exclusion Bill had been defeated in the Lords
through the brilliant advocacy of Halifax, impeached Lord Stafford ;
and the aged Catholic nobleman was executed in December.

In January, the King dissolved Parliament, and on the advice of
Laurence Hyde, the second son of Clarendon, reopened negotiations
with France ; he proposed to abandon his treaty with Spain in return

for a further grant of money, the ever-pressing need.   At the same
time he summoned a new parliament to meet in Oxford—away, he
hoped, from the threat of the London mob, managed by Shaftesbury.
But the Whigs flocked there in armed bands and parliament was again
dissolved.

Yes, the affair of Rose Alley was swallowed up by matters more
important to the nation at large—but not to Dryden. To him his
beating was a symbol of a change in himself, which had for some time
been slowly preparing and now occurred and emerged full-blown
through the sudden and violent shock of an attack by hired thugs.
Resting in his bed in Long Acre, he felt that another chapter in his life
was ended : a chapter in which there had been too much pretence, too
much self-deception, too much arrogance.   He was *not*, he knew now,
the important person he had felt himself to be in the great houses where
he had drunk with great Lords and had been unwisely boastful, believing that he was, indeed, accepted by them as an equal.   He never really
had been accepted, for—so his thoughts ran—it was certainly some
nobleman who had ordered this beating, and it was a sign of his being
put very firmly in his place that it had been done by hired thugs.
Otherwise, it would have been a challenge to a duel.

Well, all that was ended : he was a poet, and nothing else, and this
attack was perhaps designed by providence to show him that plainly.
But he already knew it, had known it since *All for Love* and *Mac-
Flecknoe*. He wished nothing more, and now, humbled yet sure, he
began to think of the poems he would write in the peace of his room,
or better still in the country round Northamptonshire . . . .

But now again fate played an ironic trick, for as Dryden happily
pondered a life of near-retirement, events were about to push him,
not merely to the forefront of that high life which he was rejecting,
but on to the very middle of the stage of English history.

CHAPTER EIGHT

The Master Poet

DRYDEN WAS NOW fifty years old; his face was slightly plumper, but his complexion was pink and fresh as ever. His fine, wavy hair was almost grey, and his large eyes had again that sleepy look that his contemporaries remarked on when he first arrived in London.

At 50, his appearance was less haughty than it had been at 40, and more comfortable. His friends and acquaintances found him more tolerant, easy of approach, friendly, but still rather slow and quiet in his conversation. He had in repose that withdrawn look associated with scholars and thinkers, but his lips and eyes were capable of breaking into a delightfully ingenuous smile.

His mode of life had changed little. When he was in London, he rose early and spent the morning working; in the afternoon he commonly went to Will's, and then on to dine with one of his friends. He normally retired fairly early and read for a while before sleeping.

His reading had become, with the course of the years, much wider in range; pure literature no longer held his entire attention. Now that his family was growing up, it was easier to settle down to his books; his eldest son, Charles, had become a King's Scholar of his father's old school, Westminster, in 1681, still under the same Dr. Busby, now an old but by no means decrepit man; his second son followed in the next year; and in 1683 his third son, Erasmus Henry, went to the Charterhouse.

Lady Elizabeth had aged more noticeably than her husband, and had become querulous, much given to *tête-à-têtes* with old friends and quarrels with the servants; she had never been interested in letters, and was even less so now. That side of Dryden's life was a nullity, but neither partner proposed to do anything about it; it was a closed book—it opened only when it was necessary to discuss matters

I

concerning the children and then sometimes led to dispute. More-over, Lady Elizabeth did not share her husband's delight in the country, she seldom accompanied him on his visits to the country houses of his friends.

His friends meant a great deal to Dryden in these years, and until the end of his life ; they were in a way a substitute for the pleasures of converse that he might in different circumstances have enjoyed at home. The friends included not merely noblemen like Dorset, Mulgrave and Laurence Hyde, the new Earl of Rochester, but well-known men of letters such as Sir George Etherege, Wentworth Dillon, Earl of Roscommon, and younger men such as Thomas Southerne, for whose first play Dryden wrote a prologue and an epilogue, Nahum Tate, Henry Dickinson (the translator of Father Simon's *Histoire Critique du Vieux Testament*), and especially, John Oldham.

At Will's, where all these men came, Dryden also met other out-standing men of his time, with whom he was on merely nodding terms. But now it was becoming the habit in any dispute on literary matters to seek—and accept—the judgment of Dryden : such was the case over the question whether a certain two lines in Creech's transla-tion of Lucretius were or were not grammatical. Dryden drew up his judgment in the form of a letter, which has been preserved. He was already becoming the grand panjandrum of letters.

Of course, like any man worth his salt, he had his enemies ; and very bitter they could be. Most of them Dryden did not now bother about ; others he took his revenge upon by immortalising them, the most equitable of all forms of revenge.

Though the clouds of civil disorder and political strife seemed to all men to be looming large in 1680, Dryden was still not directly con-cerned with them. He occupied himself with polishing the translation in verse of Boileau's *The Art of Poetry*, recently made by another of his friends, Sir William Soame, Bart., of Suffolk. Tonson tells us that Dryden kept the MS for six months and made considerable alterations in it. He rewrote, for instance, the first few lines of Canto IV :

> In Florence dwelt a doctor of renown,
> The scourge of God and terror of the town,
> Who all the cant of physic had by heart,
> And never murder'd but by rules of art . . . .

> Colds, at his presence, would to frenzies turn,
> And agues like malignant fevers burn . . . .

Dryden himself had recently been in the hands of the doctors, for he began at this time to suffer from the gout and other aches and pains. He may slyly have got his own back on some heavy-handed medico in this passage, though later he had cause to be grateful to his doctors.

A much more interesting suggestion Dryden made to Sir William was that he should substitute for the names of the French authors in Boileau's poem those of English poets. Sir William agreed and thus enabled us to glimpse Dryden's mature opinions on some English writers.

Dryden recommends, for instance, that from Butler should be learned the " buffoning grace ". Noisy bombast should be avoided —in particular (and at this point Dryden's mind must have been thinking of his own boyish dreams and poetical predilections on the banks of the Nene) do not, like Dubartas, as translated by Sylvester, " bridle up the floods, and periwig with wool the baldpate woods ". Spenser is commended as teaching the " noble art " of " writing well ". Then comes an interesting reversal of opinion :

> Then Davenant came ; who with a new found art,
> Chang'd all, spoil'd all, and had his way apart :
> His haughty muse all others did despise,
> And thought in triumph to bear off the prize,
> Till the sharp-sighted critics of the times,
> In their mock-Gondibert, expos'd his rhymes . . .
> This headstrong author, falling from on high,
> Made following authors take less liberty.

The congenial character of Davenant, the man, had faded, leaving only his poetry behind and that, to Dryden's mind in the early eighties, was thin enough. His views on Waller, however, had suffered no such diminution :

> Waller came last, but was the first whose art
> Just weight and measure did to verse impart . . . .
> His happy genius did our tongue refine,
> And easy words with pleasing numbers join . . .

Such matters occupied Dryden pleasantly enough in the early months of the new decade, and he would have been content to let a few years slide by in this civilised way. But with a family of boys ready for expensive education on his hands, money again became a problem : the falling off in income from the theatre had taken place most inopportunely.

It was the need for money which drew him half-unwillingly into the orbit of political propaganda where since 1678 there had been a furious paper warfare. From both the Tory and the Whig side, pamphlets and books on the prime questions of the day flooded the bookstalls. Political periodicals began to appear and English party journalism, in the form which we still know it, was born.

Dryden entered the field with a play, *The Spanish Friar,* which though a tragi-comedy is in effect an anti-Catholic and anti-Whig satire. It was well received, and indeed held the stage for 100 years, but its immediate success was no doubt due to the fact that it canalised the fear and hatred of Roman Catholicism, then at its height owing to the discovery of the Popish Plot. A " protestant play for a protestant patron ", wrote Dryden in his dedication to Lord Haughton. But the play—though reversing his recent dictum about the need for tragedy to be single-minded—is full of life, tricked out with charming songs (for which Purcell wrote the music), and has the lively character of Friar Dominic to keep it going. Pedro thus speaks of him :

> I met a reverend, fat, old gouty friar—
> With a paunch swollen so high, his double chin
> Might rest upon it ; a true son of the church ;
> Fresh-coloured, and well-thriven on his trade—
> Come puffing with his greasy bald-pate choir,
> And fumbling o'er his beads in such an agony
> He told them false, for fear. About his neck,
> There hung a wench, the label of his function,
> Whom he shook off, i'faith, methought, unkindly.
> It seems the holy stallion durst not score
> Another sin before he left the world.

The Prologue is lively, too—as often with Dryden it is amusingly rude to the audience, referring to them as " fickle sovereigns " ; speaking of fashion he writes :

> So we, grown penitent, on serious thinking,
> Leave whoring and devoutly fall to drinking.
> Scouring the watch grows out-of-fashion wit :
> Now we set up for tilting in the pit . . . .

He adds, thinking of the Rose Alley " ambuscade " of which all his audience knew :

> A fair attempt has twice or thrice been made,
> To hire night-murth'rers, and make death a trade.
> When murther's out, what vice can we advance,
> Unless the new-found pois'ning trick of France ?
> And when their art of ratsbane we have got,
> By way of thanks, we'll send them o'er our Plot.

Political matters soon took an even more serious turn, and Dryden was called on to help in his capacity of Historiographer Royal. He produced a reasonable, but scarcely remarkable, prose-pamphlet called " His Majesty's Declaration defended in a letter to a friend ; being an answer to a seditious pamphlet called a letter from a person of quality to his friend concerning the King's late declaration touching the reasons which moved him to dissolve the two last parliaments at Westminster and Oxford ".

But it was obviously not here that his value really lay. In prose propaganda he was easily excelled by such men as L'Estrange and Minshull. His patrons, such as Ormonde, Halifax and Hyde, who all had the ear of the King, knew *MacFlecknoe* and brought it to Charles's eye. So it was that in 1681 the King himself asked Dryden to write a poem satirising the Whig party and in particular its leader, Shaftesbury, already arrested and soon to be impeached.

The poem was the first part of *Absalom and Achitophel*, and appeared in November, 1681, a few days before judgment was to be delivered in Shaftesbury's trial on charges of high treason.

ii

Absalom and Achitophel was written for the King and so it is as consummate a work of tact and artifice as it is of art. For Dryden was faced by several tricky problems in obeying His Majesty's command. He was not merely to lampoon the King's enemies, he was also to praise the King's friends—each in precisely the relationship in which he stood towards His Majesty. And the situation was by no means clear-cut ; it was ever liable to change of emphasis and shape. Moreover, one of the principal persons to be represented was the Duke of Monmouth whose illegitimacy was as undeniable as his paternity ; he, as we have seen, had become the protegé of the Whigs, and in particular of Shaftesbury, and he was the Whig " candidate " for the succession against the Roman Catholic Duke of York. But his father still loved him : there was the difficulty. His character could not be subject to an all-out attack—yet his actions were to be condemned.

There was another consideration. For such a work to be politically effective, it had to present not merely a series of pictures of personalities, but the whole situation and in as serious a manner as it deserved ; the situation, after all, could easily deteriorate to the point where political struggle became civil war.

Compared with this, the problems facing Dryden in writing MacFlecknoe had scarcely existed. To complicate matters still further, no solution could safely be offered ; that depended on events themselves, and Charles's solutions were always ad hoc, unpredictable, and frequently involved a change of front liable to make a political satirist look ridiculous if not to involve him in most serious personal consequences.

The right style and the right machinery were, therefore, essential. It was clear that it had to be an elevated style, for the persons and events with which he was to deal were for the most part aristocratic and weighty ; the thing was not a tavern brawl, nor the main persons Shadwells or Settles.

How an Old Testament machinery first suggested itself to Dryden we do not know ; it may have been because Charles from the early days in his reign had called himself David (and the theme had been taken up by the poets, including Dryden himself), partly for the witty comparison, and partly because contemporary preachers, such as Joseph Hall, were in the habit of drawing the moral from the story of King David of letting no man " look to prosper by rebellion ". In conjunction with this, the analogy between David's indulgent attitude to his son and that of Charles to Monmouth must have appeared irresistible.

The use of Biblical stories for allegorical and satirical works was not, of course, new. A satire upon the Catholics called *Achitophel or the Picture of a Wicked Politician* by Nathaniel Carpenter, published in 1627, has been mentioned in this connection : but much more recently—in 1679—had appeared John Caryll's *Naboth's Vineyard : or the Innocent Traitor*, which was a Catholic attack on the judges in the trial of the Popish " plotters ". This, moreover, employed heroic couplets in an heroic style with reflective and exclamatory passages. In 1680, also, as Mr. Jack has pointed out, there was D'Urfey's *The Progress of Honesty* in which the rebellion of " the long-ear'd rout " against " Titus the Second, a King of ' god-like clemency ' " is described. In this Shaftesbury's followers are given names drawn from the Old Testament— Shaftesbury himself is sometimes called Hophni, sometimes Achitophel, and always " chief advocate for Hell ".

All these gave Dryden clues, but it was his own superb judgment and wit which eventually produced the immortal poem itself—that and the determination not to fuss or fume, but to make every line and couplet tell and at the same time please the reader.

The poem begins by most skilfully leading up to the fact that Absalom (Monmouth), one of the principal characters, was illegitimate ; in order to excuse his father's seeming immorality, Dryden wittily sets his tale at a time " before polygamy was made a sin " when " man on many multiplied his kind ", and when it was laudable —according to the *piety* of those times—for a king to impart " his vigorous warmth " to wives and slaves alike, thus scattering his Maker's image throughout the land.

Of this progeny Absalom was the bravest and the most beautiful. Absalom's feats in war, and his failings, are mentioned, as well as his father's fondness for him, unruly though he sometimes was.

Then the favourite subject of the rebellious British is introduced :

> The Jews, a headstrong, moody, murm'ring race,
> As ever tried th' extent and stretch of grace ;
> God's pampered people, whom, debauch'd with ease,
> No King could govern, nor no God could please.

Reference is made to their changeableness, and how, after the death of Saul (Cromwell) and the retirement of foolish Ishbosheth (Richard

Cromwell), they had brought back banished David—and now again wished to change.

But—not *all* Israel wanted another change ; it is only the " factious crowd ". The sober citizens " Well knew the value of a peaceful reign ", having looked backwards " with a wise affright ".

Next come the Jebusites (Roman Catholics) and the Popish Plot— " Bad in itself, but represented worse ". The plot failed but it had a most dangerous consequence for it stirred up faction, and it enabled leaders, who felt themselves ignored or overlooked, to play upon public disorder and to attempt to oppose the power of the throne for their own selfishly ambitious ends.

At this point, Dryden introduces his first and perhaps most famous character—Achitophel (Shaftesbury) himself. And here—if it had not been observed in the opening lines—is the epic, almost Miltonic touch : Dryden himself said that satire was undoubtedly a species of heroic poetry, and *Absalom* was partly Dryden's substitute for the poem that he never wrote, in his age perhaps could not write, on the Black Prince :

> Of these false Achitophel was first ;
> A name to all succeeding ages curst :
> For close designs and crooked counsels fit . . .

The lines are famous ; but how carefully in his characterisation Dryden trod the line between the too personal (which in this case might have eventually been dangerous) and the too general (the fault of a great deal of British satire both before and after Dryden). Achitophel is Shaftesbury, but he is also any politician of a certain type of any time.

But apart from all that, these words slide into the mind with that rightness and sense of illumination found in all great poetry. Indeed some lines are scarcely felt as satire, for the poetic effect outweighs the satiric intent :

> And all to leave what with his toil he won,
> To that unfeather'd two-legg'd thing, a son ;
> Got, while his soul did huddled notions try ;
> And born a shapeless lump, like anarchy.

There is about those lines a smell of decay, of some steamy obscenity being hidden in sordid hugger-mugger ; there is an air of mediaeval scholasticism about " the fiery soul, which, working out its way, Fretted the pigmy body to decay ", and more than a suspicion of the arcane, astrological, slightly perverted mediaeval superstitions which we connect with the name Nostradamus.

Shaftesbury, we are told, " usurp'd a patriot's all-atoning name " ; but—and here Dryden's cleverness not only as political writer unwilling to go too far, but also as a character writer—Shaftesbury must be praised for his work as Lord Chancellor " Swift of despatch and easy of access " : if only he had been content to serve the Crown thus !

But he seizes the opportunity of the Plot to stand " at bold defiance with his prince "—assisted, we are again informed, by the notorious British instability :

> For govern'd by the moon, the giddy Jews
> Tread the same track when she the prime renews ;
> And, once in twenty years, their scribes record,
> By natural instinct they change their lord.

Achitophel, however, needs a chief, for he knows his power depends too largely on the whim of the Crown :

> That kingly pow'r, thus ebbing out, might be
> Drawn to the dregs of a democracy.

So he addresses himself in persuasive speeches to the subversion of Absalom (Monmouth). He appeals to Absalom to head the rebels. In the course of this sly and cunning attempt, Achitophel is made to dismiss—as some of his party in fact did—the theory of the divine right of kings :

> And nobler is a limited command,
> Giv'n by the love of all your native land,
> Than a successive title, long and dark,
> Drawn from the mouldy rolls of Noah's ark.

Dryden and the more intelligent Tories knew, of course, that the divine right of kings was an idea thought up in Renaissance times to assert the power of the King over the Pope. In the course of time it had, indeed, gained mystical accretions, but it was still primarily of value in defending the supreme rights of the King against the extreme

Roman Catholics, particularly the Jesuits, who still insisted on the Pope's supremacy, and against Republicans who believed that kings held power by the will of the people, and could equally be deposed by them.

Achitophel, in fact, is suggesting to Absalom that, though he cannot be king by divine right, he may be by the acclaim of the people. Absalom is by no means impervious to Achitophel's suggestions ; and Dryden in part excuses him :

> Desire of pow'r, on earth a vicious weed,
> Yet, sprung from high, is of celestial seed :
> In God 'tis glory ; and when men aspire
> 'Tis but a spark too much of heavenly fire.
> Th'ambitious youth, too covetous of fame,
> Too full of angel's metal in his frame,
> Unwarily was led from virtue's ways . . . .

But he does not succumb immediately ; in reply to Achitophel, he speaks of David's mildness and of his uncle's rights to the throne ; but then Achitophel speaks again, and he is subtly introduced with the heightened, inverted, Miltonic words :

> Him staggering so when hell's dire agent found . . .

The suggestion of Achitophel's connections with the powers of evil serves to excuse Absalom's ultimate surrender.

Dryden turns to consider the men of more moderate opinion—some of them patriots still in their hearts—who are nevertheless in favour of " laying honest David by ". Among them are the old Parliament-arians and, worst of all, the Sects :

> A numerous host of dreaming saints succeed,
> Of the true old enthusiastic breed.

But most of them, Dryden continues with an air of great fairness, are men who :

> . . . think too little, and who talk too much.
> These out of mere instinct, they knew not why,
> Ador'd their fathers' God and property :
> And, by the same blind benefit of fate,
> The Devil and the Jebusite did hate ;

> Born to be sav'd, even in their own despite,
> Because they could not help believing right.
> Such were the tools . . . .

But there were others, and among them some princes of the land.
Chief amongst these was Zimri (Buckingham)—

> A man so various, that he seem'd to be
> Not one, but all mankind's epitome :
> Stiff in opinions, always in the wrong ;
> Was everything by starts, and nothing long ;
> But in the course of one revolving moon,
> Was chymist, fiddler, statesman and buffoon :
> Then all for women, painting, rhyming, drinking,
> Besides ten thousand freaks that died in thinking.
> Blest madman, who could every hour employ,
> With something new to wish or to enjoy !
> Railing and praising were his usual themes ;
> And both (to show his judgment) in extremes :
> So over-violent, or over-civil,
> That every man, with him, was God or devil.
> In squandering wealth was his peculiar art :
> Nothing went unrewarded but desert.
> Beggar'd by fools, whom still he found too late.
> He had his jest and they had his estate.
> He laughed himself from court ; then sought relief
> By forming parties, but could ne'er be chief ;
> For, spite of him, the weight of business fell
> On Absalom and wise Achitophel :
> Thus, wicked but in will, of means bereft,
> He left not faction, but of that was left.

The " character " of Achitophel had been straightforwardly evil in
the epic mode ; Zimri is from the first shown in a different, " lower "
way, and eventually is openly made fun of through wit and epigram.
This, too, exactly fitted Zimri's individual position *vis-à-vis* His
Majesty ; it is a perfect example of the principle of decorum.

Ten years later in his *Discourse concerning Satire* Dryden described
his aim and methods thus : " The character of Zimri in my *Absalom*
is, in my opinion, worth the whole poem : 'tis not bloody, but 'tis

ridiculous enough ; and he for whom it was intended was too witty
to resent it as an injury. If I had rail'd, I might have suffer'd for it
justly ; but I manag'd my own work more happily, perhaps more
dext'rously. I avoided the mention of great crimes, and applied myself
to the representing of blind sides, and little extravagancies : to which
the wittier a man is, he is generally the more obnoxious ".

After Zimri comes a number of minor portraits including the famous
Shimei (Slingsby Bethel, the Republican and London magistrate), and
Corah (Titus Oates). They are contemptuous—a mixture of irony,
scorn and name-calling.

Before turning to the loyal characters, Dryden again refers to the
foolishness of the Israelites (British) and then makes his great statement
on the dangers of constitutional change—a statement in which his mind
and his feelings were equally engaged :

> Nor is the people's judgment always true :
> The most may err as grossly as the few ;
> And faultless kings run down, by common cry,
> For vice, oppression, and for tyranny . . . .
> Yet, grant our lords the people kings can make,
> What prudent man a settled throne would shake ?
> For whatsoe'er their sufferings were before,
> That change they covet makes them suffer more.
> All other errors but disturb a state,
> But innovation is the blow of fate.
> If ancient fabrics nod, and threat to fall,
> To patch the flaws and buttress up the wall.
> Thus far 'tis duty : but here fix the mark,
> For all beyond it is to touch our ark.

This was the maturity of Dryden's thought ; it is the epitome of
that political sobriety which being stubbornly opposed to all change
yet insists that there are certain principles which it is dangerous to
abandon. It is that view of politics which is essentially opposed to
politics, believing that life is of more importance.

Turning to the men who are loyal to the King, Dryden names the
chief of these as being, to his mind, the Duke of Ormonde—" large
was his wealth, but larger was his heart ". Jotham (Halifax), and
Hushai (Hyde, Earl of Rochester) are others " honourably " mentioned.

None of these characters, of course, can stand by the great Achitophel and Zimri—partly from the nature of things (Satan is a more interesting figure than God in *Paradise Lost*), partly because, as Dryden admitted, he found it much easier to write severely than otherwise.

The poem ends with a versification of Charles's declaration of his reasons for dissolving the last two parliaments, and the optimistic couplet :

> Once more the Godlike David was restor'd,
> And willing nations knew their lawful lord.

As he remarked in the preface to the poem : " The conclusion of the story I purposely forbore to prosecute . . . . The frame of it was cut out but for a picture to the waist ; and if the draft be so far true, 'tis as much as I design'd ".

Absalom and Achitophel is without doubt a great poem ; its lines are those of a master-craftsman and they are made to last.   Yet if we ask what *sort* of a poem it is, it is not easy to reply.   For it is a series of pictures in which, though action is often hinted at, nothing really occurs ; there are touches of the epic and the narrative about it and it contains passages of undoubted satire.   But it is neither wholly epic, nor satire, nor narrative.   One can only conclude somewhat lamely that *Absalom*, artfully constructed for the purposes of an ephemeral political propaganda, is a poem *sui generis*.

There is one more point to be made.   As a propaganda poem, we should not expect to find in it much personal revelation, although it is revealing enough of the craftsman and of the writer's own political ideas.   Yet in one respect the poem is very personal indeed, for from beginning to end there is a strong undercurrent of sexuality combined, though less often, with a tendency towards blasphemy.   Both—and this is the significant point—are irrelevant to the matter of the poem and to its success.

Sexuality is, of course, inherent in the opening lines of the poem, and there it has its uses and its relevance, but in accounting for Absalom's beauty and bravery, it is not really necessary to suggest that it may have been due to the fact that his father " got him with a greater gust ".   We hear continually of " warm excesses ", of the Devil " pimping ", of things " debauched ", of " womens' lechery ", of a " pleasing rape ", of the " well-hung Balaam " ; petitioners are " unsatiate as the barren womb " and the images of loathsome diseases are plentiful.

Blasphemy, too, is never very far away.   In *Annus Mirabilis*, it may be recalled, Dryden changed certain blasphemous lines in later editions, and here we have the lines :

> For Shimei, though not prodigal of pelf,
> Yet lov'd his wicked neighbour as himself.
> When two or three were gathered to declaim
> Against the monarch of Jerusalem,
> Shimei was always in the midst of them . . . .

This coarseness of mind can be detected also in the Prologue and Epilogue Dryden wrote in the same year (1681) for " the first play acted at the Theatre Royal this year " ; it is also visible in the satires that followed the first part of *Absalom and Achitophel*.

There is, of course, a great amount of sexuality and bawdiness in many of Dryden's comedies, though this may partly be due to the fact that that was what his audiences liked.   But the special, somewhat obsessional, coarseness of the satirical poems is not quite the same sort of thing, and it must have a different explanation.

When Dryden began his series of political poems, he was fifty, a time when men often feel a waning of their physical powers without, however, a corresponding diminution of their sexual desires ; the tone of the undercurrents in these satirical poems is that of impotence, or fear of impotence, accompanied by an irrepressible upsurge of unhealthy images.   So far the explanation is simple and even trivial.   But it becomes more difficult when we consider that *Religio Laici*, written in the middle of this satirical period, shows no trace of sexual undercurrent.

It may be that the coarseness of the satires is an expression of his inner distaste for his task, perhaps for his subject, too, and that when he is writing a poem to please himself his mind is free and clear.

But whatever Dryden's private thoughts about his work, the public was delighted with *Absalom*.   Its success was enormous, seven London editions being required within two years, and two more in Dublin.

A few days after its publication, Shaftesbury was acquitted of high treason—as it was almost certain would happen in view of the Whig bias of the London grand jury which tried him ; this did not affect the propaganda value of *Absalom* which served as useful a purpose in cheering up the Tories as it did in damaging the Whigs.

But the Whigs, of course, rejoiced at the acquittal, and Shaftesbury had a great popular triumph. A medal was struck to commemorate the acquittal ; on one side it bore the face of Shaftesbury, drawn by George Bower, and on the other a view of London, the Bridge and the Tower with the sun rising over it and about to disperse a cloud. The word " Laetamur " appeared round the edge. It was fashionable for the Whigs to wear this at their breasts.

The Tories felt that some counter-blast should be made, and none better to make it than John Dryden. Indeed it was rumoured that the King himself had suggested the idea to his Poet Laureate, saying: " If I was a poet, and I think I am poor enough to be one, I would write a poem on such a subject, in the following manner ". *The Medal* was published less than four months after *Absalom*.

The Medal is prefaced with a broadly amusing " Epistle to the Whigs " : " You might have spared one side of your medal ", he suggests, " the head would be seen to more advantage if it were plac'd on a spike of the Tower . . ." He deals contemptuously with various replies that had been made to *Absalom*, and asks only that the same writers should be employed in answering *The Medal*. More seriously he says : " Give us leave to enjoy the government and the benefit of laws under which we were born, and which we desire to transmit to our posterity . . . . All good subjects abhor the thought of arbitrary power, whether it be in one or many ; if you were the patriots you would seem, you would not at this rate incense the multitude to assume it . . ."

Indeed, *The Medal* is in general a much more personal, and far graver, poem than *Absalom* ; part of it is devoted to a further attack on Shaftesbury ; the more interesting part is an argument against Whiggism and Republicanism, in which again we hear the warning voice :

> Our temp'rate isle will not extremes sustain
> Of pop'lar sway or arbitrary reign.
> But slides between them both into the best
> Secure in freedom, in a monarch blest.

Once more his mind dwells on sexual and depraved or diseased imagery ;

> But what thou (Shaftesbury) giv'st, that venom still remains ;
> And the pox'd nation feels thee in their brains.
> What else inspires the tongues and swells the breasts
> Of all thy bellowing renegado priests . . .

Here are no striking characters and few witty lines—except perhaps "Chop up a minister at every meal". But grimness and cynicism there is in plenty :

> For what can power give more than food and drink,
> To live at ease and not be bound to think ?

And there are striking, emotive lines :

> A tyrant theirs ; the heav'n their priesthood paints
> A conventicle of gloomy sullen saints ;
> A heaven like Bedlam, slovenly and sad . . . .

The fame and grandeur of his satirical poems called forth a great number of virulent replies : most of them he ignored as they deserved to be ; one or two he replied to, devastatingly but without bitterness.

One thing, however, did upset him in this time of feverish party strife. Not without pathos, he tells us that in this year he has spoken to only four men of the opposite party : " We have been acquaintance of long standing, many years before this accursed Plot divided men into several parties : I dare call them to witness whether the most I have at any time said will amount to more than this, that *I hoped the time would come when these names of Whig and Tory would cease among us, and that we might live together as we had done formerly* . . . They have severally owned to me that all men who espouse a party must expect to be blackened by the contrary side ".

iii

Dryden valued his friendships and the easy intellectual commerce with men of varied knowledge and ideas. But it was difficult to be the greatest political satirist of the day and yet remain the hail-fellow-well-met of Will's Coffee House.

His fame and his politics did not, however, affect his relations with his family and in particular with his sons. Families have a way of existing and demanding attention despite the fluctuating fortunes of their heads. So in this *annus mirabilis*—the year of the second part of *Absalom*, the *Religio Laici*, and a play—Dryden is being worried by his young sons. John, for instance, is home from Westminster, where he is a King's Scholar, suffering from a cold and whooping-cough. He recovers only after great care and the best advice. Dryden writes to Dr. Busby : " The truth is, his constitution is very tender; yet his desire of learning, I hope, will enable him to brush through the college ".

He takes the opportunity of mentioning his eldest son, Charles, whom he hopes—with somewhat suggestive emphasis—" may also deserve some part of your good opinion, for I believe him to be of virtuous and pious inclinations ". Dryden signs himself " Your most obedient servant and scholar ".

John's mother also writes to Dr. Busby, begging a favour. After promising that she and her husband will see that John goes to church regularly while he is away from school, she writes (the spelling is her own) : " In the mean time, will you pleas to give me leave to accuse you of forgetting your prommis conserning my eldest sonn, who, as you once assured me, was to have one night in a weeke alowed him to be at home, in considirasion both of his health and cleanliness. You know, Sir, that promises mayd to women, and espiceally mothers, will never faille to be cald upon ; and thearfore I will add noe more, but that I am, at this time, your remembrancer, and allwayes, honnord Sir,

                    Your humble servant, E. Dryden "

Poor woman, she was now bereft of her sons' company, her husband was often away, and even when he was at home always occupied with his books and his writing ; she fussed and fretted and wondered whether the boys were washing their necks and changing their linen often enough. Yet perhaps she was right to be anxious about them, for they all died before her.

A few months later, Dryden's half-expressed fears were justified : Charles was expelled from Westminster—Dryden believed wrong-fully. His expulsion concerned some obscure matter of school

discipline.   Dryden writes respectfully but very firmly to Dr. Busby ;
he seeks an explanation—and a reconciliation.   Presumably he had it,
for Charles went back to Westminster and eventually proceeded to
the University.

Meanwhile, Dryden had been asked to write a sequel to *Absalom and
Achitophel*.   He had declined, partly because he felt that he had already
had his say, partly because he was now busy with *Religio Laici*.   He
agreed, however, to oversee another poet who was hired to carry out
the task.   This was the Irishman, Nahum Tate, later to become Poet
Laureate and to collaborate with Brady in a famous metrical version of
the Psalms.   Tate was on the Tory side, not very distinguished but a
capable enough versifier, his best work being *Panacea—a poem on tea*.

Dryden revised his work in the second part of *Absalom*, and also
himself wrote some lines in reply to one or two of the critics of his
political poems.   This section of the poem is amongst Dryden's
finest satirical production, for it includes his famous portraits of Settle
(Doeg) and Shadwell (Og).

Elkanah Settle, the brilliant boy of the previous decade whose first
plays had delighted the Court, had not followed up his success ;
indeed he had been reduced to writing " drolls " for Bartholomew
Fair, arranging pageants for the City merchant companies and proces-
sions, with fireworks, for the annual Whig celebration of the burning
of the Pope which had horrified Dryden when he first came to London.
Settle had also taken up with Shaftesbury, and, as one of his opponents
put it, from being " an arrant knave, a despicable coward and a
prophane atheist " he became, in the Whig propaganda counsels at
least, " a Cowley, a man of honour, a hero and a zealous upholder of
the Protestant cause and interest ".

In his rôle as " zealous upholder ", Settle unwisely tried to reply to
the first part of *Absalom and Achitophel* on, so to speak, Dryden's terms,
that is, he used the same application of scripture and tried to parody
Dryden's own lines.   Dryden himself he abuses in a long paragraph—
though innocently enough he had referred in the preface to Dryden as
" so famous an author " and to himself as " a minor poet ".

That innocence dictates Dryden's tone in his Doeg portrait.   But
the innocence becomes in Dryden's hands an almost sublime stupidity ;
and—well, Dryden enjoyed himself.

He begins prophetically : he will deal with Doeg and Og,

> Who, by my Muse, to all succeeding times
> Shall live, in spite of their own dogg'rell rhymes.

Then he launches against Settle that superb piece of comic irony :

> Spiteful he is not, though he wrote a satire,
> For still there goes some *thinking* to ill nature ;
> He needs no more than birds or beasts to think ;
> All his occasions are to eat and drink . . .

> Let him rail on, let his invective Muse
> Have four and twenty letters to abuse,
> Which if he jumbles to one line of sense,
> Indict him of a capital offence.

It is contemptuously good-humoured ; there is none of that " smear " technique he had employed a few lines earlier on Ferguson and Forbes and the Rev. Samuel Johnson, nor of that sexual-toned abuse he was so fond of :

> Can dry bones live ? or skeletons produce
> The vital warmth of cuckoldizing juice ?
> Slim Phaleg could, and, at the table fed,
> Return'd the grateful product to the bed.

But Shadwell was a different matter. Shadwell knew Dryden very well, he was and had always been a Whig, and it was natural that he should be employed by the Opposition in the wordy warfare of this time, though it is not certain which of the political pamphlets is to be ascribed to him.

It is, however, fairly certain that a poem called *The Medal of John Bayes*, which appeared in May, 1682, following Dryden's *The Medal*, is by Shadwell ; it stands out from the purely political warfare for it is largely concerned with a personal attack on Dryden himself, an attack moreover which shows an intimate personal knowledge.

There were, of course, plenty of other personal attacks on Dryden, but they use the stock charges, known to all London—his early verses on Cromwell (charges made, for example, in " An Elegy on the Usurper O.C., by the author of *Absalom and Achitophel,* published to

show the loyalty and integrity of the poet "), the ignominy of Rose
Alley, or stories repeated from *The Rehearsal*.

The Medal of John Bayes contains statements about Dryden which
are so different as likely to be in essence true. The description of Dryden
as " cherry-cheeked " is pointless as abuse, but excellent from the point
of view of a libeller who wishes to establish the verisimilitude of
other more outrageous statements.

Yes, Shadwell was a different proposition, and Dryden's response to
him is different—and magnificent : as Professor Nichol Smith says,
his portrait of Og " vibrates with contempt ; it suggests even physical
aversion ". Above all it is rollickingly funny :

> Now stop your noses, readers, all and some,
> For here's a tun of midnight work to come,
> Og, from a treason-tavern rolling home.
> Round as a globe and liquored every chink,
> Goodly and great he sails behind his link.
> With all this bulk there's nothing lost in Og,
> For ev'ry inch that is not fool is rogue :
> A monstrous mass of foul corrupted matter,
> As all the devils had spew'd to make the batter . . . .
>
> Drink, swear and roar, forbear no lewd delight
> Fit for thy bulk, do anything but write . . . .

There is a tremendous gusto in it, and a poetry equalled but never
excelled in English by Pope and by Byron.

The second part of *Absalom and Achitophel* was published early in
November, 1682—three weeks after an unauthorised publisher had
issued the *MacFlecknoe*, written four years before. It was a bad winter
for Shadwell ; but he had his revenge, and he did not wait long for it.

In October of that year was presented a political play, *The Duke of
Guise,* based on the play which Dryden had projected soon after the
Restoration but had laid aside on the advice of his friends. The play
now acted was written partly by Dryden, partly by his friend Nat Lee.
Based on a parallel between the situation in England and the Guisard
League in France, it had been held up in performance by Arlington,
the Lord Chamberlain, until the King had so far suppressed his love for
Monmouth (" the Duke of Guise ") as to have him arrested ; the Duke

of York, recalled from his exile in Scotland in March, was now the greatest single influence on his brother—and against Monmouth, his nephew and rival. Moreover, the Whigs had sustained a fatal blow in the September when the King's partisans managed at last to secure the election of Tory sheriffs : Shaftesbury himself fled and died in the next January in Holland. The Rye House Plot was to come, but the worst dangers were over.

When next year Dryden defended his play from Whig attacks, he denied that any parallel existed between his Duke and Monmouth ; this was plainly untrue. What was, however, true was that Dryden certainly drew no parallels between the King and Henry III of France as various pamphleteers pretended.

In the " Vindication " of his play Dryden again refers to Shadwell, who had joined in the attacks on *The Duke of Guise* : " Og ", he jovially says, " may write against the king, if he pleases, so long as he drinks for him, and his writings will never do the government as much harm as his drinking does it good ; for true subjects will not be much perverted by his libels, but the wine-duties rise considerably by his claret ". He then retails the story of Shadwell's drunken fall down a tavern stair " where he broke no ribs because the hardness of the stairs could reach no bones ; and for my part, I do not wonder how he came to fall, for I have always known him heavy : the miracle is, how he got up again. I have heard of a sea captain as fat as he, who, to escape arrests would lay himself flat upon the ground and let the baillifs carry him to prison if they could . . . ." Thus, as Mr. Van Doren says, did Dryden cheerfully shed the venom of his enemies.

CHAPTER NINE

The Labyrinth of Life

YET BEHIND all this joviality and behind the virility and cleverness of the satiric couplets of the year 1682, there was, as we have seen, another Dryden—the Dryden who resented being involved in politics, and who wanted above all to clarify his own ideas on life and on the meaning of life, and philosophy and religion. It has been said that *Religio Laici*—which was published in November 1682—is an example of the way politics and religion were intertwined in the seventeenth century ; it is true enough, but the calm, easy reflectiveness of the poem is also a picture of the real, inner Dryden.

Religio Laici is Dryden at last coming to grips with the basic problems of his own life and beliefs. The immediate occasion of it—it was a purely personal one—was the publication by Henry Dickinson, a young friend, of a translation of Father Richard Simon's *Histoire Critique du Vieux Testament*. Simon was a scientific student of the Bible who claimed to have made various discoveries calculated to undermine the uncritical belief in the word of the sacred text which was a central point of belief in Protestantism ; it was to that extent a work of Roman Catholic propaganda, though Simon himself was a quite disinterested student. His attitude is summarised by Professor Bredvold :

" The First Book is a history of the Hebrew text from the time of Moses ; we learn that Moses could not have written all the books attributed to him, that we sometimes have in the Old Testament only abridgements of longer works now lost, that the manuscripts are all imperfect and there is no wholly reliable tradition for their interpretation, that readings are often doubtful, and the whole matter full of difficulties and obscurities. The Second Book points out the faultiness of all translations, from the Septuagint down to those made by the Protestants ".

Dryden accepted Simon's criticism as valid : but then, where was one as a Protestant ? Where lay the seat of authority in religion ? Not in Reason certainly : he had studied and eventually rejected Hobbes and deism, and makes his position clear in that perfect exordium to the poem, where indeed (as Gray claimed) are " thoughts that breathe and words that burn " :

> Dim as the borrow'd beams of moon and stars
> To lonely, weary, wand'ring travellers,
> Is Reason to the soul ; and, as on high
> Those rolling fires discover but the sky,
> Not light us here ; so Reason's glimmering ray
> Was lent, not to assure our doubtful way,
> But guide us upward to a better day.
> And as those nightly tapers disappear
> When day's bright lord ascends our hemisphere.
> So pale grows Reason at Religion's sight,
> So dies, and so dissolves in supernatural light.

Scripture is also a help, but nothing more. Again some men say that truth must be sought and found in church tradition ; Dryden's view is :

> Such an omniscient church we wish indeed ;
> 'Twere worth both Testaments ; and cast in the creed.

The " partial Papists " claim to be such a church, but without justification ; indeed their claims have, in times of ignorance, led to great abuses :

> While crowds unlearn'd, with rude devotion warm,
> About the sacred viands buzz and swarm,
> The fly-blown text creates a crawling brood,
> And turns to maggots what was meant for food.

Best, then, where there are disputes on " points not clearly known ", to leave them alone ; it is much better to curb " private Reason " than to disturb the public peace. Obscure points don't really matter, " But common quiet is mankind's concern ".

While he does not support the Roman Church's claim to infallibility, he does not pretend to find omniscience either in the Church of

England.   He is far more opposed to the Puritans than to the Papists.
But above all, he genuinely wants to *know* ;   and what he is really
after is the secret of the universe :

> But what, or who, that Universal HE ;
> Whether some soul encompassing this ball,
> Unmade, unmov'd ; yet making, moving all ;
> Or various atoms' interfering dance
> Leapt into form, (the noble work of chance)
> Or this great all was from eternity ; . . . .

It is the poem of an honest and enquiring layman, well acquainted
with the various and contradictory ideas and philosophies of his time ;
but it is an uncomfortable poem, posing many questions and leaving
only a void for the answers.   Unfortunately he did not share the
willingness of Sir Thomas Browne (whose book may have suggested
the title of Dryden's poem) to rest in honest doubt ; at one time he
was able to do so, but not now—now the questions he posed began to
carry an overcharge of his own emotions and spiritual needs.   Soon
his poetry will be reflecting the " dark side of the moon " which every
man must face in his time, though he may deny it and try to obliterate
it ; this happened to the worldly Dryden as it had done to the licentious
Rochester.   The ponderings of *Religio Laici* were a prelude to this,
just as the poem itself is a prelude to a more personal poetry, a poetry
written for himself, which his changing outlook demanded.   For
problems which other men solve by plunging into social work, into
sport or into the work of a church had to be solved by Dryden in
words : he was wholly a poet, and one of whom it might be well said
that he could not think save in verses.

How strong was his need to write for himself may be judged from
the fact that *Religio Laici* made very little noise in the world when it
was first published, and consequently very little money ; Dryden was
well aware of the likelihood of that when he wrote it, for none had a
keener nose for the market.   Nor was it true that he had made enough
money as some thought from *Absalom and Achitophel* and *The Medal* to
permit him to indulge himself in this way ; those poems earned him
fame and gratitude but little else.   " If I am a mercenary scribbler ",
he wrote in the Vindication of *The Duke of Guise*, denying charges of

being hired to write political propaganda, " the Lords Commissioners of the Treasury know best ".

Very soon he was to write other poems for himself, though he sought to present them in such a way that they would also command a considerable sale.   But before he can do that he must recoup himself for the months " wasted " on *Religio Laici* ; he began to write letters to his patrons and to talk to the shrewd Tonson.

ii

For some time Dryden had been receiving only about half the salary due to him from his posts as Poet Laureate and Historiographer Royal; his revenue from the theatre had almost stopped ; he had suffered, thus, a diminution in his income at a time he could least afford it (his family calls being ever greater), and moreover at a time when he might well have expected to have had some official acknowledgment of his efforts in the crisis so recently passed.

So, in the summer of 1683, he writes to his friend and patron, Laurence Hyde, Earl of Rochester, First Lord of the Treasury :

" I know not whether my lord Sunderland has interceded with your Lordship for half a year of my salary ; but I have two other advocates, my extreme wants, even almost to arresting, and my ill-health, which cannot be repaired without immediate retiring into the country. A quarter's allowance is but the Jesuit's powder to my disease ; the fit will return a fortnight hence. If I durst, I would plead a little merit, and some hazards of my life from the common enemies ; my refusing advantages offered by them, and neglecting my beneficial studies for the King's service ; but I only think I merit not to starve . . . I have three sons growing to man's estate ; I breed them all up to learning beyond my fortune ; but they are too hopeful to be neglected, though I want ".   He asks for some small sinecure post, and continues : " 'Tis enough for one age to have neglected Mr. Cowley and starved Mr. Butler ". He speaks of writing something by His Majesty's command (this was a translation of Maimbourg's *History of the League*), and cannot leave for the country to carry out this order until he has secured his family from want.

Hyde acted, and from this time Dryden received regularly about half of the salary due ; but no sinecure, nor, as far as is known, were further grants made to him. Writing his *Threnodia Augustalis* after Charles's death three years later, Dryden could not help observing amid all his plaudits and praises that that " gay harmonious quire, like angels ever young ", the poets whom Charles had favoured, had not been extravagantly paid for their songs :

> Tho' little was their hire, and light their gain,
> Yet somewhat to their share he threw . . . .

But some small hope Dryden now saw in the translation of the classics. About 1680 he had contributed to a little volume of translations published by Tonson, called *Ovid's Epistles, translated by several hands.* In February, 1684, Tonson brought out a volume called *Miscellany Poems*, containing new editions of *MacFlecknoe, Absalom and Achitophel*, and *The Medal*—all still without the author's name, but authorised by him—, many of Dryden's Prologues and Epilogues, and four short translations by Dryden from Theocritus, Ovid and Virgil.

The *Miscellany*, which was somewhat of an experiment, was an immediate success. To Tonson it was clear that the best part of the *Miscellany* had been the poems and translations by Dryden, and he wished that in a new collection Dryden should be at least the active editor if not the sole contributor.

But Dryden in that summer of 1684 was away in the country again, this time with his two sons, Charles and John, and he was not well, suffering from a " hectic fever ". Tonson sent him two melons and a letter with the news that his *History of the League* is being widely commended ; he asks what he thinks of the idea of reprinting Lord Roscommon's *Essay on Translated Verse.*

Dryden in his reply thanks Tonson for the melons and says he is now much better in health, that his son John has also been ill but is now mending, though Dryden's servant " with over care of him " has himself fallen ill of the same distemper, " so that I am deep in doctors, 'pothecaries, and nurses ". Tonson's " friend ", Charles (Dryden's eldest son), is well. Dryden mentions the preparation of an opera, *Albion and Albanius ;* says that in the new *Miscellany* he will not insist on the inclusion of his *Religio Laici*, and agrees with Tonson that nothing but new matter should be included.

He goes on : " But I must add also that since we are to have nothing but new, I am resolved we will have nothing but good, whomever we disoblige. You will have of mine, four odes of Horace, which I have already translated ; another small translation of 40 lines from Lucretius; the whole story of Nisus and Eurialus, both in the fifth and ninth of Virgil's Aeneid : and I care not who translates them beside me ; for let him be friend or foe, I will please myself, and not give off in consideration of any man. There will be forty more lines of Virgil in another place to answer those of Lucretius : I mean those very lines which Montaigne has compared in those two poets ; and Homer shall sleep on for me,—I will not meddle with him ".

A tall order in view of the fact that Dryden, as he tells us, had retired to the country to " unweary myself after my studies, not to drudge ". But then it had been his habit for some years, as we have seen, to retire to the country in the summer and to do the major part of his work there.

He now settled happily to his task, and as usual talked about it afterwards—in the Preface to his *Miscellany*, which came out in 1685, entitled *Sylvae, or The Second Part of Poetical Miscellanies*. The Preface is one of Dryden's most genial performances. After speaking of the more obvious difficulties of the translator—with his usual sideglance at the deficiencies of the well-known work of " Uncle Ogleby " —he claims that it is not sufficient for a translator to be able " to judge of words and style, but he must be a master of them too ; he must perfectly understand his author's tongue, and absolutely command his own. So that, to be a thorough translator, he must be a thorough poet. Neither is it enough to give his author's sense in good English, in poetical expressions, and in musical numbers ; for, tho' all these are exceeding difficult to perform, there yet remains a harder task ; and 'tis a secret of which few translators have sufficiently thought. I have already hinted a word or two concerning it ; that is, the maintaining the character of an author, which distinguishes him from all others, and makes him appear that individual poet you would interpret . . . ."

This was particularly a problem with the translation of Lucretius who, among other difficulties, " was so much an atheist, that he forgot sometimes to be a poet ". Therefore, Dryden continues in translating him, " I laid by my natural diffidence and scepticism for a while, to take up that dogmatical way of his, which, as I said, is so much his character, as to make him that individual poet ".

Diffident though he was, Dryden was never shy in print, and makes no bones about the reason why he has chosen to translate " The Nature of Love " from Lucretius's fourth book—" the objection arises from the obscenity of the subject ". Well, says Dryden, the reason I translated it is " without the least formality of an excuse, I own it pleas'd me; and let my enemies make the worst they can of this confession ". After all, he adds, " I am not yet so secure from that passion, but that I want my author's antidotes against it ".

The Lucretius translations are in fact the *pièce de résistance* of *Sylvae*. The four *Idylls* of Theocritus are pleasant enough, but they cannot be said to be adequate representations of the Sicilian poet's " incomparable sweetness " ; there is, as Mr. Van Doren has remarked, too much of the trumpet note about Dryden's versions. The Horatian *Odes* are even less successful ; Dryden was no miniaturist, and he " required more space than Horace ever would allow ".

But the Lucretius is magnificent—as a translation and, in parts certainly, as an original poem through which the translator's own peculiar genius shines. No one who reads Dryden's version of the part of Lucretius's third book " Against the Fear of Death ", can believe otherwise, nor that these words represent anything but his strongest and deepest feelings. Dryden, as Mr. Van Doren says, has " learned much from Lucretius. This poem on the fear of death is Dryden's own ".

iii

The fact of death and the personal and speculative problems associated with it were much in Dryden's mind in these latter years of the reign. It was this, in part, which accounts for the new seriousness of his verse. This was the " dark side of the moon ".

Accidental circumstances, as well as his own age, forced those facts into Dryden's consciousness : he had felt the first twinges of mortality in his own limbs ; friends and relations had begun, in the natural course of events, to die, and—though he might deny that he was yet secure from the passion of love—his natural powers had begun to run more sluggishly.

Among friends who died was the young poet John Oldham, struck down at the early age of 30 ; for him Dryden wrote the lovely lines " To the Memory of Mr. Oldham " which were prefixed to an edition of Oldham's *Remains in Verse and Prose.*

These are perhaps the first fruits of Dryden's new preoccupation with the sources of life, and with death ; they do not yet tackle the mystery, but they are a most beautiful and imperishable statement of a man's sorrow for his friend, more poignant than *Lycidas* because less considered and less lengthy :

> Farewell, too little, and too lately known,
> Whom I began to think and call my own . . . .
> Once more, hail and farewell ; farewell, thou young,
> But ah too short, Marcellus of our tongue ;
> Thy brows with ivy, and with laurels bound ;
> But fate and gloomy night encompass thee around.

The lines from the third book of Lucretius's poem, however, reject the meaning of that marvellous and lugubrious last line ; they reject also the speculations and the charnel-house fancies of Donne and of the Elizabethans :

> And therefore if a man bemoan his lot,
> That after death his mold'ring limbs shall rot,
> Or flames, or jaws of beasts devour his mass,
> Know he's an unsincere, unthinking ass . . . .

Not for Lucretius or Dryden :

> Th'avenging horror of a conscious mind,
> Whose deadly fear anticipates the blow . . . .

but rather the feeling that death is a happy release from a world which ultimately begins to pall.

This is a rational and common-sense point of view consonant with an Augustan ideal if not Augustan practice. But, then, Dryden goes on —and whose is the " anxious mind " in this passage if not his own ?

> And thou, dost thou disdain to yield thy breath,
> Whose very life is little more than death ?
> More than one half by lazy sleep possess'd ;

> And when awake, thy soul but nods at best,
> Day-Dreams and sickly thoughts revolving in thy breast.
> Eternal troubles haunt thy anxious mind,
> Whose cause and cure thou never hop'st to find ;
> But still uncertain, with thyself at strife,
> Thou wander'st in the labyrinth of life.

Dryden is deeply concerned ; the desire to know the secret of the universe has given way before a raging desire to know the secret of himself and his own existence.   It has been too easily supposed that he was unaware of " eternal troubles ", or unaffected by them.

More than that, the " anxious mind " demands, if not a solution—which Dryden thought impossible to be found—then an escape, an easing, a new *modus vivendi* to fit the new awareness.   The emergence from what Dryden aptly called " the labyrinth of life " will depend on the cast of mind, the personal situation and the contemporary ethos.

He put his problem and that of many others in these words :

> O, if the foolish race of man, who find
> A weight of cares still pressing on their mind,
> Could find as well the cause of this unrest,
> And all this burden lodg'd within the breast ;
> Sure they would change their course, not live as now,
> Uncertain what to wish or what to vow.
> Uneasy both in country and in town,
> They search a place to lay their burden down . . . .
>
> Then would he search more deeply for the cause ;
> And study nature well, and nature's laws :
> For in this moment lies not the debate,
> But on our future, fix'd, eternal state ;
> That never-changing state, which all must keep,
> Whom death has doom'd to everlasting sleep.

A man cannot long remain in such a state of metaphysical " anxiety ", although he has his absorbing work, his young friends and admirers round him, and his position in society.   It was not long before Dryden found his solution, one that we cannot feel was totally unexpected. There were signs enough—in *Religio Laici* where he had approached the standpoint of *credo quia impossibile ;* in Lucretius where he shows his agony and yet rejects Lucretius's stoicism ; in his overwhelming need for a " place to lay his burden down " and where he, even he, would be understood and comforted. Dryden in his perplexity of mind must have thought that there were fortuitous, but curiously significant, signs in the outer world, too. Soon after the translations came out in January, 1685, King Charles had a stroke ; on February 6th he died. It was quickly noised abroad that shortly before his death, the monarch had called into his bedchamber the aged Roman Catholic priest who had helped him escape from Cromwell after the battle of Worcester ; from him the King received Extreme Unction. And—his successor, all being well, was already an overt Roman Catholic.

Dryden, it seems, was away from London when the King died, staying at Linstead Lodge, the seat of Lord Teynahm, near Sittingbourne in Kent. And—Lord Teynham and all the Roper family were avowed Roman Catholics.

It was full of such thoughts, such spiritual stresses and doubts that Dryden returned to London. But before he made a final decision, he had a duty to perform as Poet Laureate ; and so with many other and weightier matters on his mind, he sat down to write a poem in memory of Charles. It was not a good poem ; he was too distracted, and too short of time. His tribute to the monarch is somewhat flaccid ; only when he comes to direct observation is there life in the verse, for instance when he describes how for a brief time after the stroke it was thought the King might yet recover :

> The drooping town in smiles again was dress'd,
> Gladness in every face expressed,
> Their eyes before their tongues confess'd.
> Men met each other with erected look,
> The steps were higher that they took . . . .

When he comes to deal briefly with the new King, he paints a most curious picture of what he expected the future to be like :

> So James the drowsy genius wakes
> Of Britain long entranc'd in charms,
> Restiff and slum'bring on its arms :
> 'Tis roused, and with a new-strung nerve, the spear already shakes.

No, Dryden's mind was elsewhere ; and it was with a sense now not of anxiety or fear that he awaited political events about which nearly all men had the gloomiest forebodings—but of boredom and perhaps of anger that such matters might disturb the quiet of his mind as it wrestled with the problems of his own soul.

CHAPTER TEN

"Be Thine the Glory"

THE ACCESSION to the throne of the United Kingdom of James Stuart, Duke of York—Roman Catholic whose exclusion had been sought by a majority of his subjects, open supporter of the high Tories whose name was anathema to the Whigs and to many other powerful men—took place surprisingly in an atmosphere of great calm. The seas of blood, for long predicted, did not flood his way to the throne. His opponents were silent ; his supporters, though jubilant, preserved a moderate mien ; and the greater part of the population tacitly showed itself ready to give him his chance. Indeed, the matter-of-factness of the population, the sweet reasonableness were extraordinary—perhaps, to acuter observers, suspiciously so, and too reminiscent of what proverbially precedes the storm.

The calm was partly because the Whigs were, for the time being, a spent force ; their motives and plans had been too starkly exposed to the public gaze ; they were discredited. Their "treason" had *not* prospered, so everyone called it treason. Moreover, moderate politicians of both parties were giving the new King their support : they were not ready to face the alternative of civil war, and, worst of all, disruption of the commerce of the land. George Savile, Marquess of Halifax, had expressed a general attitude in his *Character of a Trimmer* circulated anonymously the year before James's accession. Halifax had opposed the Exclusion Bill, but at the same time he sought to put statutory limitations on a Roman Catholic monarch. His real aims were to safeguard the people from riot and bloodshed and to ensure the sanctity of property. It was a simple doctrine—deceptively simple —but the majority of Englishmen in 1685 wished no more.

The new King seemed determined to fulfil their desires. The day after his accession, this bigoted middle-aged man whose hauteur and impatience were a by-word, told his Privy Council in lamb-like words that he " would make it his endeavour to preserve this government in Church and State as it is now by law established ". Shrewder observers could not really believe it, but so much did they hope it was true that they convinced themselves that it might be.

So the coronation, which took place on April 23rd, 1685, passed off easily and to the acclamations of the crowds. The King, indeed, did not take the Communion which was normally part of the service, but the rest of the rites were carried out with dignity by Sancroft, the Archbishop of Canterbury, and his assistants. The General Election which quickly followed was a triumph for the King, and even the boroughs returned members of strong Royalist sympathies. The new Parliament at once voted large sums of money for the King.

All this Dryden observed with satisfaction from his seat at Will's ; it seemed as though his forebodings had been fanciful, and that at last the " moody, murm'ring race " had learned its lesson. He did not feel, however, that he was called on to celebrate the coronation, as he had done that of Charles some twenty-five years before ; he was too old now to feel that " bliss was it in that dawn to be alive ", nor were the circumstances similar ; there was no feeling that the chains had at last fallen off, as there had been in 1660, and that all life lay before him, full of exciting possibilities. This was a sober affair of one King lawfully succeeding another ; Dryden felt that what he had said of the new King at the end of *Threnodia Augustalis* was sufficient, at least from the point of his view of his duty as Poet Laureate.

His duty to his pocket and his family was a different matter. The change of government had not improved his financial situation ; indeed, James had deprived him—it was typical of his cheese-paring spirit—of the annual butt of canary wine, which he had been granted by his original letters patent in the previous reign. So Dryden once more tried his luck on the stage.

Before Charles's death, he had begun to work on a masque which was intended as a *lever de rideau* to an opera to be called *King Arthur*. This masque he now expanded into a self-contained opera, *Albion and Albanius*, in which were allegorically represented the restoration of the Stuarts, their victory over the Whigs, and the succession of James to the throne. The scenery was lavish and the stage-machines more than usually ingenious, but the verse was of indifferent quality and the music intolerably bad. Moreover, Dryden had offended the musicians, first by choosing a Frenchman, M.Grabut, as his composer, and secondly by paying him compliments in the prelude to the opera ; this was regarded as an insult to Purcell and other composers of the English school. The actors were equally disappointed by the poorness of their lines ; and the management were positively furious at the opera's lack of success, since the elaborate scenery had cost a great deal, and now seemed likely to put them into debt.

The opera dragged on for five days with ever-decreasing audiences until on the sixth day, the Saturday, it was abruptly terminated, never again to be produced, by news of the landing at Lyme Regis by the Duke of Monmouth, the Protestant pretender to the throne, at the head of 150 men. This *coup de grâce*, though it was the result of an event which caused Dryden great perturbation, at least allowed the abysmal failure to fade quietly away—though not completely unobserved, for one wit went into print to suggest that the failure of the opera may have been due to Dryden's having written the music and Grabut the words.

The Monmouth rebellion was soon quelled, not so much because Monmouth lacked support—thousands of peasants flocked to his banner in the west country—but because of poor staff-work, resulting in a failure to co-ordinate Whig forces in other parts of the country. Monmouth was defeated, a month after his landing, at the night battle of Sedgemoor, and there followed the ignoble episodes of Lord Chief Justice Jeffreys' " bloody assizes ", said to have made " the country look like a shambles ". Monmouth himself was taken prisoner, pleaded with his uncle to spare him, but without avail, and like his grandfather, ended his life on the scaffold.

The whole country heaved a sigh of relief, and went through the mental motions of washing its hands of the business ; it was distasteful, it was dangerous, and it was also old-fashioned—a " last flash " from that England which had, it was felt, reached its nadir in the Civil War, and vanished altogether in 1660.

But in that belief the country was wrong. Monmouth's rebellion was a portent of something that even as late as July, 1685, seemed impossible : the victory of the Whigs. It marked also the change in King James which was to make that victory inevitable, for the decision to have his nephew beheaded and the ease with which the threat to his throne had been defeated induced in him a giddy and frenetic *folie de grandeur.* The bigotedness, vanity and hauteur he had held in check for a few months after his accession now reappeared in full force ; he determined willy-nilly to impose Roman Catholicism on his subjects. Defying the statute, he appointed Roman Catholics to key positions in the army ; he purged his Privy Council of all possible sources of opposition (including the moderate Halifax), admitting instead numbers of Roman Catholic peers ; he tried to repeal the Test Act and the Habeas Corpus Act, and when there were murmurs from the Royalist parliament he had it prorogued.

At this time Dryden was again resolutely turning his face away from politics and from public themes altogether ; as though to make up for the unmusicality of *Albion and Albanius,* he was composing one of the most musical—and least political—of his long poems, the ode " to the pious memory of the accomplish'd young lady, Mrs. Anne Killigrew ". Dryden had never met Miss Killigrew, who was a daughter of the Rev. Henry Killigrew ; she had died at an early age and, apart from her domestic virtues, her only claim to fame lay in a handful of poems—the family were given to writing, and her uncles, Thomas and William, were both well-known dramatists.

Like two other of Dryden's poetic " subjects ", Lord Hastings and John Oldham, she had succumbed to smallpox. But Dryden's feelings in the nature of things could hardly be deeply involved as they had been with Oldham. So in a strange way when he wrote his ode about Miss Killigrew it was as though he had been liberated—from the grief and emotion that had affected him in writing about Oldham, from political and social considerations that strictly prescribed his form and content in the satires, from the weighty personal matters of a poem such as *Religio Laici.*

Dryden soared, positively soared, in this fantastic ode. His note throughout is exalted and majestic, beginning very high—

> Thou youngest virgin-daughter of the skies . . . .

and ending higher still :

> There thou, sweet saint, before the choir shalt go,
> As harbinger of heav'n . . . .

In between he ranges from earth to Heaven which he links by means of the well-established convention that earthly poetry partakes of the divine. Miss Killigrew is first depicted singing in the ethereal regions to which she has been called ; there is rejoicing in Heaven ; this "music of the spheres" suggests, by comparison, the inferiority of earthly poetry :

> O gracious God ! how far have we
> Profan'd thy heav'nly gift of poesy !
> Made prostitute and profligate the Muse,
> Debas'd to each obscene and impious use,
> Whose harmony was first ordain'd above
> For tongues of angels, and for hymns of love !
> O wretched we ! why were we hurried down
> This lubric and adult'rate age,
> (Nay, added fat pollutions of our own),
> T'increase the steaming ordures of the stage ?
> What can we say t'excuse our *second fall* ?
> Let this thy *vestal*, Heav'n, atone for all :
> Her Arethusan stream remains unsoil'd,
> Unmix'd with foreign filth, and undefil'd ;
> Her wit was more than man, her innocence a child !

How skilfully Dryden leads the fantasy forward to an apologia for "lubric" verse—with more than half an eye on his own—and back again to the deified Anne, "born to the spacious empire of the Nine" ! Now he tells us of her triumphs in poetry and in painting :

> Thus nothing to her genius was denied,
> But like a ball of fire the further thrown,
> Still with a greater blaze she shone,
> And her bright soul broke out on ev'ry side . . .

Then there is a swift change of theme and of cadence ; Anne, seen at the beginning only as a wraith treading "with seraphims the vast abyss", is now brought to earth :

> Now all those charms, that blooming grace,
> The well-proportion'd shape, and beauteous face,
> Shall never more be seen by mortal eyes :
> In earth the much-lamented virgin lies !

For a moment we are switched to the sea where Anne's " warlike brother " :

> His waving streamers to the winds displays . . . .

He does not yet know of his loss :

> But look aloft, and if thou kenn'st from far
> Among the Pleiades a new kindled star ;
> If any sparkles than the rest more bright,
> 'Tis she that shines in that propitious light.

From sea and stars, Dryden rises to still more exalted realms, more distant now not merely in space but also in time—to the Judgment Day :

> When in mid-air the golden trump shall sound,
> To raise the nations under ground . . .

And on that day it shall be the sacred poets who first leap from their tombs " For they are cover'd with the lightest ground " :

> And straight ,with inborn vigour, on the wing,
> Like mounting larks to the new morning sing.
> There thou, sweet saint, before the choir shalt go,
> As harbinger of heaven, the way to show,
> The way which thou so well hast learned below.

The brilliance and sustained power of the poem are obvious ; but what is the meaning of it ? So dazzling is the performance that the critical faculties tend to lie quiescent, as though beaten into silence : the effect is not different in type from that produced by very different means in an early poem by Keats, or, a more exact parallel, in *Kubla Khan*. Even though the images have a greater clarity, the exquisite cadences finer and more sharp, the ode adds up, in a literal, prosaic sense, to very little.

It has, indeed, been suggested by Professor E. M. W. Tillyard, that it is really a description of the late seventeenth-century world-view, a mixture of the " great chain of being " with humanistic and Renaissance ideals, tempered by the doubts induced by the scientific advances of the century ; that it is dominated by the principle of decorum extended to almost metaphysical lengths ; and that it bespeaks Dryden's

" faith in the value of good manners and of an ordered way of life ". There is certainly truth in all these suggestions, but they are inadequate to describe the fullness and fantasy of the poem and our feeling about it—just as J. Livingstone Lowes's *Road to Xanadu*, though stimulating, is less adequate as a response to *Kubla Khan* than other, less involved, pieces of criticism.

The ode to Miss Killigrew is really a fantasy on contemporary themes, the emptying of a well-read and clever mind, much after the manner of the Surrealist poets of the nineteen-twenties—but with this big difference : that the end-product is filtered through the genius of a master-craftsman, with music in his fingers and magic in his rhymes.

The poem was for Dryden an opportunity of releasing tensions, letting his imagination run free from the miasma of doubt and death that had recently overwhelmed it, and throwing aside the strictness of the heroic measure. It must be remembered that though the ode form appears strict enough to us, it was to the late seventeenth century, under Cowley's influence, as to the Augustans, very much what *vers libre* was in the early years of this century—something bold, wild and almost shocking.

ii

Writing the ode to Miss Killigrew released Dryden from the purely ratiocinative element of his mental composition which, though it had been the source of his greatest poetry and was to be once again, had in the years immediately preceding the death of King Charles gone stale, and, combined with his age, had produced the melancholy reflections of the Lucretius translation, and the acrid and unhealthy sexuality of the imagery of *Absalom and Achitophel*, and *The Medal*. It had been in a sense a purge for his vapours, or, as we now say, a sublimation of his unconscious complexes.

He benefited from it immediately, starting a round of visits to friends all over the country—to Knole, the Kentish home of his old patron, the Earl of Dorset, to Staffordshire, and of course to North-amptonshire. His happiness is evident in the next poem he wrote, the gayest of all his productions : this is *A letter to Sir George Etherege*, a reply to a rhyming despatch from the author of *The Man of Mode*, who had lately gone as His Majesty's Minister to Ratisbon.

despatch had been addressed to the Earl of Middleton, the Secretary of
State—an excellent custom which our rhyming envoys might revive.
The Earl feeling himself unable to reply adequately had asked Dryden's
assistance. Dryden, remembering no doubt other and less happy
occasions when he had worked for a Secretary of State, obeyed with
pleasure ; Etherege was an old friend ; Dryden had written a prologue
to his *The Man of Mode ;* even in that satirical poem, *MacFlecknoe*,
he had gone out of his way to praise :

> Let gentle George in triumph tread the stage,
> Make Dorimant betray, and Loveit rage ;
> Let Cully, Cockwood, Fopling, charm the pit,
> And in their folly shew the writer's wit . . . .

A new verse form seemed to demand a new metre, and Dryden chose
that of *Hudibras*, which he thought " gave a boyish kind of pleasure ",
and was thus very suitable for his purposes here ; it also called for a
new style, and this is what he pulled out of the bag ; he is addressing
the new ambassador :

> You can be old in grave debate,
> And young in love-affairs of state ;
> And both to wives and husbands show
> The vigour of a plenipo.
> Like mighty missioner you come
> Ad Partes Infidelium . . . .

A touch, perhaps, of W. S. Gilbert ?   Or a private cabaret with Noël
Coward ? He continues that such " Dutch delights " as drinking
" Rhenish rummers " do not suit Etherege's English taste—and why :

> For why to leave a whore or play
> Was ne'er your Excellency's way.
> Nor need this title give offence,
> For here you were his Excellence,
> For gaming, writing, speaking, keeping,
> His Excellence for all but sleeping . . . .

There was a fatal irony in this, for some five years later His Excel-
lency, lighting some guests down the stairs of his apartment in Ratisbon after a party, fell and broke his neck.

The gaiety and good-humour of Dryden in these middle years of the decade were no flash-in-the-pan, nor were they superficial. There was, too, a deeper reason for them than writing a new sort of poem, The profound psychological and mental upheavals which had begun at about the time of the writing of the *Religio Laici*, ended—or were resolved—in the event which is recorded in the diary of John Evelyn, who on January 19, 1686, wrote : " Dryden the famous play-writer, and his two sons . . . . were said to go to mass ".

" Anything, tho' never so little, which a man speaks of himself, is too much ", Dryden said later, and his writings are singularly free from autobiographical passages. But in the matter of his conversion to Roman Catholicism he has to some extent broken the rule, and given us in *The Hind and the Panther* considerable autobiographical material —and moreover, as if foreseeing the doubts and bewilderment of future generations about this change of religion, he carefully calls attention to this material in his address to the reader at the beginning of the poem. He says, though his attitude of reserve is still in evidence : " What I desire the reader should know concerning me, he will find in the body of the poem, if he have but the patience to peruse it ".

Few writers have given full weight to the lines to which Dryden draws special attention. In this matter which was so radically important for him, it is best to let him speak for himself :

> But, gracious God, how well dost thou provide
> For erring judgments an unerring guide !
> Thy throne is darkness in th'abyss of light,
> A blaze of glory that forbids the sight.
> O teach me to believe thee thus conceal'd,
> And search no further than thyself reveal'd ;
> But her alone for my director take,
> Whom thou hast promis'd never to forsake !
> My thoughtless youth was wing'd with vain desires,
> My manhood, long misled by wandr'ing fires,
> Follow'd false lights ; and, when their glimpse was gone,
> My pride struck out new sparkles of her own.
> Such was I, such by nature still I am ;
> Be thine the glory, and be mine the shame.
> Good life be now my task ; my doubts are done :
> (What more could fright my faith, than three in one ?)

Can I believe eternal God could lie
Disguis'd in mortal mould and infancy?
That the great Maker of the world could die?
And after that trust my imperfect sense,
Which calls in question his omnipotence?
Can I my reason to my faith compel,
And shall my sight, and touch, and taste rebel?
Superior faculties are set aside;
Shall their subservient organs be my guide?
Then let the moon usurp the rule of day,
And winking tapers show the sun his way;
For what my senses can themselves perceive,
I need no revelation to believe.
Can they who say the host should be descried
By sense, define a body glorified?
Impassible, and penetrating parts?
Let them declare by what mysterious arts
He shot that body thro' th'opposing might
Of bolts and bars impervious to the light,
And stood before his train confess'd in open sight....

Why choose we then like *bilanders* to creep
Along the coast, and land in view to keep,
When safely we may launch into the deep?
In the same vessel which our Saviour bore,
Himself the pilot let us leave the shore,
And with a better guide a better world explore....

Rest then, my soul, from endless anguish freed:
Nor sciences thy guide, nor sense thy creed.
Faith is the best ensurer of thy bliss....

This may not be a great credo, not even particularly good Roman
Catholic theology, but it is sufficient apologia and it is magnificent
poetry.   The lines ring with autobiographical truth, as of a man who
has passed through doubt and spiritual—yes, spiritual—troubles and
emerged happily and confidently at the further side.   They leave
nothing for a biographer to add.

The poem is directly autobiographical in one other place, for Dryden
also recalls the period of his overweening pride—with disgust, yet with
an admission that the germ still lies within him:

And, last, a long farewell to worldly fame.
'Tis said with ease, but, O, how hardly tried
By haughty souls to human honour tied !

O sharp convulsive pangs of agonising pride !
Down then thou rebel, never more to rise,
And what thou didst, and dost, so dearly prize,
That fame, that darling fame, make that thy sacrifice . . .

Here speaks Dryden from his deepest, questioning self ; it is the only place in all his poetry where he talks so strongly and beautifully of his own profoundest emotions. This *is* Dryden, plain, in the 57th year of his journey through life. And—

Be thine the glory, and be mine the shame.
Good life be now my task ; my doubts are done . . . .

Part of the "good life", his "task" as he saw it, was to help propagate the religion by which his own doubts had been answered, and in whose calm certainty he now rested. The larger part of *The Hind and the Panther* is devoted to that end, as was his defence of a paper by Anne Hyde, the first wife of James II, announcing her adoption of Catholicism, and his translation from the French of the *Life of St. Francis Xavier* by the Jesuit, Bouhours.

The method he uses in *The Hind and the Panther* is part satirical, part propagandist and part exegetical. The plot is simple, and not without a touch of absurdity. A gentle hind—said to have been suggested to Dryden by the white deer in the park of his Catholic patron Lord Clifford at Ugbrooke in Devonshire—represents the Roman Catholic Church ; a fierce but beautiful panther stands for the Church of England, and the two discuss religious matters, ending of course in a dialectical victory for the hind.

The subject, Dryden insists, was not imposed on him, nor even suggested, by any man ; he felt it to be his duty to write it, even though he had many hindrances, and his health was not of the best. He himself divides it into three parts : " The *first part,* consisting most in general characters and narration, I have endeavour'd to raise, and give it the majestic turn of heroic poesy . . . ."

Magnificent as this part is with its immortal opening lines—how good Dryden was at opening lines ! —

> A milk-white hind, immortal and unchang'd,
> Fed on the lawns, and in the forest rang'd ;
> Without unspotted, innocent within,
> She fear'd no danger, for she knew no sin . . .

it cannot really be said to be heroic poetry in spite of such lines as :

> Such wars, such waste, such fiery tracks of dearth . . .

Certainly Milton was in his mind as he wrote ; these lines are a memory of some in the third book of *Paradise Lost* :

> If, as our dreaming Platonists report,
> There could be spirits of a middle sort,
> Too black for heav'n, and yet too white for hell,
> Who just dropp'd halfway down, nor lower fell.

But the essence of this first part lies in the autobiographical lines, already mentioned, and the machinery precludes the heroic since there has to be lines such as :

> The lady of the spotted muff began . . .

and such nearly satirical, *Absalom*-like couplets as :

> Souls that can scarce ferment their mass of clay ;
> So drossy, so divisible are they . . . .

One striking thing in this first part, compared with almost all Dryden's earlier poems, is the direct observation of nature and the countryside.   It is as though his love of the country, so long repressed in his verse, had at last burst forth.   It appears in such a simile as :

> As, where in fields the fairy rounds are seen,
> A rank, sour herbage rises on the green ;
> So, springing where these midnight elves advance . . .

or,

> As, where the lightning runs along the ground,
> No husbandry can heal the blasting wound ;
> Nor bladed grass nor bearded corn succeeds,
> But scales of scurf and putrefaction breeds . . . .

The second part of the poem, Dryden says, "being matter of Dispute, and chiefly concerning church authority, I was oblig'd to make as plain and perspicuous as possibly I could ; yet not wholly neglecting the numbers, tho' I had not frequent occasions for the magnificence of verse . . . ." The verse, indeed, is highly competent for the exegetical purpose it serves, but is inevitably of lesser interest today. The third part, " which has more of the nature of domestic conversation, is, or ought to be, more free and familiar than the two former "—and so it is, containing as it does various satirical portraits including that of Gilbert Burnet, formerly Professor of Divinity in Glasgow, preacher at the Rolls Chapel, and now self-exiled to Holland as a result of his Low Church tenets. Burnet was always more the intriguer than the divine, and his power among the clergy of the Church of England had been great ; he was to reap his reward at the court of William and Mary—and his memorial in these lines :

> ' God save King Buzzards ! ' was the gen'ral cry.
> A portly prince and goodly to the sight,
> He seem'd a son of Anak for his height :
> Like those whom stature did to crowns prefer ;
> Black-brow'd and bluff, like Homer's Jupiter ;
> Broad-back'd and brawny-built for love's delight,
> A prophet form'd to make a female proselyte.
> A theologue more by need than genial bent ;
> By breeding sharp, by nature confident.
> Int'rest in all his actions was discerned ;
> More learn'd than honest, more a wit than learn'd ;
> Or forc'd by fear, or by his profit led,
> Or both conjoin'd, his native clime he fled ;
> But brought the virtues of his heav'n along,
> A fair behaviour and a fluent tongue . . . .

Two other personal references are worth noticing in the poem. In an admittedly somewhat obscure passage, Dryden makes a thinly-veiled attack on a Roman Catholic priest, the Jesuit Father Petre, one of the King's chief advisers. Petre was known to be the *eminence grise* whose influence on the King was always to extreme courses, and whom the moderate Catholics feared. The tragic end of the Swallows in Dryden's poem represents their fears. and was an accurate forecast of what was shortly to happen. Dryden, in fact, though he has joined an authoritarian church, is preserving his intellectual independence ; and this tends to confirm that what he sought in religion was satisfaction for his soul—his possession of which has often been doubted—rather than for his ratiocinative powers.

The other reference is to the suggestion, made already in his own time, that his conversion had been for pecuniary rewards. As we have seen, no such rewards came to him—only the certainty that his championship of the Catholic faith would inevitably damage him when James died and the Protestant succession was resumed. So this claim is justified :

> Now for my converts, who, you say, unfed,
> Have follow'd me for miracles of bread ;
> Judge not by hearsay, but observe at least,
> If since their change their loaves have been increas'd.

The Hind and the Panther was published simultaneously in London and at a printing press maintained by the King at Holyrood in Edinburgh for the dissemination of tracts favourable to the Roman Catholic cause. It passed rapidly through three editions. From this point of view it was a success, but in reality a *succès de scandale* ; it was a poem everyone read and everyone condemned. For it appeared at the worst possible moment from the point of view of the religion it supported and the King whose religion it was.

In the middle of 1687, as a recent historian has remarked, even the King's " most trusted advisers saw that he was blowing the lid off the stove ". His proposed repeal of the religious Test Acts had met with widespread opposition ; his second Declaration of Indulgence caused Archbishop Sancroft and six bishops to petition the King to withdraw, since they considered his power to dispense with the penal laws was illegal. In reply, the King put them in the Tower.

In the meantime, Prince William of Orange, husband of Mary, King James's elder daughter, who had earlier unsuccessfully offered to barter his support for James against an assurance of his succession to the English throne, entered into negotiations through an envoy with certain English politicians, the chief of whom was Danby, the scheming and wily Yorkshireman, released from prison at the beginning of the reign. In January, 1688, King James demanded the return of six regiments serving in Holland under Prince William's command ; William was faced with war with his implacable enemy Louis XIV, and felt this was the last straw and that he must, for the safety of his own country, know on which side the British would range themselves in the hostilities. Soon in the Dutch ports preparations were being made for a naval invasion ; leading Whig and Tory politicians wrote a joint letter of invitation to William ; and in December, 1688, King James fled the shores of Britain.

In the hubbub of these closing months of the reign, Dryden is almost lost to view. He was, of course, still writing—for example, his *A Song for St. Cecilia's Day* for a musical society which had begun an annual celebration of November 22, the feast of the patron saint of music ; the ode was set to music by an Italian composer, Draghi, and published as a broadside. It is another example of Dryden's growing delight in using words to bring out their innate sound and power ; but it has neither the subtlety nor the sweep of the ode to Anne Killigrew, nor the sheer magnificence of the *Alexander's Feast* ten years later. He also wrote *Britannia Rediviva*, the least successful of all his poems, to celebrate the birth of a son to the King. For the rest, he continued to visit Will's and his friends in the country ; sometimes he rode up to the camp on Hounslow Heath where the King annually concentrated the army ; more often he remained at home with his books, and now, in the autumn and calm of his mind, it was increasingly to the great Romans to whom he turned—Juvenal, Ovid and, above all, Virgil.

On February 6, 1689, a Convention Parliament ceased quarrelling about the future government of the country, and declared William and Mary King and Queen, thus tumbling all Dryden's prospects in the dust, ensuring that his bread-and-butter even would be a matter of doubt, and flinging him among that minority who from now on would be known as Jacobites. Over those Jacobites soon broke a positive storm of satires, libels and pasquinades ; Dryden was scarcely less caught in this torrent than were Father Petre or the Papal envoy, Mgr. Adda.

Dryden had for some time contemplated a move from Long Acre. Now he began to put his books together, the furniture assembled over

eighteen years, and, to the accompaniment of Lady Elizabeth's
querulous voice, said farewell to the house where his years of fame had
been spent, many of his best works written, and where he had watched
his sons grow up.

As he and Lady Elizabeth clambered into the coach, and rumbled the
short distance to the newly laid-out Gerrard Street where he had taken
the fifth house at the east end of the south side, what were his thoughts ?
That the centre chapter of his life was at an end ?   That this move was
so different from that earlier one when he had followed the handcart
with his books and few clothes across Lincoln's Inn Fields to the lodgings of Sir Robert Howard ?   Or that a new, challenging era was
opening when again he would have to face the world and make his
mark, almost as he had had to do in 1660 ?

But now at least he had attained an equanimity ; his mental doubts
and his spiritual unease were at an end.   He could even smile, as he
unpacked " in the ground room next the street " in his new house,
when he discovered among his books—inserted no doubt by some
" well-wisher "—a new printed squib : " The address of John Dryden,
Laureate, to His Highness the Prince of Orange ".

> What is't for thee, great prince, I will not sing ?
> No bounds shall stop my Pegasean flight,
> I'll spot my Hind and make my Panther white . . . .

He could smile—the smile of a man whose Hind is forever " milk-
white . . . . immortal and unchang'd ".

CHAPTER ELEVEN

" *The Virgil of our Age* "

THE FIRST leaves of Autumn are falling in the garden of Lord Leicester's great mansion as the front door of a new house on its northern side opens, and two old gentlemen carefully descend the steps into the street. Behind them, an old woman with streaky grey hair, close-set eyes, and a discontented expression closes the door with a bang ; the shorter, more portly, of the two men, who is carrying a sheaf of papers, sighs.

The two slowly turn the corner into Little Newport Street, and make towards the Strand ; then the taller, who has an air of authority and an assertive way of pushing his chin forward, remarks : " You are to have Mrs. Bracegirdle and Mrs. Mountfort this time—not a patch on Nelly Gwyn nor on Annie Reeves. Pah, they can't act no more ! "

" Dear Robert ", says his plump, rubicund companion, " they never *could* act, those women. You forget the trouble I had with *The Conquest of Granada* . . . " " The trouble *you* had ! The trouble is, John, to be frank, that you read your things so abominably badly at the first shot that you depress 'em. You read as if you were one of my clerks at the Exchequer telling over His Majesty's profit and loss account ! "

John smiles indulgently. Robert has not changed a little bit since the days at the Blue Anchor, or the time when they had that little tiff in print about his opinion on—what was it ? To rhyme plays or not to rhyme them, or something of that sort : still as positive as ever, old Robert, but as good a brother-in-law as one could hope to have and now head of the Exchequer.

And so the two old gentlemen pass into the portals of the theatre, the familiar smell of carpentry and paint, the bustle and hustle of the preparations for yet another play by John Dryden, his *Amphitryon*.

It is not his first play since the Revolution—the *new* Revolution, that is. His *Spanish Friar* had been revived for the very first visit the new Queen paid to the theatre—the shy daughter of James II who dotes on her cold husband and whose compensation for a loveless life has been the writing of fulsome letters to a girlhood friend. It had been thought that this play with its strongly Protestant bias and its fun at the expense of the Catholic Orders would be exactly the thing. Unfortunately there were other passages in it about a female usurpation of a throne, and on that first night there was a positive swish of silks in the theatre as everyone turned to observe the reactions of Her Majesty. The Earl of Nottingham, who was present, wrote to a friend afterwards : " Some unhappy expressions put her in some disorder, and forced her to hold up her fan, and often look behind her, and call for her palatine and hood, and anything she could next think of ; while those who were in the pit before her turned their heads over their shoulders, and all in general directed their looks towards her, whenever their fancy led them to make any application of what was said ".

That had not greatly helped Dryden's changed position *vis-à-vis* the Court, though to be fair there had been as yet no marks of ill-favour, no vindictiveness. It was true that he had lost his posts as Poet Laureate and Historiographer Royal at the Revolution, but that had not been unexpected. It was, indeed, a bitter blow that his old friend, Charles Sackville, Earl of Dorset, now Lord Chamberlain, had been the instrument of his deprivation, but Dorset had not merely expressed his honest regret, he had helped him financially. " I must ever acknowledge ", Dryden wrote, " to the honour of your Lordship, and the eternal memory of your charity, that since this revolution, wherein I have patiently suffered the ruin of my small fortune, and the loss of that poor subsistence which I had from two kings, whom I have served more faithfully than profitably to myself—then your Lordship was pleased, out of no other motive than your own nobleness, without any desert of mine, or the least solicitation from me, to make me a most bountiful present, which at that time, when I was most in want of it, came most reasonably and unexpectedly to my relief. That favour, my lord, is of itself sufficient to bind any grateful man to a perpetual acknowledgment, and to all the future service to which one of my mean condition can be ever able to perform. May the Almighty God return it for me, both in blessing you here, and rewarding you hereafter ! "

Dorset, whatever his morals had been, *was* a generous and loyal friend : Dryden never forgot the £100 note he found under his plate when he dined one Christmas day at Knole House, Dorset's home in Kent. Indeed, despite the torrent of abuse, Dryden had found nothing but kindness from his old friends. Mulgrave helped him, too. As Dryden said in dedicating to him his translation of the *Aeneid* : " Will you give me leave to acquaint the world that I have many times been oblig'd to your bounty since the Revolution ? Tho' I was never reduced to beg a charity, nor ever had the impudence to ask one, either of your Lordship, or your noble kinsman the Earl of Dorset, much less of any other ; yet when I least expected it you have both remember'd me ".

All this helped to blunt the edge of the ironical fact that the man who had taken Dryden's place as Poet Laureate was the man whose heavy shadow had lain over his life since Cambridge days, that Og who :

> . . . . from a treason tavern rolling home.
> Round as a globe and liquored every chink,
> Goodly and great he sails behind his link . . . .

Dryden could now see the reversal of fortune as somehow inevitable, a proper revenge almost, for the pride and laughing scorn with which he had treated him in *MacFlecknoe* and in *Absalom and Achitophel*. Apart from that, Shadwell had suffered, perhaps far more than Dryden was now suffering, during the previous reign, as he said in his epistle dedicatory to *Bury Fair* (1689). He was a Whig, and : " I never could recant in the worst of times, when my ruin was designed, and my life was sought, and for near ten years I was kept from the exercise of that profession which had afforded me a competent subsistence ". Under the government of James, he had been silenced as a " non-conforming poet ". Well, he was no poet anyhow, but his comedies had their merits, and when he hastened at the Revolution to congratulate the Prince of Orange, and then his Queen in laudatory poems, Dorset could hardly do other than present him to the King as the most likely among the Whigs for the post of Poet Laureate.

Nor could Dryden, being a fair-minded man, really begrudge him his moment of triumph in the prologue to *Bury Fair* when he wrote :

> Those wretched poetitos, who got praise
> For writing most confounded loyal plays,
> With viler, coarser jests than at Bear-garden,
> And silly Grub-street songs worse than Tom-farthing.
> If any noble patriot did excel,
> His own and country's rights defending well,
> These yelping curs were straight loo'd on to bark,
> On the deserving man to set a mark . . . .

But Shadwell's triumph was short-lived ; in 1692, he took an over-dose of the opium to which, as well as to liquor, he was greatly addicted, and was succeeded as Poet Laureate by that cipher Nahum Tate, and as Historiographer Royal by the critic, Thomas Rymer.

Meanwhile Dryden had returned to the attack on the theatre with his new tragedy, *Don Sebastian*. He had taken great pains with this play in which he went back to the style of the heroic drama, the drama of his great successes almost twenty years before. The dedication is, naturally enough, about the moderate use of political victory and the liberality of considering the friend rather than the cause. It was addressed to his near neighbour, the Earl of Leicester, a Whig and perhaps even a Republican, who apparently took note of the sentiments of the dedication and rewarded the fallen poet generously. In the prologue Dryden addressed some hopeful words to his audience :

> . . . . there's no pretension
> To argue loss of wit from loss of pension.
> Your looks are cheerful ; and in all this place
> I see not one who wears a damning face.
> The British nation is too brave to show
> Ignoble vengeance on a vanquish'd foe.
> At least be civil to the wretch imploring,
> And lay your paws upon him without roaring . . . .
> Jove was alike to Latian and Phrygian ;
> And you well know, a play's of no religion.

Flatteringly persuasive enough, but *Don Sebastian* was not at first a success, though it was by no means due to " damning faces " in the audience ; that audience, indeed, was much more of Dryden's easy opinions now than it ever had been, and much more inclined to take

pleasure where they could find it rather than to " stiffness of opinion "
which, as Dryden said in the dedication to this very play, " is the effect
of pride, and not of philosophy. . . . True philosophy is certainly of a
more pliant nature ". It could scarcely be otherwise in a nation where
the old differences between Whig and Tory were already in flux under
the impetus of the formation of new monied classes. It was at this time,
as Mr. G. N. Clark has said, that " England was becoming not only a
business nation, but a nation with a growing capitalist class and a
growing class of wage-earners who owned nothing except their labour
power ". William's government contained both Whigs and Tories
—just as did the group which still supported the King " over the water"
(now optimistically awaiting the " call " in Calais).

No, the failure of *Don Sebastian* was due to purely technical reasons
—it was too long, for one thing ; but after certain alterations were
made it became one of the most popular of all Dryden's plays, holding
the stage for many years after his death. It could hardly not succeed,
for it contains excellent scenes, good, straightforward dialogue, and
verse full, indeed, of Shakespearian cadences, yet still with the unique
Dryden lilt :

> The genius of your Moors is mutiny ;
> They scarcely want a guide to move their madness ;
> Prompt to rebel on every weak pretence ;
> Blustering when courted, crouching when oppressed ;
> Wise to themselves, and fools to all the world ;
> Restless in change and perjured to a proverb.
> They love religion sweetened to the sense ;
> A good, luxurious, palatable faith.

But it was no use pretending : he had gone back to the theatre only
because of hard necessity ; his heart was no more in it than when he
had said farewell to the stage ten years before. Indeed, he could not
refrain from repeating some of his reasons for his dislike in the preface
to *Don Sebastian* : " Having been longer acquainted with the stage
than any poet now living, and having observed how difficult it was to
please ; that the humours of comedy were almost spent ; that love and
honour (the mistaken topics of tragedy) were quite worn out ; that the
theatres could not support their charges ; that young men without
learning set up for judges, and that they talked loudest who understood

least ; all these discouragements had not only weaned me from the
stage, but had also given me a loathing of it ".

The loathing remained . . . sometimes it led him to indiscretion, as
frustration often does. There was the affair of the prologue he wrote
for a revival of Fletcher's *Prophetess*. This contains reflections on the
way the government was throwing money away on a useless war.
Dorset had to forbid a second performance.

Dryden's frustration in the theatre had, however, another and more
useful outcome : it led him back again to translation. This was an
instinctive reaction, and his instinct was correct ; it was a translator
of poetry that his latter years were to be most usefully employed, and
most satisfactorily rewarded.

Meanwhile, there was *Amphitryon*, and long hours in the theatre.
The cast liked the comedy, with its roots in Molière and Plautus, but
its wholly Drydenesque conversation and wit—and the charming
songs : " Celia, that I once was blest " and " Fair Iris I love, and hourly
I die ". Now, too, he made up for the supposed slight on the great
Purcell by his choice of Grabut as his composer in *Albion and Albanius*.

He chose Purcell to compose the music for the songs, and added
an *amende honorable* in the dedication : " Mr. Purcell, in whose
person we hav eat length found an Englishman equal with the best
abroad ".

When the play opened, the audience endorsed the opinion of the
cast, and *Amphitryon* was one of Dryden's greatest successes. By
dedicating it to Sir William Leveson Gower, one of the leading lights
of the Revolution, Dryden took out a sort of insurance policy against
possible misconstructions. In the prologue he glances at the fact that
he is no longer permitted to write the satire that had made his fame in
the previous decade :

> The lab'ring bee, when his sharp sting is gone,
> Forgets his golden work, and turns a drone :
> Such is satire, when you take away
> That rage in which his noble vigour lay.
> What gain you by not suffering him to tease ye ?
> He neither can offend you, now, nor please ye . . . .

Encouraged by the success of *Amphitryon*, Dryden now took out of
his drawer the sketches he had made for an opera (to which *Albion and*

Albanius was originally intended only as a *lever de rideau*), and in collaboration with Purcell began to prepare it for the stage. But there were many difficulties ; *King Arthur* had after all originally been intended, at least in part, as a celebration of the discovery of the Rye House Plot. It had to be altered and Dryden altered it, but he could not forbear to complain that " not to offend the present times, nor a government which has hitherto protected me, I have been obliged so much to alter the first design, and take away so many beauties from the writing, that it is now no more what it was formerly, than the present ship of the Royal Sovereign, after so often taking down and altering, is the vessel it was in the first building ". The opera, Dryden tells us, was shown in manuscript to the Queen by his " first and best patroness ", the Duchess of Monmouth, and approved. It was a great success, but a musical rather than a poetic success. Dryden himself admits that : " My art on this occasion ought to be subservient to his (Purcell's). . . . A judicious audience will easily distinguish betwixt the songs wherein I have complied with him, and those in which I have followed the rules of poetry, in the sound and cadence of the words ". In fact, where he has followed poetic rules the result is far better. Such lines as these were excellent from Purcell's point of view but hardly from ours :

'Come if you dare ', our trumpets sound ;
'Come if you dare ', the foes rebound :
'We come, we come, we come, we come ',
Says the double, double, double, beat of the thund'ring drum . . . .

But, on the other hand, this song has become part of the English heritage of poetry :

Fairest isle, all isles excelling,
Seat of pleasures and of loves ;
Venus here will choose her dwelling,
And forsake her Cyprian groves . . . .

Well, opera has always been an " impossible " form, which makes the fact that there are operas which are great works of art the more surprising and remarkable. But the remarks of Charles de St. Denis, Seigneur de St. Evremond, one of Dryden's acquaintances, remain generally true : " An opera is an odd medley of poetry and music wherein the poet and the musician, equally confined one by the other, take a world of pain to compose a wretched performance ".

St. Evremond . . . that curious French gentleman, sometimes on the fringes, sometimes at the very centre of English society, from 1661 when he first arrived as an exile from his native country until his death at the age of 90 in 1703.   Dryden had met him casually in the company of Cowley, Hobbes and Waller in the very early years of the Restoration.   Then he had vanished, and as suddenly reappeared with a pension of £300 from Charles and his friendship, first, with Mlle. de Kérouaille, Duchess of Portsmouth, and then, oddly enough, with Mme. de Mazarin, her rival.   " His eyes ", we hear, " were blue, keen and full of fire, his face bright and intelligent, his smile somewhat satirical ".   But in 1692 these features were overshadowed by an enormous " wen at the root of his nose ".   He was a great conversationalist, a believer in the more delicate and pleasant arts of intercourse. And he wrote, equally delicate, light things—essays, three or four plays, some verses ; always in French, for he had not deigned to learn English.

Dryden never took him seriously—he did not ask to be so taken ; but he read him, and listened to him at the dinner parties of his noble friends, and learned from him that there was an art of civilised living just as there was of civilised poetry.   Dryden says in his *Life of Plutarch* that as early as 1683 he had been " casually casting his eye on the works of a French gentleman, deservedly famous for wit and criticism ". Now in 1692, Dryden writes a " character " of St. Evremond, prefixed to a translated selection of his essays.   It is not really a " character " in the seventeenth-century sense, but rather an introduction, more common today, by a distinguished man of letters to work by a less distinguished one.   Indeed, the very phrases Dryden uses have a wholly twentieth-century ring. (Did he remember, as he wrote them, the blurbs he had composed at the start of his career for Herringman at the Blue Anchor ? Did he observe how far he, and with him English prose, had come in that thirty years ?)

He says that St. Evremond's thoughts are " the standard of judicious thinking and graceful speaking "—there is an Augustan ring about that ; " he generally dives into the very bottom of his authors ;

searches into the inmost recesses of their souls, and brings up with him those hidden treasures which had escaped the diligence of others "— that is surely pure twentieth century.

The Augustan ring was no accident ; it is as symbolical of Dryden turning his back on the past and looking towards the future as was the fact that the opera *King Arthur* ended, as Scott says, " all the hopes which the world might entertain of an epic poem from Dryden on the subject of King Arthur ", the Black Prince, or on any other subject. The time for that had come and gone for personal reasons and because of the penury of King Charles ; but now it was also too late in the history of the English sensibility.   As Dryden put it : " The guardian angels of monarchies and kingdoms are not to be touched by every hand ; a man must be deeply conversant in the Platonic philosophy to deal with them ; and, therefore, I may reasonably expect that no poet of our age will presume to handle those machines for fear of discovering his own ignorance ".

The time of hope for a restoration of the Stuart line and the Roman Catholic religion had also departed, though Dryden did not know it. Indeed, it appeared to him as he stumped home from the theatre one night in 1692 that there were again favourable signs.   Large numbers of Tory politicians, dissatisfied with the trend of events under William, were turning their thoughts to the " king over the water " ; and Dryden, in choosing a subject for his next and penultimate play, relaxed his caution and picked on the story of the Spartan, Cleo-menes.   This did not require much wresting by critics to suggest Jacobite purposes.   Before the presentation of *Cleomenes* whispers of its tendentiousness caused its suspension ; it ultimately did appear— and was a failure, not because of its possible political allegories, but because it was dull.   Part of it was written by a young friend of Dryden, Thomas Southerne, an Irishman who had had a varied career in law and in the army.   Southerne, for whose plays Dryden had earlier written prologues, was a man of strong principles (his play *Oroonoko* contains a passionate plea for the abolition of the slave-trade), and also an extremely clever man of the theatre, not only as play-wright, but as producer and businessman.   Unlike such earlier theatrical friends as Nat Lee, who had gone mad, and the pathetic Thomas Otway (to whom, though scarcely a friend, Dryden also referred in favourable terms), Southerne was immensely practical : he made a fortune out of theatrical management, and retired to enjoy it to a ripe old age.   Years later Pope summed him up delightfully :

> Tom, whom heav'n sent down to raise
> The price of prologues and of plays.

It was his practicality that recommended him to Dryden ; it was Southerne's genuine admiration for a great man which made them the best of friends throughout this last ten years of the century. When Southerne's play *The Wives' Excuse* was a failure, Dryden wrote some consolatory lines :

> But rest secure, the readers will be thine . . .

adding the advice :

> The standard of thy style, let Etherege be ;
> For wit, the immortal spring of Wycherley.
> Learn after both, to draw some just design,
> And the next age will learn to copy thine . . . .

A few days later Dryden might have set him different standards, for at Will's Southerne introduced to him a young gentleman from the Middle Temple, called William Congreve. Congreve, born in Yorkshire, had like Southerne been educated at Trinity College, Dublin ; he was a young man of great personal charm, and when Dryden read in manuscript his first play, *The Old Bachelor*, he knew immediately that, in spite of a too-evident Jonsonian influence, he was in the presence of a genius. Congreve's feeling for the old poet was just as immediate, and strong.

Dryden made a few alterations in *The Old Bachelor* ; it was produced in 1693 and was a great success. Another Congreve play, *The Double Dealer*, produced in the same year, was a failure ; in spite of its miraculous stagecraft, and its dramatic prose, the like of which had never been heard before on the English stage, its characters were drawn with an honesty too brutal for the audience's taste : Congreve's complete lack of sentimentality, his piercing eye, was too much for an audience not yet able to see life in his perspective, not to appreciate his greatest gift—an incomparable sense of style.   As Dryden privately put it in a letter : "The women think he has exposed their bitchery too much ; and the gentlemen are offended with him for the discovery of their follies ".

It so happened that Dryden, too, had just had a resounding failure with his last play (as with his first) ; *Love Triumphant*, in which he had gone back to the style of the Spanish dramas of his youth, deserved to fail, and not all his protestations in his dedication of it in its printed form to the Earl of Salisbury (a relation of Lady Elizabeth) can excuse its badness. His enemies were, of course, delighted. One of them wrote :

> A reverend grisly elder first appeared,
> With solemn pace through the divided herd ;
> Apollo, laughing at his clumsy mien,
> Pronounc'd him straight the poets' alderman.
> His labouring muse did many years excel
> In ill inventing, and translating well,
> Till ' Love Triumphant ' did the cheat reveal . . . .

It was an unhappy ending to his dramatic career, yet he had somehow foreseen it ; the prologue to the play, which he had written as his farewell to the stage, was full of cynicism and not lacking a very human touch of bitterness :

> So now this poet, who forsakes the stage,
> Intends to gratify the present age . . .
> Here's nothing you will like ; no fustian scenes,
> And nothing, too, of—you know what he means.
> No double-entendres, which you sparks allow,
> To make the ladies look they know not how . . . .
> But here's a story, which no books relate,
> Coin'd from our own old poet's addle-pate . . .
> He dies, at least to us, and to the stage,
> And what he has he leaves this noble age.
> He leaves you, first, all plays of his inditing,
> The whole estate which he has got by writing . . .
> To his worst foes he leaves his honesty,
> That they may thrive upon't as much as he.
> He leaves his manners to the roaring boys,
> Who come in drunk, and fill the house with noise.
> He leaves to the dire critics of his wit,
> His silence and contempt of all they writ . . . .

He would in a way miss the theatre—the little chats with the actors, for instance, Doggett, known as " Solon ", who had acted the comic part in *Love Triumphant*, and had been assiduous in visiting Dryden at home " to consult with him concerning his own character ", as Dryden chattily told one of his correspondents.   But—in the upshot, had the theatre been anything more than his bread-and-butter, his stint ?   Such moments of self-examination are often severer than is necessary ; and Dryden must have known that *All for Love* was worth all the years of labour, but he knew, too, that that play had been the result of playing truant from his stint, for it was the only play he wrote for himself.   No, at this poignant moment of farewell, he could only think of the years wasted, and could recall nothing but the querulous voices of his critics whom yet in his heart he despised :

> Tho' he pretends no legacy to leave you,
> An old man may at least good wishes leave you.

Then with an upsurge of his essential good-nature and kindness and sympathy—" He was of a nature exceedingly humane and compassionate . . . His friendship, where he professed it, went much beyond his professions "—he thought of how much bitterer a blow had been the failure of his second play, after the success of his first, to the young man Congreve.   So when he wrote a poem as preface to the published version of that failure, *The Double Dealer*, he flew determinedly in the face of general opinion, and his words to Congreve are as moving and instinct with deep feelings as those he had written ten years before on the death of young John Oldham :

> In him all beauties of this age we see,
> Etherege his courtship, Southerne's purity,
> The satire, wit and strength of Manly Wycherley.
> All this in blooming youth you have achiev'd,
> Nor are your foil'd contemporaries griev'd.
> So much the sweetness of your manners move,
> We cannot envy you, because we love . . .
> O that your brows my laurel had sustain'd ;
> Well had I been depos'd, if you had reign'd ! . . .
> Already I am worn with cares and age,
> And just abandoning th'ungrateful stage ;

> Unprofitably kept at Heav'n's expense,
> I live a rent-charge on his providence :
> But you, whom every Muse and Grace adorn,
> Whom I foresee to better fortune born,
> Be kind to my remains ; and O defend,
> Against your judgment your departed friend !
> Let not the insulting foe my fame pursue,
> But shade those laurels which descend to you ;
> And take for tribute what these lines express :
> You merit more ; nor could my love do less.

Dryden had, as we have seen, that prime gift of the true critic : he recognised genius at first glance. He had that even rarer gift in literary men—the readiness to acknowledge another's genius. With all this went a modest and sympathetic nature which makes friendship easy—combined with the discrimination that will avoid extending friendship to those who will abuse or scorn it.

ii

In 1692, Tonson published a translation of the satires of Juvenal and Persius ; those of Juvenal were translated by Dryden assisted by his two elder sons, by Tate, the Laureate, Bowles, Stepney, Hervey, Power, Creech, and by Congreve ; the translations of Persius were the work of Dryden alone. To the translations—which did what they were meant to do, that is to make money, and ran quickly into a second edition—Dryden prefixed a long " Discourse concerning Satire ", addressed to his old friend, the Earl of Dorset. It was the first of a number of rambling reflections on literature and authors and on himself which he wrote in the last decade of the century, happily belying his promise that as " the tattling quality of age . . . is always narrative . . . this is the last time I will commit the crime of prefaces, or trouble the world with my notions of anything that relates to verse ".

In the " Discourse concerning Satire ", he is looking back over his life as a poet, and sees himself at the time of the *Essay of Dramatic Poesy* as " sailing in a vast ocean, without other help than the polestar of the ancients, and the rules of the French stage among the moderns ". He thanks Dorset for his help at that time and ever since. He speaks (as we have already seen) of his desire to write an epic, but now it is too

late, for " age has overtaken me, and want, a more insufferable evil,
thro' the change of the times, has wholly disenabled me ".   He does
suggest, however, that future poets might well search the Old Testament for epic machinery : " Christian poets have not hitherto been
acquainted with their own strength . . . The perusing of one chapter in
the prophecy of Daniel, and accommodating what there they find with
the principles of Platonic philosophy, as it is now Christianis'd, would
have made the ministry of angels as strong an engine for the working
up heroic poetry, in our religion, as that of the ancients has been to
raise theirs by the fables of their gods . . . ."

He speaks again of Milton, and says that his subject in *Paradise Lost*
is not that of an heroic poem, " properly so call'd.   His design is the
losing of our happiness ; his event is not prosperous, like that of all
other epic works ; his heavenly machines are many, and his human
persons are but two ".   No man, indeed, has copied the manner of
Homer ; he has his flats, certainly, but they are due to his getting " into
a track of scripture ".   His " antiquated words " were his choice, and
in that he imitated Spenser as Spenser imitated Chaucer ; such words
can properly be revived " when either they are more sounding, or
more significant, than those in practice ", but they should be explained
and used only with moderation.   He will not justify Milton's blank
verse because " whatever causes he alleges for the abolishing of rhyme
. . . . his own particular reason is plainly this, that rhyme was not his
talent ".   Even in his youth, Dryden maintains, " his rhyme is always
constrain'd and forc'd . . . at an age when the soul is most pliant, and
the passion of love makes almost every man a rhymer tho' not a poet ".
It is a strange opinion to have of the author of *Il Penseroso* and *L'Allegro*:
of all the possible explanations, none is satisfactory except that which
attributes a lapse of memory to Dryden.

Of Donne he had spoken recently (in his dedication of his elegy,
Eleonora) saying that he was " the greatest wit, tho' not the greatest
poet of our nation . . ."   He goes on to make a further criticism here :
" Would not Donne's *Satires*, which abound with so much wit, appear
more charming, if he had taken care of his words, and of his numbers ?
. . . . I may safely say it of this present age, that if we are not so great
wits as Donne, yet certainly we are better poets ".

Donne like Cowley had wanted the saving grace of a sense of

decorum. Donne " affects the metaphysics, not only in his satires, but in his amorous verses, where nature only should reign ; and perplexes the minds of the fair sex with nice speculations of philosophy when he should engage their hearts and entertain them with the softnesses of love. In this (if I may be pardon'd for so bold a truth) Mr. Cowley has copied him to a fault ; so great a one, in my opinion, that it throws his *Mistress* infinitely below his *Pindarics* and his latter compositions, which are undoubtedly the best of his poems . . ." A little later, in the preface to *The Fables*, Dryden was to give the final, and fair, *quietus* to this " darling of his youth " : " One of our late great poets is sunk in his reputation, because he could never forgo any conceit which came his way, but swept like a dragnet, great and small . . . He must always be thought a great poet, he is no longer esteem'd a good writer ; and for ten impressions, which his works have had in so many successive years, yet at present a hundred books are scarcely purchas'd once a twelvemonth ; for, as my late Lord Rochester said, tho' somewhat profanely, ' Not being of God, he could not stand '." Dryden's masters now, as he was to acknowledge in the dedication of his translation of the *Aeneid*, were older and greater poets.

Much of his discourse is naturally concerned with satire, and we have already observed his views upon lampoons, classical satire and his own work in *Absalom and Achitophel*. With regard to the merits of Horace and Juvenal, his opinions have altered slightly. In 1685, he wrote that Horace's satires are " incomparably beyond " Juvenal's ; now he is not quite so sure. Many considerations, he says, seem " to incline the balance on the side of Horace, and to give him the preference to Juvenal, not only in profit, but also in pleasure. But, after all, I must confess that the delight which Horace gives me is but languishing. Be pleas'd still to understand, that I speak of my own taste only ; he may ravish other men ; but I am too stupid and insensible to be tickled. Where he barely grins himself, and, as Scaliger says, only shows his white teeth, he cannot provoke me to any laughter. His urbanity, that is, his good manners, are to be commended, but his wit is faint ; and his salt, if I may dare to say so, almost insipid. Juvenal is of a more vigorous and masculine wit ; he gives me as much pleasure as I can bear ; he fully satisfies my expectation ; he treats his subject home : his spleen is rais'd, and he raises mine : I have the pleasure of concernment in all he says . . . The meat of Horace is more nourishing ; but the cookery of Juvenal more exquisite : so that, granting Horace to be the more general philosopher, we cannot deny that Juvenal was the greater poet, I mean in satire ".

Dryden was always ready to admit his changes of taste ; in this case, the change may have been due to the fact that he himself was a great satirist frustrated by circumstances from writing the satire on the new age that he alone could have done, and thus all the more interested in the keener and more " masculine " satire of Juvenal than in the urbanity of Horace. But—what phrases, what brilliance of perception, brilliantly and yet modestly expressed !

Two more points : Dryden thinks it worth while in this discourse to refer to the audience he has in mind for his translations. Barten Holyday, the early seventeenth-century translator of Juvenal and Persius, " wrote for fame, and wrote to scholars ; we write only for the pleasure and entertainment of those gentlemen and ladies, who, tho' they are not scholars, are not ignorant : persons of understanding and good sense, who, not having been conversant in the original, or at least not having made Latin verse so much their business as to be critics in it, would be glad to find if the wit of our two great authors be answerable to their fame and reputation in the world ". It is the phrase " persons . . . not having been conversant in the original " which suggests that a change has occurred : Dryden's early poems had been addressed to an audience capable of picking up a classical allusion without difficulty ; the new reading public, as Dryden was aware of it, came from a different level of society—the successful tradesmen now coming into their own and shortly to be provided for by that successful tradesman, Daniel Defoe, and by the go-between of the learned and the unlearned, Joseph Addison, already in London after a brilliant career in Oxford. It was, however, a reading public which still had an immense respect for poetry and particularly classical poetry ; it was after all this public which after the turn of the century made Pope's fortune by buying in great quantities his translations of the *Iliad* and the *Odyssey*.

A final point : Dryden makes here one more personal statement, a defence of his moral character. " More libels have been written against me, than almost any man now living ; and I had reason on my side to have defended my own innocence. I speak not of my poetry which I have wholly given up to the critics : let them use it as they please ; posterity, perhaps, may be more favourable to me ; for interest and passion will lie buried in another age, and partiality and prejudice be forgotten. I speak of my morals which have been suffi-ciently aspers'd : that only sort of reputation that ought to be dear to every man, and is to me. But let the world witness for me, that I have often been wanting to myself in that particular ; I have seldom answer'd any scurrilous lampoon, when it was in my power to have exposed my enemies ; and, being naturally vindictive, have suffer'd in silence, and possess'd my soul in quiet.

" Anything, tho' never so little, which a man speaks of himself, in my opinion, is still too much ; and therefore I will waive the subject..."

He did not entirely succeed in concealing his personal feelings ; for next year, in his dedication of *Examen Poeticum* (*The Third Miscellany*) to Lord Radcliffe he could not forbear making a further remark on those who slandered him : " Ill writers are usually the sharpest censors ... The corruption of a poet is the generation of a critic : I mean of a critic in the general acceptation of this age, for formerly they were quite another species of men. They were defenders of poets, and com-mentators on their works ; to illustrate obscure beauties ; to place some passages in a better light ; to redeem others from malicious interpretations ; to help out an author's modesty, who is not ostenta-tious of his wit . . ."

And then quite suddenly the façade vanishes ; the old poet throws off the mask, and a bitter *cri de coeur* is given forth : " 'Tis a vanity common to all writers, to overvalue their own productions ; and 'tis better for me to own this failing in myself than the world to do it for me. For what other reason have I spent my life in so unprofitable a study ? Why am I grown old in seeking so barren a reward as fame ? The same parts and application which have made me a poet might have rais'd me to any honours of the gown, which are often given to men of as little learning and less honesty than myself. No government has ever been, or ever can be, wherein time-servers and blockheads will not be upper-most. The persons are only chang'd, but the same jug-glings in state, the same hypocrisy in religion, the same self-interest and mismanagement will remain for ever. Blood and money will be

N

lavish'd in all ages, only for the preferment of new faces, with old consciences ".

It was all true : politics were (and are) like that ; Dryden was well qualified for the academic post he had thought of a decade before, and would now have been spending his declining years in the comfort and quietude of a college cloister rather than in the hurly-burly of writing to live. Yes, it was true—but at the bottom of it all was that appalling moment of self-revelation when he saw his life to have been spent in seeking so barren a reward as fame. Fame ! the will-o'-the-wisp that had danced through his life, and that was connected so closely in his mind with what he regarded as his overweening sin, pride. And pride was not so easily conquered ; he put it all in a single sentence in his dedication of the *Aeneid:* " A man is humbled one day, and his pride returns the next ".

Only God could throw out pride—that at least he knew now—and it was God he called upon in his paraphrase of the hymn, *Veni Creator Spiritus :*

> Proceeding Spirit, our defence,
> Who dost the gift of tongues dispense,
> And crown'st thy gifts with eloquence !
> Refine and purge our earthy parts ;
> But, O, inflame and fire our hearts !
> Our frailties help, our vice control,
> Submit the senses to the soul . . . .
> Make us eternal truths receive,
> And practice all that we believe . . . .

And as he wrote, and was a little comforted, there came into his mind the lines he had written six years before :

> O sharp convulsive pangs of agonizing pride !
> Down then thou rebel, never more to rise . . .

It was not to be supposed that a dedication containing such forth-right sentiments would recommend itself either to him to whom it was addressed, Lord Radcliffe (who had married a natural daughter of Charles II), nor to the government then in power. Lord Rad-cliffe realised neither that it would be Dryden's dedication only that preserved his name to future generations, nor that the trans-lations themselves—of part of Ovid's *Metamorphoses* and from the sixth book of Homer's *Iliad*—were fine examples of Dryden's art. Dryden himself, in a letter from the country whence he retired for a short time soon after the publication of the *Miscellany*, tells Tonson plainly : " I am sure you thought my Lord Radcliffe wou'd have done something : I guessed more truly that he cou'd not ".

Worse still, the governement of William and Mary took the outburst on governments in general as applying to them. " About a fortnight ago ", Dryden continues in his letter, " I had an intimation from a friend by letter that one of the secretaries, I suppose Trenchard, had informed the Queen that I had abus'd her government (those were the words) in my Epistle to my Lord Radcliffe ; and that thereupon she had commanded her historiographer, Rymer, to fall on my plays ; which he assures me he is now doing. I doubt not his malice from a former hint you gave me ; and if he be employ'd I am confident it is of his own seeking ; who, you know, has spoken slightingly of me in his last critique " (*A Short View of Tragedy*) " and that gave me occasion to snarl again. In your next let me know what you can learn of this matter ".

The " snarl " against Rymer had also been in the dedication to Lord Radcliffe ; Dryden had referred to " another sort of insects, more venomous than the former ; those who manifestly aim at the destruction of our poetical church and state ; who allow nothing to their countrymen, either of this or of the former age. These attack the living by raking up the ashes of the dead ; well knowing that if they can subvert their original title to the stage, we who claim under them must fall of course. . . ."

When Rymer's tragedy, *Edgar,* failed, he " snarled " again at " Shakespeare's critic . . . to find his faults, and yet himself make worse ". . . .

> A precious reader in poetic schools,
> Who by his own examples damns the rules.

Again in his poem on Congreve, he puts Tom Rymer on a par with Tom Shadwell ; and well says in a letter to Dennis : " Shakespeare had a genius for it (tragedy) ; and we know, in spite of Mr. Rymer, that genius alone is a greater virtue (If I may so call it) than all other qualifications put together. You see what success this learned critic has found in the world, after his blaspheming Shakespeare. Almost all the faults which he has discovered are truly there ; yet who will read Mr. Rymer, and not read Shakespeare ? For my own part I reverence Mr. Rymer's learning, but I detest his ill-nature and his arrogance. I indeed, and such as I, have reason to be afraid of him, but Shakespeare has not ".

In the end, Dryden forgave Rymer and referred to him with respect : was that, perhaps, because he remembered how much he had learned from him of the classical drama twenty years before ?

iii

But mostly these middle years of the decade were happy ones for Dryden ; sunbeams seem to play over his movements, whether in the country or in London, and there is an air of contentment about him, in his letters as in the great work he now began, the translation of Virgil's *Georgics* and the *Aeneid*. It is true that the beams came from a sun already slowly sinking, and that always there were not too far distant shadows—the shadow of shortage of money, the shadow of the departure of his three sons, barred by their religion from most posts at home, to Italy where they took posts in the Pope's entourage.

Yet life *was* good—and varied, so varied indeed that sometimes, as Dryden jogged away once more from London on another country visit, or as he sat at Will's meeting yet another young man of promise, it seemed as though his life had become a kaleidoscope containing brilliant figures, who danced before him delightfully, but at a distance, for whom he was the central figure. And beyond them, an ever-changing backdrop, lay the fine, new streets of London, the beautiful houses of his friends, the sloping lawns and fruitful orchards of country mansions, the woods and streams of England, the rivers in which he fished, the rustics who saluted him, and the clever men and the rich nobles who wrote for his advice and who sought out the company of England's greatest living poet.

Now he is tripping out of town with his publisher Tonson—parsimonious, red-haired, freckled-face and ugly ; they visit Northamptonshire, and after Tonson goes back to town Dryden stays on at the house of his friend, Sir Matthew Dudley, at Clapton Manor, only two miles from Titchmarsh. What matter that Sir Matthew is often away in his calèche and, Dryden writes to Tonson, " I suspect a wooing " ?

(He was right ; Sir Matthew was paying his court to Lady Mary O'Brien, daughter of the Earl of Thomond, who lived some twenty miles away at Great Billing.) What matter, too, if one night he is " obliged to sit up . . . out of civility to strangers who were benighted, and to resign my bed to them " ? No matter at all, for he spends his day fishing with Sir Matthew's son, William—and as a matter of fact it was lucky he *had* fished that day " for if I had not taken a lusty pike, they must have gone supperless to bed, four ladies and two gentlemen : for Mr. Dudley and I were alone, with but one man and no maid in the house ". He was rather proud of his fishing ; when someone told him that Tom D'Urfey, the play and song writer, was a good fisherman, Dryden commented " *He fish !*—he cannot even write ! "

Then Dryden is again at Gerrard Street in the front room ready, though he is in the midst of his labours on Virgil, to carry on a long correspondence with his new friend, William Walsh. Walsh, the son of a Worcestershire squire, is somewhat of a dandy, but a dandy with a fine taste in poetry ; he has been at Wadham College, Oxford, and then on the continent, in Naples and Venice. That was what first made him interesting to Dryden who says that Walsh " had improved himself by travelling ". Walsh had begun by sending Dryden a poem with an unsigned letter, asking him to " Deal frankly with me, Sir, and let me know without any compliment your real thoughts . . . ."

Dryden saw through this at once, but he wrote back desiring to know more of the young man. They met at Will's (on one occasion there, as Walsh remembered, Dryden stated that there were not more than twenty good epigrams in Martial), and then Walsh went back to Abberley in Gloucestershire. Soon he is asking Dryden for a preface for his *Dialogue Concerning Women ;* Dryden obliges, and Walsh is delighted. He boasts of his intimacy with the great poet in a letter to one of his lady friends, and says that very few people have had, as he has had, their verses corrected by Mr. Dryden. The two became more friendly still, and Dryden chats to Walsh of all manner of things : he has been to the theatre to see D'Urfey's new farce, " but his luck has left him ; it was suffered but four days ; and then kicked off for ever. Yet his Second Act was wonderfully diverting ; where the scene was in Bedlam : and Mrs. Bracegirdle and Solon were mad : the singing was wonderfully good, and the two whom I nam'd sung better than

Redding and Mr. Ayloff whose trade it was ; at least our partiality
carried it for them.   The rest was woeful stuff, and concluded with
catcalls of which the two noble Dukes of Richmond and St. Albans
were chief managers . . ."   There is news of the war (the King of
France has left Versailles and is believed to be going to Flanders " and
intends to offer battle ") ; Mr. Wycherley's poems are not coming out
before Michaelmas ; and, oh yes, it has been so hot in Rome, he hears
from his sons, " that they could only stir out morning and evening ;
and were already in the midst of peas and cherries ; 'tis quite contrary
here where we have had nothing but rain, cold weather, and a late
Spring time without any hope of any Summer ".   Yes, and the cider
you sent was " perfectly good ".

Again, Walsh is writing a defence of the English method of writing
tragedies with a comic underplot ; " and ", says Dryden, " not only
all present poets, but all who are to come in England, will thank you
for freeing them from the too servile imitation of the Ancients ".   But,
Dryden adds, I fear that this is not your real opinion and that you are
writing this out of consideration for " my irregular way of tragi-
comedies, in my doppia favola . . . I will never defend that practice,
for I know it distracts the hearers.   But I know, with all, that it has
hitherto pleased them for the sake of variety, and for the particular
taste which they have for low comedy ".

Ten of our ships, laden with corn, are said to have been seized and
carried into France.   What other news ?   A minor thing : " I have
undertaken to translate all Virgil ; and as an essay have already
paraphrased the third Georgic, as an example ; it will be published in
Tonson's next Miscellanies, in Hilary term.   I propose to do it by
subscription ; having an hundred and two brass cuts with the coat of
arms of the subscriber to each cut ; every subscriber to pay five guineas;
half in hand besides another inferior subscription of two guineas, for
the rest whose names are only written in a catalogue printed with the
book . . ."

After a time the correspondence between them languished and by
accident they seldom met : when Walsh was in town, Dryden seemed
to be in the country, and vice-versa ; but the friendship remained,
and Dryden repeatedly said that, in his opinion, Walsh was " the best
critic of our nation ".

Walsh was a sweet-natured man ; he it was who encouraged the young, deformed Pope to pursue classic correctness of versification, and thus became a living link between the two great poets. Another of Dryden's correspondents, however, far from being sweet-natured, had a quite frightening reputation, and when Dryden received a first letter from him, he delayed some time in answering it. It was from John Dennis. Dennis had been expelled from Caius College, Cambridge, for stabbing a fellow-student ; he had come to London and written bitter and vituperative pamphlets in the Whig interest ; he was known for his ill-temper and jealousy. A letter from such a man naturally raised doubts in its recipient. Yet the letter seemed genuine enough, and full of praise for Dryden's poems of which he said : " When at any time I have been dejected by disappointments, or tormented by cruel passions, the recourse to your verses has calm'd my soul, or raised it to transports which made it contemn tranquillity . . ." Perhaps if he had continued to read Dryden's verses he would not now be embalmed in *The Dunciad*.

Dryden's reply is chatty and confidential, but there is no sign of the warmth of feeling with which he wrote to Walsh ; and the correspondence lapsed.

Another correspondence intervened—that with Tonson. For the poet and his publisher were no longer quite so friendly as they had been; it is perhaps a not unusual result of mixing business and pleasure. Dryden seems to have felt that the financial arrangements made between them for the translation of Virgil were unfavourable to him, but being short of money he was obliged to accept them. The bargain had been sealed, as was the custom, over a glass in a tavern, and Congreve was present ; but Tonson was slow at paying, and when he did pay it was in gold, then a much-depreciated currency owing to the custom of chipping pieces off the coins. Dryden writes to him brusquely : "Some kind of intercourse must be carried on betwixt us while I am translating Virgil. Therefore I give you notice that I have done the seventh Aeneid in the country ; and intend some few days hence to go upon the eighth : when that is finished I expect £50 in good silver, not such as I had formerly. I am not obliged to take gold, neither will I ; nor stay for it beyond 24 hours after it is due . . . I desire neither excuses nor reasons from you : for I am but too well satisfied already.   The notes and prefaces shall be short ; because you shall get the more by saving paper ", he witheringly concludes.

Tonson replied apologetically, but did not change his terms or his methods in the slightest.   He sent the money in silver as requested— but in shillings and sixpences, and Dryden found that they, too, were not negotiable, so he sent them back.   Dryden writes bitterly : " Upon trial I find all of your trade are sharpers, and you not more than others ; therefore I have not wholly left you ... Let me hear from you as speedily as you can ".

Dryden wants to buy two of Mr. Tompion's famous watches to send to his sons in Rome, but Mr. Tompion will not take gold.   " But he will take a goldsmith's bill for two and twenty pounds which is their price.   I desire you wou'd give him such a bill, and abate it out of the next £50 which you are to pay me when Virgil is finished . . . . Mr. Tompion's man will be with me at four o'clock in the afternoon, and bring the watches, and must be paid at sight.   I desire you there- fore to procure a goldsmith's bill, and let me have it before that hour, and send an answer by my boy ".

He asks Tonson to meet the Towcester carrier who lodges at the "Castle" in Smithfield and collect the rents from his Northamptonshire estate from him.   " If I were not deeply engaged in my studies, which will be finished in a day or two, I would not put you to this trouble ..."

Sometimes Tonson went really too far ; he insisted, for instance, that Dryden should dedicate his Virgil to King William.   Dryden refused, as obdurately as he had refused to write an elegy on the death of Queen Mary in 1694.   Tonson at once became even less co-operative than before ; one day he refused point-blank to do Dryden some small service, and the poet sat down and gave these three lines to a messenger with the injunction : " Tell the dog that he who wrote these can write more ".   The lines were :

> With leering looks, bull-faced and freckled fair,
> With two left legs, and Judas-coloured hair,
> And frowsy pores that taint the ambient air.

Tonson hastened to comply—but in the end got his own back, for although he did not get the desired dedication to the King, he cun- ningly altered each picture of Aeneas to resemble His Majesty whose hook-nose was one of his most notable features. Some wit wrote of this trick :

> Old Jacob, by deep judgment swayed,
> To please the wise beholders,
> Has placed old Nassau's hook-nosed head
> On poor Aeneas' shoulders.
>
> To make the parallel hold tack,
> Methinks there's little lacking ;
> One took his father pick-a-back,
> And t'other sent his packing.

Dryden, for all his tweaking of Tonson's ear, was half afraid of him ; after all, it was his livelihood that was at stake in these exchanges. One day at home Dryden was entertaining a young man, Henry St. John, later to become famous as Viscount Bolingbroke ; St. John heard some-one else enter the house. Dryden broke off his conversation and said to him : " This is Tonson ; you will take care not to depart before he goes away : for I have not completed the sheet which I promised him ; and if you leave me unprotected, I shall suffer all the rudeness to which his resentment can prompt his tongue ".

But — Tonson had to be tolerated, not only because he was, as Dryden admitted, a good publisher by comparison with the others, but also because he could, for instance, push a play Dryden's second son, John, had written, *The Husband his own Cuckold*, and he could expedite the letters between Dryden and his sons in Rome—although he was not always careful about the agents he chose, as Dryden complained in a letter to him. After the first exuberant flush of their trip together into the country, Dryden's attitude changed ; in the end it was that of a nervous man towards his dentist.

And so from Gerrard Street, where he slaves at his translations, conducts his business affairs, meets his aristocratic or more utilitarian friends, writes his letters and suffers from the moodiness of his wife, he passes about four in the afternoon along Little Newport Street, into Long Acre and so to the house with the sign of the rose on the corner in Covent Garden. Sometimes Congreve or Southerne accompanies him from his house ; on one occasion, when he was in the country, they met him four miles out of London, and thence bore him in triumph back to Will's where a company of young poets, poetasters, dramatists and pamphlet writers awaited him, the Grand Cham of literary London in the fullness of his age.

As he enters the upstairs room, the buzz of talk dies down ; those who are standing make way as he passes to a seat near the balcony, for it is summer-time ; those who are sitting at the tables against the walls stare up curiously ; even the men immersed in the game of shovel-board stop their play for a moment.   So this is the great Dryden, short, tubby, wigless, with his wavy grey locks playing about his forehead and his eyes modestly downcast . . . What he has seen, what he has written, this man—and what he is writing now, something for all England to be proud of, one great poet translating another !

His escorts, Congreve and Southerne, nod their greetings to acquaint-ances, and then pull a big elbow-chair forward for Dryden, who quietly seats himself, takes out an enormous snuff-box (he is said to make his own snuff of which he is inordinately fond) and offers a pinch to one or two of the young men who have drifted as unostentatiously as possible towards his chair.

A dark-browed man with an apron pushes his way without ceremony through the men round the balcony—all talking, no drinking is bad for trade—and inquires Mr. Dryden's wishes. This is William Erwin, " Will " in fact, who in spite of the fame of his coffee house has had to seek sanctuary from his debtors, and is only recently free again. Mr. Dryden smiles faintly and will take a glass of wine ; Congreve follows his example, but Southerne orders a glass of ale with ginger and nutmeg in it : " Bad for your liver ", comments Dryden and immediately feels a twinge of his gout.

Julian, " Secretary to the Muses ", pushes his obsequious way for-ward, his hands full of copies he has made of the latest lampoons ; he is roughly pushed back from the presence by a young man with a some-what portentous air, already perhaps a trifle drunk, but never forgetful of the arts that make a man welcome in company, and particularly the company of the great. Joseph Addison spends his days and his nights in the coffee house, but he never forgets his attentions to the great. Dryden he has celebrated (or propitiated) in some fulsome verses :

> Prevailing warmth has still thy mind possessed,
> And second youth is kindled in thy breast . . . .
> Thy lines have heightened Virgil's majesty,
> And Horace wonders at himself in thee . . . .

In return, he is to be allowed to write the arguments of the books of the *Aeneid,* and an essay on the *Georgics;* his assiduity elsewhere will also in a year or two gain for him a travelling bursary to the continent and high preferment in the civil service. But, in spite of his flattery and his occasional pomposities, Dryden likes him ; it is difficult not to like the young Addison, ever ready to render a service, clever, widely-read and already possessing a developed judgment—if only he wouldn't try to make his friends keep the same late hours and drink the same deep potations as he does himself !

The room is a-buzz again now with a thousand topics of the day : the King's statement in Parliament that there had been a plot to assassinate him at Turnham Green ; the Whig " Junto's " desire to create a new East India Company ; the hopes of peace ; the latest play and the latest lampoon. The little knot of people round Dryden are talking of poetry and the classics and of satire ; the ball passes easily from hand to hand, rather as an offering to Dryden than from a desire to exchange views. Then Dryden says in his quiet voice : " If anything of mine is good in the satirical way, 'tis my *MacFlecknoe* ; and I value myself the more on it, because it is the first piece of ridicule written in heroics". There is a respectful pause ; then a shy voice from the back of the little group says that it is indeed a fine poem, but he had not imagined it to be the first that was ever written that way. Congreve peers past the outraged Addison ; Southerne sits up shocked ; a young man with short, coarse hair and country clothes is revealed, blushing in his confusion at having been so bold as to address the great man. But Dryden raises his eyes and smiles on the youth (Congreve noting to himself that the old poet is " of a very easy, of very pleasing access ") ; he asks him how long he has been a dealer in poetry and who did he imagine had written so before ? The youth, emboldened by his calm voice, names Boileau's *Lutrin* and Tassoni's *Secchia Rapita.* " 'Tis true ", Dryden replies, " I had forgot them ". (Congreve observes to himself : " He was extreme ready, and gentle in his correction of the errors of any writer, who thought fit to consult him and full as ready and patient to admit of the reprehensions of others, in respect of his own oversights or mistakes "). The young man, whose name is Lockier, sighs with relief ; and is overjoyed when Dryden asks him to chat again with him another day. They become friends, and Lockier, later to become Dean of Peterborough, never forgets his evenings at Will's.

But not all evenings there pass quite so calmly. Sometimes one of those poetasters or pamphleteers with a grudge against Dryden and a feeling of being left out takes a seat at one of the side-tables, and after a few drinks with some of his friends begins to make loud remarks about " the lordly leader of his bleating troops ", and demands to know why the great man always looks sober when everyone else is becoming gayer every moment. Sometimes there is another sort of unpleasantness. There is a young man, tall and with flashing blue eyes, who often comes into Will's and as by right makes his way immediately into the inner circle of Dryden, Congreve and Addison. Until recently he has been secretary to Sir William Temple at Moor Park in Surrey, now he is attempting to write, and imperiously demanding the name of poet. Unfortunately neither his temper, which is short, nor his poetry, which is vague and undistinguished, earn him the name by right ; he has shown some of his odes to Dryden, to whom he is distantly related, and Dryden, unforgivably, has told him : " Cousin Swift, you will never be a Pindaric poet ". Already Swift has taken his revenge in the Introduction to *The Tale of a Tub* (as yet unpublished), and will do elsewhere. He shows his attitude plainly enough in his conversation, but at Will's in the nineties, no one suspects that he is any more than an ambitious, disgruntled and bad-tempered young man, cut out *faute de mieux* for a country parsonage in Ireland. Yet his presence is curiously oppressive, as though there were a dynamo buzzing away inside him, and storing up electricity for which as yet there is no use ; he disturbs Dryden, though he makes no comment ; everyone is relieved when he leaves. This is not the *ambience* for him, though he is to find, and be happy in, a not dissimilar one a few years hence—one in which there is no Great Man to dominate, and where wit and learning find their own level.

It is time to go, but Dryden lingers on under Addison's plea for just another " brimmer ", though he knows it is not good for his gout.

But the company is in the full flood of conviviality, with Congreve at his wittiest and Southerne roaring with laughter and slapping his hands on his fat thighs. Dryden is in process of denying that he takes a diet of stewed prunes before writing his songs ; and he is denying it with as many " I'gads " as the day that expression was first made fun of in *The Rehearsal* long, long ago. " Tho' 'tis true ", he adds, " that I am very given to damsons—preserv'd whole, mind ye, not in mash, never in mash ". (Addison is recounting a story of the King's mistress.) " Nor is it true I had blood let before my tragedies—though old Scarborough, God rest his soul, would always have been letting me blood. Now Dr. Hobbs . . . ." And Dryden falls to thinking of the other Hobbes, that witty " old bear ", who believed in blowing through his tubes and singing at night to clear himself before retiring. Hobbes—dead sixteen years or more ; Waller, his friend, and Denham, dead ; young, mad Rochester ; dear John Oldham—what a poet he might have been !—and poor Nat Lee—all gone. For a moment a wave of nostalgia, of pity, of age sweeps over him ; but it is swiftly gone, for someone is talking of the new D'Urfey play they have just seen, and expressing astonishment that even he could write so badly. " Ah, Sir ", says Dryden, " you do not know my friend Tom so well as I do ; I'll answer for him, he can write worse yet ". It is late, the " brimmers " have gone round well and truly—and everyone roars.

At that moment, the door opens and the ancient, lined visage of Sir Robert Howard appears. Dryden rises precipitately and the party breaks up. " Now, John ", says Sir Robert, linking his arm in Dryden's " this question of my play you are to alter ; as I see it, it would take you but a few weeks . . . ." " Ye are wrong, dear Robert ", the poet replies, " for to study the subject alone—The Conquest of China by the Tartars !—would take six months—and ", the two old gentlemen successfully negotiate the steps and turn into the street (did Dryden recall the ignominy of Rose Alley ?) " Well, I couldn't do it under six months ". The voices die away in the balmy air of the summer night ; two old friends are on their way to bed.

iv

As the months creep on towards July, 1697, Dryden is increasingly occupied with his Virgil, and it seems as though his whole mind is dominated by the words and the spirit of the great Roman. He goes often to stay in the country, for he suffers from catarrhal colds (" am thick of hearing ") ; one of his favourite places is Denham Court in Buckinghamshire, the country house of Sir William Bowyer to whom he is related by marriage, for it is conveniently near London. Dryden writes in a note to the Second *Georgic* : " Nature has conspired with art to make the garden at Denham Court of Sir William's own plantation one of the most delicious spots of ground in England : it contains not above five acres (just above the compass of Alcinous's garden described in the *Odyssey*) ; but Virgil says, in this very *Georgic* :

> —Laudato ingentia rura ;
> Exiguum colito "

He discusses various points in the *Georgics* with Sir William, who is something of an expert on horticulture and arboriculture. Dryden, referring to the Second *Georgic*, writes : " For want of sufficient skill in gardening, agriculture etc., I may possibly be mistaken in some terms. But concerning grafting, my honour'd friend, Sir William Bowyer, has assur'd me that Virgil has shewn more of poetry than skill, at least in relation to our more northern climates ; and that many of our stocks will not receive such grafts as our poet tells us would bear in Italy ".

Illuminating comments on natural history were made to him by another " most ingenious friend, Sir Henry Shere ". Dryden tells us that this gentleman had observed " thro' a glass hive, that the young prince of the bees, or heir presumptive of the crown, approaches the king's apartment with great reverence, and for three successive mornings demands permission to lead forth a colony of that year's bees. If his petition be granted, which he seems to make by humble hummings, the swarm arises under his conduct ; if the answer be, *le roi s'avisera,* that is, if the old monarch think it be not convenient for the public good to part with so many of his subjects, the next morning the prince is found dead before the threshold of his palace ".

It was such advice which helped him to a truer understanding of Virgil, and drew him closer to the country from which he sprang, and to which he so often felt the need to return.

But it was not only Bowyer and Shere who gave Dryden help. It seemed indeed that the whole nation, or the civilised part of it, were ready to help, to spur on the aged author in his great undertaking, and to participate by subscribing or in some other way in the production of what was felt to be the greater glory of literature and of England. It was, in a sense, the nation which had inspired him to his task in the beginning—the nation whose mouthpiece was the critic Motteux, in the *Gentleman's Journal* of March, 1694, when he wrote : " We hope that Mr. Dryden will undertake to give us a translation of Virgil ; 'tis indeed a most difficult work, but if anyone can assure himself of success in attempting so bold a task, 'tis doubtless the Virgil of our age for whose noble pen that best of Latin poets seems reserved ". As Dr. Johnson put it : " The nation considered its honour as interested in the event ". Gilbert Dolben, son of the former Archbishop of York, presented Dryden on his first announcing his intention—at a dinner party at Edward Sheldon's at which the recording Evelyn was present —with " all the several editions of Virgil, and all the commentaries of those editions in Latin ". Dr. Knightly Chetwode wrote the Life of Virgil and the preface to the *Pastorals ;* Sir William Trumball, one of the Secretaries of State, and later the friend of Pope, advised and encouraged him ; the Earl of Exeter invited him to pursue some part of his labours at his magnificent house at Burleigh in Northamptonshire. " In a village belonging to his family I was born ; and under his roof I endeavour'd to make that *Aeneid* (the seventh) appear in English with as much lustre as I could ". And Sir Robert Howard was always at hand ; Dryden talked with him about the psychology of the principal actors in *Aeneid,* for " he is better conversant than any man that I know in the doctrine of the Stoics . . . ."

All over England—and the continent, too—as the months crept on men were discussing the forthcoming translation. Dryden was now at the very pinnacle of his fame, and his name was known even among those ment to whom poets and poetry made little appeal. Letters between friends to whom Dryden was personally unknown contained mention of the translation, and as Dryden toiled on revising the last pages, such letters as this were crossing Europe—it is from Thomas Burnet of Kemney to the Electress Sophia : " We are every hour impatiently expecting the coming out of Mr. Dryden's laborious version of Virgil into English. Virgil was the most heroic poet that ever sung in the most flourishing times of ingenious arts and wit in the Roman Empire ; and Mr. Dryden (for his vast learning, perfection in our language, noble fancy, richness of thought, ripeness of age, and experience of more than 50 years in the practice, and the many triumphant pieces of his composition already extant) hath the fairest pretences to the immortal laurels of Virgil as prince of all our English poets. He is so old that it is looked upon as his leaving the world of poetry ; and if he can but make a good exit, all that ever a poet can wish for in his declining days. If it fall out other ways, they will say his Muse is at her dotage ; and ought not to be heard. However we all expect to feast ourselves upon this book when it comes forth ; then I shall show your E. Hsse the relish the best critics have of it. It is a disadvantage to be translating the best piece of poetry of the ancients, whereof the version, being but an imitation or copy, must come short of the original ; and because the author has been so many years about the work, as his last and chiefest work, our wits will criticise the same the more ".

Burnet and the world had not long to wait, for in the summer of 1697 a stately folio appeared of " The Works of Virgil : containing his Pastorals, Georgics and Aeneid. Translated into English Verse ; by Mr. *Dryden*. Adorned with a Hundred Sculptures ". The first edition was quickly sold and in a very short time a second was produced.

But what of the man who had made it ? As the last page-proofs left his hand, he felt age and exhaustion upon him, and had to call in his doctors, Gibbons and Hobbs : " That I have recover'd, in some measure, the health which I had lost by too much application to this work, is owing, next to God's mercy, to the skill and care of Dr. Gibbons and Dr. Hobbs . . ." It was in the state of near-exhaustion that he wrote his " postscript to the Reader " which is one of the most moving and beautiful pieces of prose in English, and of which Matthew Arnold rightly said : " Here at least we have the true English prose, a prose such as we would all gladly use if we only knew how ".

These are the immortal lines that Dryden, his hands dirty with printer's ink, wrote in the front room of his house in Gerrard Street in the high days of early summer in 1697 :

" What Virgil wrote in the vigour of his age, in plenty and at ease, I have undertaken to *translate* in my declining years ; struggling with wants, oppress'd with sickness, curb'd in my genius, liable to be mis-construed in all I write ; and my judges, if they are not very equitable, already prejudic'd against me, by the *lying character* which has been given them of my morals. Yet, steady to my principles, and not dispirited with my afflictions, I have, by the blessing of God on my endeavours, overcome all difficulties, and, in some measure, acquitted myself of the debt which I ow'd to the public when I undertook this work. In the first place, therefore, I thankfully acknowledge to the Almighty Power the assistance he has given me in the beginning, prosecution, and *conclusion* of my present studies, which are more happily perform'd than I could have promis'd to myself, when I labour'd under such discouragements. For what I have done, imperfect as it is for want of health and leisure to correct it, will be judg'd in after ages, and possibly in the present, to be no dishonour to my native country, whose language and poetry would be more esteem'd abroad, if they were better understood. Somewhat (give me leave to say) I have added to both of them in the choice of *words*, and harmony of numbers, which were wanting (especially the last) in all our poets, even in those who, being endued with genius, yet have not cultivated their mother tongue with sufficient care ; or, relying on the beauty of their thoughts, have judg'd the ornament of words, and sweetness of sound, unneces-sary . . . ."

The " Dedication of the Aeneid "—to his old friend, the Earl of Mulgrave, now also Marquis of Normanby—is a more light-hearted affair, mainly concerned with Virgil himself. There are even humor-ous sallies ; the critics, for example, he says make " Aeneas little better than a king of St. Swithen hero, always raining ". But it contains also a statement of his political standpoint : " I meddle not with others, being, for my own opinion, of Montaigne's principles, that an honest man ought to be contented with that form of government, and with those fundamental constitutions of it, which he receiv'd from his ancestors, and under which he himself was born ; tho' at the same time he confess'd freely, that if he could have chosen his place of birth, it should have been at Venice ; which, for many reasons, I dislike, and am better pleased to have been born an Englishman ".

The statement is slightly disingenuous coming from Dryden ; yet he is careful to speak of the *form* of government and its fundamental

o

constitutions as they have been handed down from the distant past. It is really no more than an affirmation of his belief in the British system of monarchy, and a rejection of all ideas of republicanism ; such ideas, after all, were in the minds of some of the great Whigs in the late seventeenth century.

Of the translation of Virgil, it can only be said that, in spite of faults and inequalities, it has become an English classic. The *Pastorals* are perhaps the least successful, for there Dryden's characteristic rapidity and strength are out of place ; the delicacy and shy charm of the original have vanished. Nor are the poetic undertones we look for in the *Georgics* to be found. Conversely, the *Aeneid* gains in power from the strength of the verse, and the translation—the most successful is the sixth book—often rises to heights of poetry which it is no exaggeration to call great. Some of it, not unexpectedly, reads like the forced labour it was ; we look in vain for famous things like " sunt lachrymae rerum " (which, in fact, vanishes entirely). But as a whole the *Aeneid* is a great piece of translation to which, in spite of the many since attempted, we still turn for its vigour, accuracy and general readability. If there is in it a great deal of that " poetic diction " whose artificiality dismays us in so much eighteenth-century poetry, it must be remembered that this translation was the great source-book of that diction, the work on which poets of the next generation were brought up : in 1697, the words and phrases were new-coined and seemed the very last word in freshness, correctness and sheer poetry, despite Dryden's statement that so inexhaustible was Virgil's stock of " figurative, elegant and sounding words " that he " found it very painful to vary phrases ".

Of course, there were adverse critics : it seemed impossible for Dryden to produce anything without raising a whirlwind of abuse, usually with but a thin ripple of real criticism. Such a critic was the Rev. Luke Milbourne, who though a clergyman was said to be also a rake. In " Notes on Dryden's Virgil in a Letter to a Friend ", Milbourne says that Mr. Tonson has very fairly put on the title-page " Dryden's Virgil " to warn the reader " that this is not that Virgil so much admired in the Augustaean age, an author whom Mr. Dryden once thought untranslatable, but a Virgil of another stamp, of a coarser allay ; a silly, impertinent, nonsensical writer, of a various

uncertain style ".   But Milbourne's biggest mistake was in producing his own version of the tenth eclogue and detailing its superiority to that of Dryden.   As Dryden succinctly remarked in the
Preface to *The Fables* : " His own translations of Virgil have answered
his criticisms of mine ".

Swift, too, fell upon the Dryden's work, but in a more personal and
unpleasant manner, for he made fun of the fact that Dryden had made
a triple dedication of his Virgil—to Clifford, Chesterfield, and Mulgrave, thus no doubt earning a triple fee.   It was in a way a fair criticism, but one of the shadows which darkened this happy period of his
life—and to the end—was the shortage of money.   Dryden was simply
doing what he could to make himself solvent ; it has been estimated
that his total earnings from the Virgil, including his dedications,
brought him only £1,200, compared with the £9,000 Pope earned by
his translation of Homer, and which set him up for life.   Dryden after
all was a family man, and throughout this decade was financing his
sons as well as running a town house and keeping a wife.   Financially
profitable dedications were part of the literary life of his day ; he had
no need to be ashamed of making what he could from them.

CHAPTER TWELVE

" An Old Age is Out "

ONE MORNING in the late summer of 1697 Mr. St. John paid another visit to Dryden at his house in Gerrard Street. He found the old poet red-eyed and unshaven ; his hand trembled as he grasped that of St. John, and bade him sit down. St. John enquired the cause. " I have been up all night ", Dryden explained ; " my musical friends made me promise to write them a musical ode for their feast of St. Cecilia : I have been so struck with the subject which occurred to me, that I could not leave it till I had completed it ; here it is finished at one sitting ". He put into St. John's hands the famous poem *Alexander's Feast*.

Dryden had indeed written the poem at one sitting, but since the day a fortnight before when the stewards of the musical society (including Mr. Bridgman, the son of some friends of Lady Elizabeth) had approached him at his house, he had given the subject much thought, and had worked out his ideas and made notes on the versification. The theme of the power of music upon the souls of men was an ancient one ; Dryden had often encountered it in Longinus, in Athenaeus and in Cowley's *Davideis*, which is largely concerned with just this subject, and contains the remark : " Timotheus by music enflamed and appeased Alexander to what degrees he pleased ". D'Urfey, who had written the ode for the celebrations of the society some years earlier, had employed the same swift changes of tempo as Dryden does in *Alexander's Feast*. But the idea of giving a narrative form to a music ode was new, and the working out of the idea was equally new.

In this poem, as in so many others of his, it is the irresistible swing of the verse and the endlessly varied cadences which carry the day ; the cadences are far more subtle than in the ode he had written ten years before for the same society, and though the result may be, as Mr. Van

Doren says, " only immortal ragtime ", the poem has a power to hold the reader, to raise his spirits and delight his ear which is associated only with the finest poetry. And it might well be asked whether " ragtime " can be " immortal ", for " immortal " this poem is in the affections of every new generation of readers.

It was set to music by Jeremiah Clarke and performed with great success by the society ; its success in critical circles was equally great. The young man, who later became Lord Chief Justice Marlay, took the opportunity shortly after the poem's appearance to pay his court to the author at Will's. Marlay congratulated Dryden on having produced " the finest and noblest ode that had ever been written in any language ". To which Dryden, who had already drunk a few " brimmers ", replied : " You are right, young gentleman, a nobler ode never *was* produced, nor ever *will* ".

In more subdued mood, he wrote to Tonson : " I am glad to hear from all hands that my Ode is esteemed the best of all my poetry, by all the town : I thought so myself when I writ it ; but being old I mistrusted my own judgment ".

For *Alexander's Feast*, Dryden received £40 ; he also picked up various small sums for epistles which he wrote for the plays written by two new friends—George Grenville (later Lord Lansdowne) and the young French Huguenot writer, Peter Motteux, whose appeal to Dryden in the *Gentleman's Journal* to translate Virgil we have seen.

Another poem, which certainly gained him money—perhaps as much as £500—was that " To my Honour'd Kinsman, John Dryden of Chesterton, in the county of Huntingdon, Esquire ".

But this had a deeper significance than the desire to make money, for it represented a sort of reconciliation between Dryden and the various branches of his family from whom he had been divided first by politics and then by habit for many years. John Dryden of Chesterton was the poet's first cousin, and the M.P. for Huntingdonshire, a Whig and a Protestant.

The poem refers to political matters—Dryden toned these down when he printed it in *The Fables*—but it also shows how Dryden, the old man full of cares and years, is looking at the past, and particularly at the past of his own family, and is saying to his cousin with nostalgia and pain : " After all, we come from the same stock, we share many memories, we belong to each other, as in this life we can belong to no one else, for we share the same blood ".

He begins with a somewhat envious reference to the situation of his cousin compared with his own, and in spite of the Horatian debt there is genuine feeling in :

> How blest is he who leads a country life,
> Unvex'd with anxious cares, and void of strife !
> Who, studying peace and shunning civil rage,
> Enjoy'd his youth, and now enjoys his age :
> All who deserve his love, he makes his own ;
> And, to be lov'd himself, needs only to be known . . .

Nor can Dryden forget his wife, who is more and more difficult to live with, petulant and quarrelsome :

> Lord of yourself, uncumber'd with a wife ;
> Where, for a year, a month, perhaps a night,
> Long penitence succeeds a short delight :
> Minds are so hardly match'd, that ev'n the first,
> Tho' paired by Heav'n, in Paradise were curst.
> For man and woman, tho' in one they grow,
> Yet, first or last, return again to two . . . .

Then he comes to the family, and mentions those among them who :

> With noble stubbornness resisting might :
> No lawless mandates from the court receive,
> Nor lend by force, but in a body give.
> Such was your gen'rous grandsire ; free to grant
> In Parliaments that weigh'd their prince's want :
> But so tenacious of the common cause,
> As not to lend the king against his laws ;
> And, in a loathsome dungeon doom'd to lie,
> In bonds retain'd his birthright liberty,
> And sham'd oppression, till it set him free.

But his cousin's grandsire was also his own—Sir Erasmus Dryden who had been sent to prison for refusing to give loan-money and was released on the eve of the general election for Charles I's third parliament in 1628. Dryden is feeling solidarity with his family in the past and in the present. It is his own contribution to the diverse talents of the family that he stresses in :

> Nor think the kindred Muses thy disgrace ;
> A poet is not born in ev'ry race.
> Two of a house few ages can afford ;
> One to perform, another to record.

Presenting the poem to Montagu as one he intends to put in *The Fables*, Dryden says : " In the description which I have made of a Parliament-man, I think I have drawn not only the features of my worthy kinsman, but have also given my own opinion of what an Englishman in Parliament ought to be ; and deliver it as a memorial of my own principles to all prosperity ". These are the lines :

> Well-born and wealthy, wanting no support,
> You steer betwixt the country and the court ;
> Nor gratify whate'er the great desire,
> Nor grudging give what public needs require.
> Part must be left, a fund when foes invade ;
> And part employ'd to roll the wat'ry trade : . . .
> Good senators (and such are you) so give,
> That kings may be supplied, the people thrive.
> And he, when want requires, is truly wise,
> Who slights not foreign aids, nor overbuys,
> But on our native strength, in time of need, relies . . .
> Safe in ourselves, while on ourselves we stand,
> The sea is ours and that defends the land.
> Be, then, the naval stores the nation's care,
> New ships to build, and batter'd to repair . . . .

Dryden was writing shortly after the Peace of Ryswick in 1697 ; he knew that the House of Commons was against any renewal of hostilities and therefore against attempts to maintain military forces. The King, on the other hand, could never forget his enmity to France, for which a large standing army was required. Dryden opposed that— and with him were large sections of both parties. He told Montagu in a letter that his first draft of his poem had been more strongly worded, but that his cousin had persuaded him to remove " a satire against the Dutch valour in the last war. He desir'd me to omit it (to use his own words) *out of the respect he had to his sovereign*. I obeyed his commands, and left only the praises which I think are due to the gallantry of my own countrymen ". Apart from those praises, his

stress on the importance of the navy is complementary to his opinion
about the maintenance of a large army.   There was another reason, a
more personal one, for his plea for the navy, for he had recently renewed his acquaintance with Samuel Pepys, the young man who had
made himself so useful to his cousin, Sir Gilbert Pickering, in the last
years of the Commonwealth, and who in the intervening years had
become the great architect and propagandist of the British Navy.

The two old and famous men often dined together, and freely
discussed everything between heaven and earth.   But it was not only
affairs of state that they discussed : poetry was one of their most
frequent subjects, for Pepys had the interest of all educated men of his
time in literature.   He had been from his early manhood a great
devotee of the theatre, and a great reader.   He was proud to show
Dryden his collection of books and told him of his intention to leave it
to Magdalene College at Cambridge.   What interested Dryden most
in his collection were the old ballads and popular tales ; for Dryden
shared his friend Dorset's passion for such tales as *Reynard the Fox*
and *Jane Shore*.   It was an interest that, in these last years of his life, led
him to re-read Chaucer, and with such enthusiasm that he came to
prefer Chaucer to Ovid and to Virgil—though he admitted that this
was not at all the usual view and " the vulgar judges . . . will think me
little less than mad for preferring the Englishman to the Roman ".   It is
Chaucer's naturalness that he praises—" he writ with simplicity, and
follow'd nature more closely ".   Not only that : " He is a perpetual
fountain of good sense, learn'd in all sciences, and therefore speaks
properly on all subjects : as he knew what to say, so he knows also
when to leave off, a continence which is practic'd by few writers ".
Chaucer's verse, indeed, is not regular, for we cannot believe his editor,
Speght (whose Elizabethan edition of Chaucer had been reprinted in
1687) or Rymer who say the fault is in our ears and that really there
were ten syllables to Chaucer's line not nine ; yet " there is the rude
sweetness of a Scotch tune in it, which is natural and pleasing, tho' not
perfect ".   He mentions the vast scope of Chaucer in the *Canterbury
Tales* presenting " the various manners and humours (as we now call
them) of the whole English nation in his age ", and how they are all
so subtly differentiated and with such liveliness that one can imagine
oneself meeting his people in the street.

Dryden told Pepys that he had in mind to refurbish several of Chaucer's tales, his reason being that "Chaucer, I confess, is a rough diamond, and must first be polish'd before he shines". He went on to tell Pepys, as he later told his readers, that "I found I had a soul congenial to his, and that I had been conversant in the same studies".

There were, it was true, some of his friends who did not want him to touch Chaucer—the late Earl of Leicester, for instance, who thought that Chaucer's good sense and the beauty of his thoughts might vanish no matter how skilful the modernisation might be. Dryden deferred his work on Chaucer until after Leicester's death, but only out of respect for him, not because be believed damage could be done to Chaucer. For, after all, is it not better that Chaucer should be made available to modern readers rather than remain the delight of the very few learned enough to read him in his original language ? "How few there are who can read Chaucer so as to understand him perfectly ! And if imperfectly, then with less profit and no pleasure". One can give too much veneration to "ancient words". "When an ancient word for its sound and significance deserves to be reviv'd, I have that reasonable veneration for antiquity, to restore it. All beyond this is superstition. Words are not like landmarks, so sacred as never to be removed . . . ."

With all this Pepys is in agreement, but he has one request to make : that among the pieces Dryden reversifies from Chaucer shall be his "Character of a Good Parson". The cause of his request, as Pepys afterwards explained in a letter to Dryden, was that he hoped from Dryden's poem " to fancy some amends made me for the hourly offence I bear from the sight of so many lewd originals ". Dryden obliged ; it was a sort of *amende honorable*, as Scott says, for the many slighting references in his works to venal clergymen and to the cloth in general ; Dryden sent his poem in manuscript to Pepys for his comments, saying " My Parson desires the favour of being known to you, and promises, if you find any fault in his character, he will reform it ".

ii

Dryden was now suffering from all the aches and pains which could afflict a man of his age when medical science was scarcely further

advanced than it had been in Elizabethan times : he suffered from the
gravel, from gout (so badly that sometimes he could not stand up), and
from a catarrhal deafness that had long afflicted him. Yet he was as
active, both physically and mentally, as he had ever been, and more
prolific of new ideas and new views than at any time in his life.
" A cripple in my limbs ", he writes, but : " I think myself as vigorous
as ever in the faculties of my soul, excepting in my memory, which is
not impair'd to any great degree ; and if I lose not more of it I have no
great reason to complain. What judgment I had, increases rather than
diminishes ; and thoughts, such as they are, come crowding in so fast
upon me, that my only difficulty is to choose or reject ; to run them
into verse, or to give them the other harmony of prose. I have so
long studied and practic'd both, that they are grown into a habit and
become familiar to me ".

Dryden's was one of those exceptional minds that, even in age, do
not ossify or become set in their views or their way of thinking.
Having, for example, finished the great labour of translating the whole
of Virgil's works, he gaily turned his thoughts to Homer, and not
merely from the point of view of financial reward, nor even because
his friends called on him to undertake the task. No, he has been reading Homer again, and now finds good reason to prefer him to Virgil
—not, however, for purely poetic or technical reasons, but because he
finds that where Virgil " was of a quiet, sedate temper, Homer was
violent, impetuous and full of fire ". And therefore, calmly adds
Dryden aged 67, " more suitable to my temper ". He insists upon
this point : in a letter to Montagu he says of Homer that " I find him
a poet more according to my genius than Virgil, and consequently hope
I may do him more justice in his fiery way of writing ". Nor can it
be denied with the first book of the *Iliad* (the only one he was able to
do) before us, that his insistence is justified : his Homer *is* more lively
and powerful than anything to be found in his Virgil.

He is constantly throwing off ideas—about prefaces, for example.
" The nature of a preface ", it has just struck him, " is rambling ; never
wholly out of the way, nor in it ". Or, again, is it not true that there
is a sort of *family* among poets ? " Milton was the poetical son of
Spenser, and Mr. Waller of Fairfax, for we have our lineal descents
and clans as well as other families. Spenser more than once insinuates

that the soul of Chaucer was transfus'd into his body, and that he was begotten by him two hundred years after his decease. Milton has acknowledged to me that Spenser was his original . . . ."

The Fables themselves are evidence of the breadth of his interests at this time—Chaucer, Ovid, Boccaccio, he is reading, enjoying, translating them with the same gusto and skill. And the style of *The Fables* is equally varied ; here it is satirical, there lyrical, here metaphysical, there argumentative. For example, in the verses to the beautiful Duchess of Ormond which he prefixed to his translation of *Palamon and Arcite* he is again the gallant metaphysical and the true poet who has never wholly forgotten his early love of Donne and Cowley, and now recalls it, but with a mature and entirely individual touch ;

> O daughter of the rose, whose cheeks unite
> The diff'ring titles of the red and white ;
> Who heav'n's alternate beauty well display,
> The blush of morning, and the milky way ;
> Whose face is paradise, but fenc'd from sin :
> For God in either eye has plac'd a cherubim.

Or he can become the satirist again, as contemptuous as ever, and yet more comfortably than before. This passage on the militia from *Cymon and Iphigenia* is in his best vein of satire ; it is also almost the last example of his lifelong ability to take a mental snapshot of a scene of action and to express it vividly :

> The country rings around with loud alarms,
> And raw in fields the rude militia swarms ;
> Mouths without hands ; maintained at vast expense ;
> In peace a charge, in war a weak defence ;
> Stout once a month they march, a blustering band,
> And ever, but in times of need, at hand.
> This was the morn when, issuing on the guard,
> Drawn up in rank and file they stood prepared
> Of seeming arms to make a short essay,
> Then hasten to be drunk, the business of the day.

In at least one story in *The Fables*, Dryden attains a new style altogether, and one which, if it had been written at the end of the next century, would have been regarded as typical of the early Romantic poets. This is his translation and adaptation of Boccaccio's eighth tale of the fifth day of the *Decameron*, which Dryden, having changed the names, calls *Theodore and Honoria*. This was the story which so affected the young Byron and which he recalled during a visit to Ravenna :

> Evergreen forest ! which Boccaccio's lore
> And Dryden's lay made haunted ground to me,
> How have I loved the twilight hour and thee . . . !

Wordsworth, too, told Scott that he thought Dryden's Boccaccio " the most poetical of his poems ", although his view of " poetical " was somewhat narrow. Yet Wordsworth was right in sensing in these latest poems of Dryden a new departure—something which skipped Pope and led rather to Akenside, the Countess of Winchelsea and to Gray.

" A certain ardour and impetuosity of mind, with an excellent ear " Wordsworth observed in Dryden in *The Fables* and in general. But others have found less to be admired. Mr. C. S. Lewis, in our own time, has repeated, though in different phraseology, charges made against *The Fables* when they first appeared. Mr. Lewis says, of *Sigismonda and Guiscardo* : " Dryden fails to be a satisfactory poet because being rather a boor, a gross, vulgar, provincial, misunderstanding mind, he yet constantly attempts those kinds of poetry which demand the *cuor gentil* ". Sir Richard Blackmore, a physician and would-be poet, said the same thing in other terms when he condemned Dryden for his licentiousness :

> Dryden condemn, who taught men how to make,
> Of dunces wits, an angel of a rake . . .
> . . . . debauched by Dryden and his crew,
> Turn bawds to vice and wicked aims pursue.

The element of coarseness, and not merely in its circumscribed sense of lewdness, was certainly there in Dryden. He had seen too much of honour and great men and ideals in the time of the Restoration to have much faith in them ; the last word about sexual love had, for him, been said by Wycherley or Congreve. He knew, in fact, that his views were narrow and perhaps twisted on this matter, but he knew also he could not change them ; they were too much part of him. He would, of course, defend himself as he well knew how from such silly men as Blackmore—" Quack Maurus, though he never took degrees " and so on.   But he wrote much more to the true point in his Epilogue to the revival of a play by the Elizabethan Fletcher, *The Pilgrim* :

> As for reforming us, which some pretend,
> That work in England is without an end :
> Well, we may change, but we shall never mend.
> Yet if you can but bear the present stage,
> We hope much better of the coming age.

The coming age !   Dryden smelled it all around him, and nowhere more so than in such notices in the *London Gazette*, No. 3474, of Monday, February 27, 1698 : " His Majesty being informed, that, notwithstanding an order made the 4th of June, 1697, by the Earl of Sunderland, then Lord Chamberlain of His Majesty's household, to prevent the profaneness and immorality of the stage, several plays have lately been acted, containing expressions contrary to religion and good manners : And whereas the master of the revels has represented, that, in contempt of the said order, the actors do often neglect to leave out profane and indecent expressions as he has thought proper to be omitted . . . ."   And so on and so on.   Poor Congreve was the first to suffer—Congreve who had written the greatest comedy of his time : Dryden tells Mrs. Steward : " This day was played a revived comedy of Mr. Congreve's, called ' The Double Dealer ' which was never very taking.   In the play-bill was printed—' Written by Mr. Congreve ; with several expressions omitted '.   What kind of expressions those were, you may easily guess if you have seen the Monday's Gazette . . ."

It was a new age with a new set of public morals, and that is why, when a serious spokesman for it appeared in the person of the Rev. Jeremy Collier, later a Bishop, Dryden set himself to consider his position quite seriously.   Collier's *Short View of the Immorality and Profaneness of the English Stage* was pungent, witty, sarcastic and, as Dr. Johnson said, " invigorated by the just confidence in his cause ". Collier attacked most of the living writers from Dryden to D'Urfey, quoting coarse passages from their productions so that (Johnson again) " the nation wondered why it had so long suffered irreligion and licentiousness to be openly taught at the public charge ".

To the allegations Collier made against him personally, Dryden soberly replied : " In many things he has taxed me justly ; and I have pleaded guilty to all thoughts and expressions of mine which can be truly argued of obscenity, profaneness, or immorality, and retract them . . . . It becomes me not to draw my pen in a bad cause, when I have so often drawn it for a good one. . . ."

A new age, yes, and not one in which Dryden could truly share ; an age less sturdy if more refined—the age of Pope ; an age equally licentious but more hypocritical—the age of his friend Addison and his *Spectator* ; an age of deism and religious rationalism, not " naturally sceptic and not at all bigoted " which as late as his *Life of Lucian* in 1696, Dryden thought was " if I am not much deceived, the proper character of our age ".

iii

But what did it all really matter to him ? He had had his life, and despite all, he still had it and was happy in it, though it was in a sense a life of the past. He had his friends around him at Will's and in Gerrard Street, and always there were new ones anxious to praise and help him ; he had his family, and his relatives always glad to see him and most solicitous for his welfare whenever he went into North-amptonshire ; above all he had his work, the poetry which still gave him the greatest pleasure in the world, and which was held in high regard save by a few men whom it was scarcely worth bothering about. " If they will consider me as a man who has done my best to improve the language, and especially the poetry . . ."—that, he wrote to Mrs. Steward, was all he asked.

And his immortal soul ? He had long ago made his peace with the terrors of this world and had confided his soul and its future to the Roman Catholic Church. He was not disposed to alter his decision (nor even to think about it very much), although it meant being short of money in the end. " The court ", he told Mrs. Steward, " rather speaks kindly of me than does anything for me, though they promise largely "—and in spite, he might have added, of the representations of such friends in high places as Charles Montagu, now Lord Halifax. But " perhaps they think I will advance as they go backward, in which they will be much deceived ; for I can never go an inch beyond my conscience and my honour . . . I can neither take the oaths nor forsake my religion ; because I know not what church to go to, if I leave the Catholic ; they are all so divided amongst themselves in matters of faith necessary to salvation, and, yet all assuming the name of Protestants . . . Truth is but one ; and they who have once heard of it, can plead no excuse if they do not embrace it ".

A tough, brave and trusting old man it was who jogged along so often in the coach for Oundle in these last three years—brave in facing poverty for his beliefs, trusting in those beliefs and knowing that he had at best not long before he put them to the trial, tough at his age and in his state of health in facing the rutted and pitted roads to his native county. Sometimes worried, too, not for himself, but for his sons ; Charles had had an accident in Rome. Dryden had written sending money to him and his brothers, but it was their mother who had really expressed his, and her own, fears in her postscript to his letters. Your father, she tells them in her own quaint spelling is " much at woon as to his health, and his defnesse is not wosce . . . He expresses a great desire to see my dear Charlles ; and trully I see noe reason why you should not both come together, to be a comfort to one another, and to us both, if the King of France includ Ingland in the peace ; for you doe but gust make shift to live wheare you are, and soe I hope you may doe heare ; for I will leaf noe ston unturn'd to help my belov'd sonns . . . not forgetting my sonn Harry, whose prayers I desire for a comfortable meetinge. I hope I may have some better thinges against you come, than what is sent you in that box ; there being nothing considerabell but my deare Jackes Play, who I desire in his next to me to give me a true account how my deare sonn Charlles is head dus ; for I cane be at noe rest tell I heare he is better, or rather thourely well, which I dally pray for ".

A few months later Dryden takes advice from a surgeon and sends it to Charles in Rome. Dryden asks Tonson to aid in expediting the letter for, he says : " This is a business of the greatest consequence in the world ; for you know how I love Charles : and therefore I write to you with all the earnestness of a father that you will procure Mr. Francia to enclose it in his packet this week : for a week lost may be my son's ruin ; whom I intend to send for next summer, without his brother, as I have written him word : and if it please God that I must die of overstudy, I cannot spend my life better, than in saving his ".

So the old poet jogged on towards Northamptonshire, but not now to stay always at Titchmarsh ; sometimes he stayed with his sporting kinsman, John Dryden of Chesterton, to whom he had addressed his poem. (" Exercise, I know, is my cousin Dryden's life, and the oftener he goes out will be the better for his health "). More often he stayed with Mrs. Elizabeth Steward and her husband, Elmes, at Cotterstock, a few miles away from Titchmarsh. Mrs. Steward was the daughter of Dryden's cousin, Elizabeth Pickering, who had married John Creed of Oundle, Tangier Secretary to Charles II, and was not therefore a close relation of the poet. But she was a beautiful young woman—about 26 at this time—and extremely talented, being both painter and poetess. She became very fond of the old poet, and he of her ; she cossetted him, sent him presents of his favourite dishes when he was in London, and delighted in his conversation which brought the literary and political affairs of the London world to her dinner-table.

At first, Dryden felt that his visits must incommode her, but soon he knew himself to be loved and his visits to Cotterstock became one of the highlights of the summer for him. When he passed on to Titch-marsh it was with regret ; as he wrote once to Mrs. Steward : " (At Titchmarsh) I had no woman to visit but the parson's wife ; and she, who was intended by nature as a helpmeet for a deaf husband, was somewhat of the loudest for my conversation ; and for other things, I will say no more than that she is just your contrary . . . ." Very often, too, when he got back to London he found his health deteriorated : " I came sick home, and kept my house for three weeks together ; but, by advice of my doctor, taking twice the bitter draught, with senna in it, and loosing at least twelve ounces of blood, by cupping on my neck, I am just well enough to go abroad in the afternoon . . . ."

Sometimes, of course, his pleasure in country life with the Stewards led him to what, in his state of health, were excesses. Writing to tell Mrs. Steward that he is once again about to come on a visit, he adds " a petition, that you would please to order some small beer to be brew'd for me without hops, or with a very inconsiderable quantity ; because

I lost my health last year by drinking bitter beer at Titchmarsh. It may perhaps be sour, but I like it not the worse, if it be small enough ".

His days in the peace of the Steward house at Cotterstock were wholly delightful to him. In the morning he would read or write, or perhaps sometimes he would go fishing while Mrs. Steward busied herself with the household tasks and her husband managed his estate. In the evening they would all meet and dine together, sometimes with visitors, friends of the Stewards, and often with Mrs. Steward's mother, Mrs. Creed, a great favourite of the poet and now nearly sixty years old. Mrs. Creed often spoke of her cousin's " excellent conversation ", and indeed in the delightful surroundings of Cotterstock and in the family circle where he was loved, Dryden felt himself able to talk as he talked nowhere else. And what talk it was ! Of country life, of servants, of Dryden's noble friends, of poetry and painting and music—each member of the circle had something to contribute, yet each was interested in the other's specialised knowledge. One evening after dinner the conversation turned to the origin of names, and after a while Dryden, with a bow to Mrs. Creed, spoke these lines extempore :

> So much religion in *your* name doth dwell,
> Your soul must needs with piety excel.
> Thus names, like well-wrought pictures drawn of old,
> Their owners' nature and their story told—
> Your name but half expresses : for in you
> Belief and practice do together go.
> My prayers shall be, while this short life endures,
> These may go hand in hand with yours ;
> Till faith hereafter is in vision drown'd,
> And practice is in endless glory crown'd.

On other occasions the talk turned to spirits and witches, divination and astrology. Dryden had always been interested in astrology, nor did his religious faith put an end to that interest ; indeed in his latter years he learned more about it and was able to cast horoscopes. He had cast one when Charles was ill in Rome, and told his sons of it : " Towards the latter end of this month, September, Charles will begin to recover his perfect health, according to his nativity, which, casting it myself, I am sure is true ; and all things hitherto have happened

P

accordingly to the very time I predicted them. I hope, at the same time, to recover more health, according to my age ".

For Dryden, astrology was a science, and therefore quite separate from his religion. He points out in his preface to *The Fables* that Chaucer, Virgil, Horace, Persius and Manilius were all astrologers. In adapting " The Knight's Tale ", he expanded and amplified Chaucer's astrological references. It is true that in " The Cock and the Fox " he ridicules prediction from dreams, and other doctrines from Paracelsus, but, as Scott rightly remarked, " we have good reason to suspect that, like many other scoffers, he believed in the efficacy and truth of the subject of his ridicule ".

One evening his friends had proof of Dryden's " occult " powers. His niece, Mrs. Shaw, the married daughter of his brother Erasmus, was dining at the same house as her uncle. At table, the poet whispered to her to look at the butler who was waiting to serve the guests. Mrs. Shaw was of a nervous disposition, but she replied that she could see nothing of particular note about the butler. Dryden then told her that she might depend upon it that the man would soon come to a violent death. She was shocked, but did not think any more of the conversation until, two days later, she happened again to be at the same house and was told by her friends that the butler had that morning killed himself.

Whether Dryden possessed exceptional and occult powers or not, he had certainly spent many years in reading the faces of men of the world ; as Mr. Osborn remarks, " the troubled features of a mal-adjusted country menial would have presented no deep problem to him ".

But of all these things Dryden could talk freely in the house at Cotterstock ; in London it was a different matter—there he was troubled by too many business affairs, the need to talk always of literary matters, the duties of a father and a husband. At Cotterstock he expanded and became the full human being he was. When Charles returned to England, he sometimes accompanied his father on his trips north, though he was seldom in very good health, and both father and son regularly took the waters at Barnet Wells or Epsom. (They had been advised to go to Bath but " that city is so close and so ill-situated that perhaps the air may do us more harm than the waters do us good ".) Charles, too, found the atmosphere of Cotter-stock congenial ; after one visit he wrote to Mrs. Steward that " I assure you in all my travels I never left any place with more reluctance than Cotterstock ".

How nostalgic Dryden was for the country and his relations may be gathered from the numerous letters he wrote to Mrs. Steward, and the way he tried to give her all the news in which she might be interested. Sometimes he describes his journeys in the coach—how now, a young man galloped alongside and was assiduous in going ahead to order meals because a young, well-favoured girl was travelling ; how at other times there were awkward passengers. " The coach was crowded up with an old woman fatter than any of my hostesses on the road. Her weight made the horses travel very heavily ; but, to give them a breathing time, she would often stop us, and plead some necessity of nature, and tell us, we were all flesh and blood : but she did this so frequently that at last we conspired against her ; and that she might not be inconvenienc'd by staying in the coach, turn'd her out in a very dirty place, where she was to wade up to the ankles, before she cou'd reach the next hedge . . ."

He tells her, too, how " between my intervals of physic, and other remedies which I am using for my gravel, I am still drudging on : always a poet, and never a good one. I pass my time sometimes with Ovid, and sometimes with our old English poet Chaucer ; translating such stories as best please my fancy ". Now he tells of plays and poems and the rumours of bad relations between England and Scot-land ; there are new orders against the Roman Catholics. forbidding them to hold landed property ; he has seen Dryden of Chesterton in town, and he is very pleased with the marrow-puddings she has sent—may he ask her, too, for " part of a chine of honest bacon . . . . I like them better plain having a very vulgar stomach ".

But increasingly he has to tell her of his being unwell. " I had last night at bedtime an unwelcome fit of vomiting ; and my son, Charles, lies sick upon his bed with the colic, which has been violent upon him for a week . . . I am lame at home, and have not stirr'd abroad this month at least. Neither my wife nor Charles are well . . . Congreve is ill of the gout at Barnet Wells . . . I beg your pardon for this slovenly letter ; but I have not health to transcribe it ".

iv

Yet in the front room in Gerrard Street the old man slaved on ;
money was still short, although *The Fables* had been a success. " The
town encourages them with more applause than anything of mine
deserves ", he tells Mrs. Steward, adding : " I always thought my
verses to my cousin Dryden were the best of the whole ; and, to my
comfort, the town thinks them so ; and he, which pleases me most,
is of the same judgment, as appears by the noble present he has sent me,
which surprised me, because I did not in the least expect it ". He adds
that he has corrected the lines to his cousin " with so much care that
they will now be worthy of his sight, and do neither of us dishonour
after our death ".

After our death . . . Upstairs lay his son and his wife, the one pale
and sick, the other querulous and almost disordered in her mind, now
calling upon her other two sons in Rome, now bewailing the poverty
of her state. It was necessary to work on, and Dryden set himself to
the task, although scarcely able to walk because of an infection in his
leg and suffering, too, from his gravel and his deafness.

Happily he had good friends, young men who came to see him and
proposed this and that that he might do to earn money. Congreve
was a frequent visitor, and it was as though he were another son ; his
old friend Dorset often rode up from Kent to see him ; Tonson
stumped in, sullen as ever, but now quite forgiven, to tell him of the
sales of *The Fables*. A young female writer, Miss Elizabeth Thomas,
who had approached him in the usual manner by sending two poems
for his comments, sometimes looked in from the house where she lived
with her mother in Dyot Street, St. Giles, nearby. She in part made
up for the absence of Mrs. Steward, and Dryden treated her with an
old man's gallantry. When she could not come, he wrote to her—
telling the future " Curll's Corinna " how he liked her verses, that he
found much of Orinda (Mrs. Katherine Philips) in her manner, that
she should avoid the " licence which Mrs. Behn allowed herself of
writing loosely " (though " I confess I am the last man who ought to
arraign her, who have been myself too much a libertine in most of my
poems ; which I shou'd be well contented had I time either to purge,
or to see them fairly burn'd)".

But Dryden was glad to be still working—it kept his mind from straying to the past, as it now tended to do. The work, which had been obtained through his young friend Vanbrugh, was an epilogue, a prologue and a secular masque to go with the revival of Fletcher's *The Pilgrim*. Dryden, it had been agreed, should get the profits of the third night. The prologue and epilogue he quickly finished ; they were in his best, most casually mordant style, dealing with the everyday matters then occupying London—Blackmore's and Collier's attacks on him, bear-baiting, the fops. It diverted his thoughts, and they were diverted still more when Vanbrugh, who had cast the revival, sent up to him the young man whom he had chosen to play a small part and to recite the epilogue. He did it well, and Dryden asked Vanbrugh to let him also speak the prologue. So did Collie Cibber begin his career.

But still there were moments when the Gerrard Street house was empty and when the " St. Anthony's fires " in his leg were quiet. Then his life would come back to him ; he would think of his youth, of his father and mother and the strange Puritan " saints " who had flitted in and out of the house ; he would think, too, of his cousin, Honor— she had never married and lived still at Canon's Ashby with his cousin, Sir Robert, whom he never saw ; of his early ambition and his deter- mination to be a poet and to go to London, and of his years in Sir Gilbert Pickering's house where he slept in the tiny room with the bull's-eye window ; of his meeting with Howard and his entrée, through him, into London society ; of his first play and his excitement at the marks of favour King Charles had shown him—and then of the money he had borrowed from him ; of his triumphs on the stage, his appointment as Poet Laureate, of his cynicism, his determination to succeed at whatever cost, of his pride, his overweening pride, and the blows that it suffered in *The Rehearsal*, in Rose Alley and in the calm of his room in Long Acre ; of his slow, difficult progress to belief ; of his fine poems—and the less fine ones.

And in the end what did it all amount to ? Fame—and wracking pains in his limbs ; the favour of kings—and shortage of money in his old age ; friends, the best a man ever had—and sad memories of so many already dead. And himself, his own character ? It had been neither very good, nor yet very bad ; it had had its meannesses—he had flattered where flattery was not due, and only for profit ; there had been Anne Reeves, and too much drinking at Will's, and too many licentious stories. But on the other hand, he had never been vindictive ; he had helped his friends, and often spared his enemies, and he had been a good father. He sighed : a good father, but one son lay sick upstairs, and the other two were far away from their native land, because of him—because he had put his own salvation first and they had suffered in following him. That was, indeed, the way of the world ; and yet if he by the action of his will had exiled them, had not their existence compelled him to write on and on, when perhaps he would have been happier in the church or a Cambridge college ? But then there would have been no plays and perhaps much less poetry; and—some things of his *would* certainly last, for he had put into them every skill his long apprenticeship had taught him. Perhaps that had been worth doing—or was it, again, only that writing poetry had been the greatest pleasure of his life, at once his livelihood, and his never-failing refuge from the cares and annoyances of everyday life ? Motive and will, cause and effect—life was still a labyrinth ; the why and what were not to be found ; a blind faith alone could comfort.

Now the " St. Anthony's fires " struck him again. and he heard his wife's sharp voice upbraiding her maid. He must turn to his work : a secular masque to follow Fletcher's play ! There was a certain irony in the *secular* as in the fact that the name of the play was *The Pilgrim*. He would make of it, then, something personal, which should perhaps also read ironically to the men of the eighteenth century, already like the century itself knocking on the gates.

" *Enter* CHRONOS, *with a scythe in his hand, and a great globe on his back, which he sets down at his entrance.*

> Chronos.   Weary, weary of my weight,
> Let me, let me drop my freight,
> And leave the world behind.
> I could not bear
> Another year
> The load of humankind . . .

> Janus.   Since Momus comes to laugh below,
> Old Time, begin the show,
> That he may see, in every scene,
> What changes in this age have been . . . ."

In James I's time it was all sylvan sports ; in Charles I's time it was all wars. Then it was gallantry and licence at the Courts of Charles and James. But in spite of all changes " things are as they were " and the result is nullity :

> " Momus.   All, all of a piece throughout :
>> *Pointing to* DIANA
>> Thy chase had a beast in view ;
>
>> *To* MARS
>> Thy wars brought nothing about ;
>
>> *To* VENUS
>> Thy lovers were all untrue.
>
> Janus   'Tis well an old age is out :
>
> Chronos   And time to begin a new.
>
> Chorus of All   All, all of a piece throughout :
>> Thy chase had a beast in view ;
>> Thy wars brought nothing about ;
>> Thy lovers were all untrue.
>> 'Tis well an old age is out,
>> And time to begin a new.
>
> *Dance of huntsmen, nymphs, warriors and lovers.*"

These were the last words Dryden wrote, for the pains in his leg worsened and he had to take to his bed. There his friend and doctor, Mr. Hobbs, examined him and advised an immediate amputation of his toe. This Dryden refused, and gangrene spread to his leg. He was in great pain. Again the doctor advised amputation, again Dryden refused. This time Hobbs warned him of the likely consequences, but Dryden replied " that he was an old man, and had not long to live by the course of nature, and therefore did not care to part with one limb, at such an age, to preserve an uncomfortable life on the rest ".

He asked his friends to come and see him, and Vanbrugh was able to give him good news of the success of his prologue and secular Masque. Congreve came, and Dorset and Montagu ; Southerne visited him several times, and many others sought to see him but were prevented by his doctor. The *Postboy* announced in its issue of April 30, 1700, that " John Dryden, Esq., the famous poet, lies a-dying ".

That night old Mrs. Creed, on a visit to London, arrived bringing with her the breath of the countryside he loved so well ; and it is she who has described the last scene on the evening of April 30.   She wrote : " When nature could be no longer supported, he received the notice of his approaching dissolution with sweet submission and entire resignation to the Divine will ; and he took so tender and obliging a farewell of his friends, as none but himself could have expressed ; of which sorrowful number I was one ".   And so when the friends he loved so well had withdrawn, he composed himself for the night, and at three in the morning died.

Epilogue

THE DEATH of Dryden, though it was scarcely unexpected, brought a realisation throughout the civilised world of the fact that a great man and a great poet had passed. From Paris Sir John Shadwell, the son of Dryden's late opponent, wrote : " The men of letters here lament the loss of Mr. Dryden very much. The honours paid to him have done our countrymen no small service ; for, next to having so considerable a man of our own growth, 'tis a reputation to have known how to value him . . ." Engraved copies of his portrait were printed and were avidly purchased—

> Pictures (weak images of him) are sold,
> The French are proud to have the head for gold.

In England, every scribbling poetaster who had rushed into print to attack him at the Revolution now flooded the presses with poems in his praise. His friends—Montagu and Dorset among them—obtained for him the honour of burial in Poet's Corner in Westminster Abbey, and they defrayed the expenses of a magnificent funeral which took place on May 12, 1700. It was preceded by a ceremony at the College of Physicians where his body had lain in state and where Sir Samuel Garth, physician and poet, delivered a funeral oration in Latin and that ode of Horace which begins " Exegi monumentum aere perennius " was sung.

The procession to the Abbey which followed was led by two beadles of the college in mourning cloaks and hatbands, the heads of their staffs wrapped in black crape ; there was a band of oboe and trumpet players playing a funeral march ; the hearse, hung with the arms of the Dryden family and those of his wife, was followed by a great number of the coaches of his noble friends and of his literary acquaintance, so that, as Ward reported in the *London Spy*, " no ambassador from the greatest emperor in all the universe, sent over with the welcome embassy to the throne of England, ever made his public entry to the court with half that honour as the corpse of the great Dryden did its last exit to the grave ".

In the Abbey itself the choir sang an epicedium, and the funeral rites were conducted by one of the prebends. He was interred, fittingly enough, between Cowley, his first great poetic love, and Chaucer, his last.

It was a splendid and fitting end to the life of the writer who had dominated the literary scene for so long. And yet to one man at least the whole proceeding seemed an irony. " I come ", he wrote, " from Mr. Dryden's funeral, where he had an ode of Horace sung instead of David's Psalms ; whence you may find that we don't think a poet worth a Christian burial. The pomp of the ceremony was a kind of rhapsody, and fitter, I think, for Hudibras than him ; because the cavalcade was mostly burlesque : but he was an extraordinary man, and buried after an extraordinary fashion, for I do believe there was never such another burial seen . . . . And so much for Mr. Dryden ; whose burial was the same as his life, variety, and not of a piece : the quality and mob, farce and heroics : the sublime and ridiculous mixed in a piece ; great Cleopatra in a hackney coach ".

George Farquhar, who wrote this, was a strange young man who achieved some success with his witty plays, but whose short life was full of disappointment and bitterness. Yet—" great Cleopatra in a hackney coach " ! It is not impossible to view the life of Dryden in such a light, nor to feel that his greatness rose up from uninspired foundations and amid squalid surroundings, like a noble spire above a slum.

The spire remained, a guide and landmark to every succeeding poet who has written in English ; but so, for a short time, did the uninspired circumstances which had encumbered the poet in his life. For example, he left no will, for the good reason that he had little to leave save his personal belongings and his rents from Northamptonshire, and if it had not been for his many friends his family would have been unable to afford a funeral in Westminster Abbey. His son, Charles, applied for and was granted administration of his father's estate—his mother was no longer able to do so, for the quirks and unpleasantness of her character, which had so long oppressed her husband, developed into insanity ; she lived another fourteen years, but out of the world, and her final resting place is unknown. Charles, too, ended unhappily, for in 1704 he was drowned after being seized by the cramp while swimming in the Thames near Datchet. The second son, John, died in Rome

only three years after his father.   The third son, Erasmus Henry, was
ordained a priest in Rome, was sub-prior of the convent of the Holy
Cross at Bornhem in Belgium, and returned to England soon after his
father's death.   He worked in Northamptonshire for some time as a
Catholic missioner ;   in 1710 he inherited the title conferred on his
great-grandfather, but died a few months later.   None of the sons
married, and thus the direct line of descent became extinct, and thus,
too, ended in sterility the personal life of the poet.   There was perhaps
an ironical justice in the fact that, despite the grandeur of his funeral
and his fame as a poet, no monument was erected to him in the Abbey
until twenty years later, though in the meantime many proposals
were made to such an end.   In 1720 his old friend, Mulgrave, now
the Duke of Buckingham, built a modest monument—his conscience
having, perhaps, been awakened by Pope's famous lines for an inscription on Rowe's tomb :

> Thy reliques, Rowe, to this fair urn we trust,
> And sacred place by Dryden's awful dust :
> Beneath a rude and nameless stone he lies.
> To which thy tomb shall guide enquiring eyes.

But commonplace misfortunes followed even here : the monument,
built at last, bears a simple Latin inscription—in which the year of
Dryden's birth is incorrectly given.

Yet though the chair at Will's was vacant, and then Will's itself was
closed, though his own family went mad or died prematurely, the
aura or spirit that had been Dryden the man lived on in at least two
hearts, where it remained warm and dear until they, too, died.   One
of them was a man of the town ;   the other, appropriately enough, a
woman of the country.   Congreve had loved Dryden as a son a
father, and from the day of his death he never wrote another play nor
anything in any way memorable :   he became a man of affairs, a fine
gentleman, a courtier, and in 1717 obeyed Dryden's behest of long
before—

> Be kind to my remains ; and O defend,
> Against your judgment, your departed friend !

In that year he published a complete edition of Dryden's plays, and
with it those beautiful and moving words on his friend from which we
have already quoted : " He was of a nature exceedingly humane and

compassionate . . . . His friendship, where he professed it, went beyond his professions.   He was of very easy, very pleasing access ; but somewhat slow, and, as it were, diffident in his advances to others . . . He was extreme ready and gentle in his correction of the errors of any writer who thought fit to consult him . . ."

It was the true epitaph of Will's and Gerrard Street and the theatre—all that side of his life—written by one who shared his taste for town life, for talk and " brimmers ", and for plays like *Marriage à la Mode* as much as for poems like *Religio Laici*

Another humbler epitaph was being prepared in the quiet countryside near where he had been born, where the trees still gently stirred along the banks of the Nene in which he had delighted to fish.   It was slow, amateur work with brush and pen on a wooden monument set in the middle of the north wall of the tiny chapel in the parish church of Titchmarsh—but there day after day old Mrs. Creed went with her implements and the paper on which she had laboriously composed the words which she was copying on to the woodwork.   The words told that in the church lay the remains of Erasmus Dryden and his wife, Mary Pickering, the eldest of whose sons was John Dryden, " the celebrated poet and laureate of his time.   His bright parts and learning are best seen in his own excellent writings on various subjects.   We boast that he was bred and had his first learning here ; where he has often made us happy by his kind visits and most delightful conversation.   He married the Lady Elizabeth Howard, daughter to Henry Earl of Berkshire ; by whom he had three sons, Charles, John and Erasmus-Henry ; and, after 70 odd years, when nature could be no longer supported, he received notice of his approaching dissolution with sweet submission and entire resignation to the divine will . . . . ."

Here the old lady rested her arm, and wiped a tear, and took up her labours another day.   But at last, with a wooden bust set over it, the humble monument was finished, and Mrs. Creed brought her epitaph to an end, with these words : " And it is with delight and humble thankfullness that I reflect on the character of my pious ancestors ; and that I am now, with my owne hand, paying my duty to Sir Erasmus Dryden, my great-grandfather, and to Erasmus Dryden, Esq., my honoured uncle, in the 80th year of my age.   Eliz. Creed, 1722."

Notes

THE notes that follow are not intended as, in any sense, a critical apparatus ; they are meant only to enable the reader to identify the quotations from Dryden and other writers, and to give the sources of the salient facts upon which the biography is based. Where there are differences of opinion among scholars and critics on the interpretation of certain incidents, these are mentioned along with the reason for preferring the interpretation given. The references to the work of Dryden himself are not to any particular edition ; the reason for this is that there are many editions of the poems in general use, while the complete editions of all the works—Scott's and the Scott-Saintsbury— are available only in very large libraries, and are therefore, for all practical purposes, out of reach of most readers. (The University of California is, I believe, to produce a complete edition of all Dryden's works.) The best edition of the poems is that by Professor George R. Noyes, first published in 1909 and in a revised, enlarged form in 1950 ; but this, too, is an American edition and not easily available to the ordinary reader in this country. I assume, therefore, that most readers will use, for the poems, the Globe, the Everyman, or the Oxford University Press editions, or one of the various selections ; for the plays, there are selections in the Mermaid edition, the Reynard Library edition and elsewhere ; for the prose, the handiest edition— though it is very incomplete—is the Everyman, but there are selections in many other books easily available.

It is, therefore, only when I quote from lesser known, or little reproduced works—such as Dryden's Letters, or one or two poems that have only been attributed to him—that I shall give specific data about where they are to be found. In the case of biographical detail I shall always give the precise source.

Page   **Preface**
ix.   Aubrey. *Brief Lives*, ed. Clark, 1898, I, 241.

Page	**Prologue**
xiii, l. 2	Johnson, *Lives of the Poets :* Oxford " World's Classics " edition, p. 297.
xiii, l. 4f.	The description of the aged Dryden is based on the portrait, reputedly by Kneller, owned by the Salwey family of Overton, Ludlow, Shropshire (reproduced as Frontispiece in James M. Osborn's *John Dryden : Some biographical Facts and Problems*, Columbia Univ. Press, 1940) ; the miniature, believed to be by Jonathan Richardson, now in the Dobell Dryden Collection in the Folger Shakespeare Library ; and on statements by John Wilmot, Earl of Rochester, and by Thomas Shadwell (v.s.). The " younger " portrait is that by Kneller, owned by Mr. P. C. D. Mundy of Caldrees Manor, Ickleton, Essex, and bought by him from the sale of Sneyd pictures from Keele Hall, Staffordshire.
xiii, l. 8	The shyness is attested by Congreve in his famous character of Dryden which he appended to his edition of Dryden's plays in 1717 ; and in various places by Dryden himself.
xiii, l. 13	Snuff-box. Malone's *Life of Dryden*, p. 518. Oldmixon, *Country Wit* (poems), 1696, p. 21.
xiii, l. 17	" St. Anthony's fires ." See Dryden's Letter of Fri., Dec. 29, 1699. (Scott-Saintsbury edition, 1893, Vol. XVIII, p. 171).
xiii, l. 27	Macaulay, *History of England*, 1849, Vol. II, p. 199.
xiii, l. 29	Wordsworth. Letter to Scott, Nov. 7, 1805. See Knight, *Life of Wordsworth*, 1889, Vol. II, pp. 27-29.
xiv, l. 2f.	Dryden in the country. Osborn, p. 198f.
xiv, l. 4f.	Daily habits. Scott-Saintsbury, Vol. I, p. 379.
xiv, l. 22	Flippancy. Scott-Saintsbury, Vol. I, pp. 94-95.
xiv, l. 22	*A Defence of an Essay of Dramatic Poesy* passim.
xiv, l. 36f.	*The Hind and the Panther*, Part I, II, pp. 75-76.

Chapter 1

1, l. 7f.	Sylvester. Dryden refers to this translation and these lines in particular in his correction of the translation by Sir William Soame in 1683 of Boileau's *Art of Poetry :*

Nor, with Dubartas, bridle up the floods,
And periwig with wool the baldpate woods. (See Noyes, p. 917.)

Page

1, l. 14   Poetic Blossoms, 1633,

2.   Dryden Family Tree, reproduced in part from Osborn, p. 237. with
corrections by courtesy of Mr. P. C. D. Mundy.

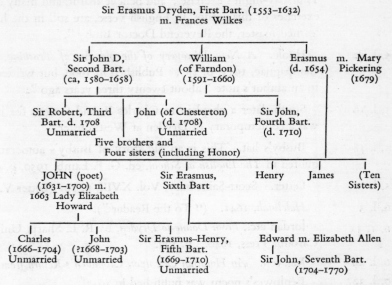

Sir Erasmus Dryden, First Bart. (1553–1632)
m. Frances Wilkes

Sir John D,   William   Erasmus m. Mary
Second Bart.   (of Farndon)   (d. 1654) Pickering
(ca, 1580–1658)   (1591–1660)   (1679)

Sir Robert, Third   John (of Chesterton)   Sir John,
Bart. d. 1708   (d. 1708)   Fourth Bart.
Unmarried   Unmarried   (d. 1710)
                     Five brothers and
                     Four sisters (including Honor)

JOHN (poet)   Sir Erasmus,   Henry   James   (Ten
(1631–1700) m.   Sixth Bart   Sisters)
1663 Lady Elizabeth
Howard

Charles   John   Sir Erasmus–Henry,   Edward m. Elizabeth Allen
(1666–1704)   (?1668–1703)   Fifth Bart.
Unmarried   Unmarried   (1669–1710)   Sir John, Seventh Bart.
                                Unmarried   (1704–1770)

2, l. 18f.   The Puritanism of the Dryden family is well established. Scott-
Saintsbury, Vol. I.   p. 22 f.

2, l. 12   Sir Erasmus.   Malone, p. 321.   Osborn p. 136.

2, l. 22   "Committee-man."   Shadwell, The Medal of John Bayes, 1682.
Osborn, p. 155 ff.

3, l. 6   Ascham.   The Scholemaster (1570).

3, l. 12   Birthplace.   Osborn, p. 269.   Dryden was born on Aug, 9., 1631,
the evidence being a horoscope preserved among the papers of Aubrey.
(Bodley MS. Ashmole 243, f. 209).   He was baptised on the 14th
August (Bodley MS. Top. Northants. C. 17. f. 167).   The fact of
early baptism makes it reasonable to assume that, though " Puritan ",
his parents were not of the extreme Baptist sect.

3, l. 22f.   Astraea Redux, 1660, II. 25-29

3, l. 32   " The bottle."   Scott, 1808 Edition, pp. 454-455.

3, l. 33   " Something slow."   Congreve, op. cit.

4, l. 5   Titchmarsh monument.   Scott-Saintsbury, Vol. XVIII, p. 225.

Page

5, l. 2   Persius. In a note to the argument of his translation of the third satire of Persius, 1692, Dryden wrote : " I remember I translated this satire, when I was a King's Scholar at Westminster School, for a Thursday-night's exercise ; and believe that it, and many other of my exercises of this nature, in English verse, are still in the hands of my learned master, the Reverend Doctor Busby ".

5, l. 12   Hoole. *A New Discovery of the old Art of Teaching,* ed. E. T. Campagnac, 1913, p. 187. Published in 1660, but written according to an author's note " about twenty three years ago ".

5, l. 16   South, later a chaplain to Charles II, and famous for his sermons, was a contemporary of Dryden at Westminster.

5, l. 18   Busby's hat. This is an old story of Busby's autocratic methods, quoted in *The English at School,* ed. G. F. Lamb, 1950, p. 45.

5, l. 25   Letter. Scott-Saintsbury, Vol. XVIII, p. 102 (Letter V, 1682).

6, l. 3   *Halelviah,* 1641. (" To the Reader ").

6, 1. 11   Jordan etc., *From Donne to Dryden,* by R. L. Sharp, Univ. of North Carolina Press, 1940. p. 177.

6, l. 26   Marvell. *An Horatian Ode upon Cromwell's Return from Ireland.*

7, l. 32.   Benlowes's poem was published in 1652.

9, l. 13f.   Templer. Scott-Saintsbury, Vol. I, p. 24.

10, l. 31   Waller's verses on *Gondibert.* " To Sir William Davenant on his first two books of Gondibert." (Waller's Poems, Muses Library, Vol. II, p. 9, ed. G. Thorn Drury).

11, l. 11   Hoddesdon. *Sion and Parnassus* .... (London, 1650),

11, l. 26   " Sawcily traduced." Shadwell, *Medal of Mr. John Bayes.*

11, l. 28   " Disobedience." Conclusion-Book, Trinity College (Malone, p. 221). " July, 19, 1652. Agreed, then, That Dryden be put out of Comons, for a fortnight at least ; and that he goe not out of the colledg, during the time aforesaid, excepting to sermons, without express leave from the master, or vice-master ; and that, at the end of the fortnight, he read a confession of his crime in the hall, at dinner time, at the three .... fellowes table. His crime was, his disobedience to the vice-master, and his contumacy in taking his punishment inflicted by him."

11, l. 31f.   Dryden's father, Erasmus, died in June, 1654.

12, l. 23   Honor Dryden, a daughter of Dryden's uncle, Sir John Dryden of Canon's Ashby, was born about 1637, and died sometime after 1707. A letter (Scott-Saintsbury, Vol. XVIII, p. 89) from the poet to Honor, written from Cambridge on May 23, year unknown, is in existence, but is of no great biographical value, being written in the usual seventeenth-century style of high-flown, rather academic gallantry, interspersed with somewhat spicy conceits.

13, l. 2   Crichton. In 1727, a Mr. Pain wrote a letter incorporating the testimony of a college contemporary of Dryden, Dr. Robert Crichton. "Dryden," he said, "was two years above him, and was reckoned a man of good parts and learning while in college : he had to his knowledge read over and very well understood all the Greek and Latin poets : he stayed to take his bachelor's degree, but his head was too roving and active, or what else you'll call it, to confine himself to a college life, and so he left it and went to London into gayer company, and set up for a poet, which he was as well qualified for as any man ". (Christie, " Biographical Introduction " to *Select Poems by Dryden*, 1883 edition, p. xvi.).

14, l. 8   **Chapter 2**

The "Minor post". Dryden was often accused by his contemporaries after the Restoration of having worked for the Commonwealth ; Shadwell, op. cit, refers to him " as being clerk to Noll's Lord Chamberlain " i.e., Sir Gilbert Pickering. On Oct. 19, 1657, Mr. John Thurloe, Secretary of State, paid Dryden £50, and Dryden receipted the document. (Masson, *Life of Milton*, 1859-1880, V. pp. 375-376). A document in the Public Records Office gives a list of minor government employees who were given an allotment of mourning cloth to be worn at Cromwell's funeral. The passage contains the following names, preceded by the cloth allowances they applied for and the amount they received :

9	6	Mr. John Milton	
9	6	Mr. Merville (Marvell)	} Lattin Secryes
9	6	Sir Philip Meadows	
		Mr. Sterry	
9	0	Mr. Drayden.	

As Dryden received no cloth, it may be deduced that, although he believed being cousin to the Lord Chamberlain that he should apply, it was judged that his position in the Government service was so lowly that his request could not be granted.

14, l. 14   Sir Gilbert Pickering. For his character, see Scott-Saintsbury, Vol. I, note to p. 30.

14, l. 22   For Dryden's personality, or lack of it, at this time see Shadwell's *Epistle to the Tories*, the preface to his *The Medal of John Bayes ;* also " A Letter from a Gentleman to the Hon. Edward Howard, Esq ; Occasioned by a Civiliz'd Epistle of Mr. Dryden's before his Second Edition of his Indian Emperor ", by R.F. (1668) ; and the discussion of these sources in Osborn, op. cit., pp. 161-162, and 168f.

14, l. 28ff.   For the details of Pickering, his wife and Pepys in London I am indebted to *Samuel Pepys* by Arthur Bryant.

17. l. 33f.   ' A fox." *Fables*—" The Cock and the Fox ".

18, l. 6f.   " No government." From the Dedication to *Examen Poeticum*, 1693.

19-20   Gifford, Herringman and Dryden's " blurbs ", see Osborn, op. cit., 171-183.

22, l. 11f.   Howard. Shadwell in one of his plays refers to him as " Sir Positive At-all ", and as a young man his character seems to have been determined and brusque, as well as slightly supercilious.

22, l. 19   Charleton, Osborn, pp. 172-175.

27   Dryden living with Howard. Letter-books of Sir Andrew Henley, British Museum, Sloane 813, f. 71. The address of Howard is given and " the serge bed Mr. Dreiden useth " is mentioned. (" Serge " bed must refer to the coverlet or hangings).

29   Wild. *Essay of Dramatic Poesy.* Scott-Saintsbury, Vol. I, p.37.

33, l. 26f   Epistle Dedicatory to the *Duke of Guise,* 1682.

Chapter 3

34, l. 10   Eachard, " Some Observations upon the Answer to an Enquiry ", 1672. Quoted by Sharp, pp. 143-144.

35, l. 3-4   Osborn. p. 231.

35   *The Royal Society,* 1660-1940, by Sir Henry Lyons, 1944, p.55. *The Senecan Amble* by George Williamson, Chapters 9 and 10. These give details of Dryden's connection with the Society.

Page

35, l. 30f.   " Mere poets." " Preface to notes and observations on the Empress of Morocco ".

36, l. 2   " A new nature." *Essay of Dramatic Poesy*, 1668.

36, l. 9   " Trade which like blood . . ." *Annus Mirabilis*, 1666, second stanza.

38, l. 11   " Academy." Dedication to *The Rival Ladies*, 1664.

38-39   Glanvill, Canes, Owen, etc. See *The Intellectual Milieu of John Dryden* by Louis I. Bredvold, Univ. of Michigan Press, 1934, chapters 2 and 3.

40, l. 2   Dryden and fair sex. Scott-Saintsbury, Vol.I, p. 73.

40, l. 27   Lady Elizabeth. " Bad writer." See Letters, Scott-Saintsbury, Vol. XVIII, p. 135.

41, l. 6   Lady Elizabeth's Letter to Chesterfield. Scott-Saintsbury, Vol. I, note to pp. 74-75.

42, l. 2   " Ultimo Novembris." Scott-Saintsbury, Vol. I, note to p. 74. (Exchequer. Osborn, p. 194.)

43, l. 22ff.   Nokes. Scott-Saintsbury, Vol. I, p. 92 note.

44, l. 18f.   Cowley's reaction. Johnson's *Life of Cowley*.

47   Popularity of Heroic plays. Preface to *The Conquest of Granada*.

48, l. 6   " The Censure of the Rota," Oxford, 1773. Scott-Saintsbury, Vol. I, p. 133.

48, l. 12   Epic. Dedication of *The Aeneid*.

48, 2. 17   " Imitation in little." Preface to *The Conquest of Granada*, 1672.

Chapter 4

51, l. 13   " The discourse." Dedication of *The Assignation*, 1673.

52-54   Trip down the river. *Essay of Dramatic Poesy*.

60, l. 8   Sir Robert Long. Catalogue of Collection of Autograph Letters and Historical Documents formed by Alfred Morrison, II (1885), 46.

62, l. 26   Blood-letting. Shadwell op. cit.

66, l. 14   Loan to King. Osborn, p. 194 and 98.

Chapter 5

67, l. 29   Money-lenders. Ashley, *England in the Seventeenth Century*, 1952.

68, l. 28   Rochester. Books on him by V. De Sola Pinto and by Charles Williams. D.N.B. article.

70   Dryden and Theatre. Osborn, p. 184ff.

71, l. 8f.   Anne Reeves.   Scott-Saintsbury, Vol. I, 73.   Osborn p. 89.

71, l. 34   Dryden's patent is printed in full in Scott-Saintsbury, Vol. XVIII, pp. 197-200.   73, l. 2ff.   Mr. P. C. D. Mundy writes : " According to Bell, in 1670 his salary was £200 a year increased to £300 a year in 1685.   He had £120 a year from the Blakesley farms, increased to £200 on his mother's death.   Malone suggests that his income, except for 18 months when the playhouses were shut, was equal to £600 a year in 1800 value, and, from 1670 to 1676 equal to £1,500 a year.

74, l. 5   Flecknoe.   Osborn, p. 98.

76, l. 35   Prof. D. Nichol Smith, *John Dryden* (*Clark Lectures*), 1950.

78, l. 24   " Neglected poet."   It has been the fashion to deny that *Paradise Lost* was neglected on its first appearance ; for instance, Mr. John Bailey in *Milton*, 1915, speaks of his being praised by Dryden and Dorset, and of the poem's selling 1,300 in the first eighteen months after publication.   But Dorset in such a matter would be likely to rely on the opinion of his friend, Dryden, and there is scarcely a mention elsewhere of the poem until Dryden's long campaign for Milton neared its end.   It was only in the eighteenth century that Milton began to be thought worthy of imitation, and not until the nineteenth that he began to be appreciated—apart from Dryden—for his true worth.

Chapter 6

80   Windsor party.   C. E. Ward, Publications of the Modern Language Association, 1936, pp. 786-88.   Shadwell op. cit : " At Windsor in the company of several persons of quality, Sir G(eorge) E(therege) being

80, l. 27
83-84
87-88

present ".   On this occasion, according to Shadwell, the company was at a loss one afternoon as to how it should amuse itself, and Dryden supplied the answer : " Let's b . . . . each other ".

Buckingham and *United Kingdoms*.   D.N.B.

Letter to Rochester.   Scott-Saintsbury, Vol. XVIII, p. 91.

Visit to Milton.   Aubrey, in the notes he sent to Anthony Wood, adds Dryden's name to the short list of Milton's " familiar learned acquaintance " and tells the story of " tagging " his verses, as well as the fact that Dryden told Aubrey of Milton's pronouncing the " R "

Page

hard. There is also *The Monitor*, No. 17, 6-10 April 1713 (pointed out by G. Thorn-Drury in " The Review of English Studies " (Jan, 1925), Vol. I, p. 80 : " Mr. Dryden who went in company with Mr. Waller to make a visit to Mr. Milton . . ." And in the Preface to the *Fables*, Dryden wrote : " Milton has acknowledg'd to me, that Spenser was his original ". Aubrey also adds that " Mr. Milton received him civilly ".

88, l. 17   " Anchovies." Scott-Saintsbury, Vol. I, 46.p. 1

88-89   Epic. *Discourse concerning Satire* (prefixed to Juvenal and Persius translations). Preface to *Aureng-Zebe*. Scott-Saintsbury, Vol. XVIII, p. 115f. (letter to John Dennis).

90-91   Mackenzie. *Discourse concerning Satire*. (Also for the question of " turns ").

94, l. 31   Schoolmaster. Settle in *Absalom Senior* (1682) implies that Dryden wished to become Provost of Eton. Dryden and the wardenship of All Souls is discussed by Noyes, in the biographical sketch prefixed to his edition of the Poems, lvi-lvii. In 1687, the man who was appointed certainly considered Dryden a serious rival for the post.

95   *An Essay upon Satire*. General scholarly opinion today is that Mulgrave was certainly the author of this poem, in which only some lines were written by Dryden though more were probably corrected by him. It was written about 1675, and first printed in 1680. The poem is printed by Noyes, p. 913-916.

96, l. 32ff   Rochester. *Collected Works*, ed. Hayward (1926). This letter has been thought to establish Rochester as the author of the beating of Dryden in Rose Alley. But the assault took place in December, 1679, whereas it has recently been shown that the letter cannot have been written later than the Spring of 1678 and was probably written two years earlier, in the Spring of 1676. (Dryden's aspersions in the preface to *All for Love*, March, 1678, seem to have been ignored by Rochester.) It seems, therefore, much more likely that the beating was ordered by one of the Royal mistresses, probably the Duchess of Portsmouth, as the contemporary, Luttrell in his *Brief Historical Relation of State Affairs* (Oxford ed. 1857, Vol. I, p. 30), suggested. See end of next chapter. For this view of the affair, see " Review of English Studies ", XV (1939), and XVI (1940), 177, 178.

Page   **Chapter 7**

98, l. 6   Harriott. Osborn, op. cit., prints a letter giving the information
                about Harriott, which was given to Alexander Stephens by Lady
                Dryden in 1798 in reply to his enquiries about Dryden.   A copy of
                the letter was preserved by one of Dryden's descendants, Percy Dryden
                Munday, and permission given by him to Osborn to reproduce it.
                (Osborn, p. 235f.)

98, l. 12   Elmes.   Osborn, pp. 200 and 264.

99   " Heads of an Answer to Rymer."   Osborn, p. 267f.

105-106   Ian Jack, *Augustan Satire*, London (1952).

109, l. 25   Country visit in summer of 1679. Osborn, p. 200f.

110-112   Rose Alley. See note on p. 96 I. 32ff.

                Chapter 8

114, l. 19   Creech's translation.   Dryden's decision in this question is printed
                in Scott-Saintsbury, Vol. XVIII, p. 96f.

114, l. 30   *The Art of Poetry*, printed in Noyes, p. 916ff.

117ff.   Background of *Absalom and Achitophel*. The most brilliant and
                scholarly treatment of this poem that I have come across is that by
                Ian Jack, op. cit.

120   Letter to Busby. Scott-Saintsbury, Vol. XVIII, p. 99. Lady
                Elzabeth's letter is on the same page as a footnote.

                Chapter 9

134   Richard Simon.   Bredvold, pp. 98-107.

137   Letter to Hyde.   Scott-Saintsbury, Vol. XVIII, p. 103f.

138   Dryden's reply to Tonson.   Scott-Saintsbury, Vol. XVIII, p. 105f.

                Chapter 10

148f.   Killigrew Poem.   Professor E. M. W. Tillyard in *Five Poems*
                (London, 1948) has given a brilliant analysis of this poem in pp. 49-66 ;
                but as I have said in the text the poem itself still escapes that analysis.

Page

158, l. 24   A recent historian. Ashley, *England in the Seventeenth Century* (1953)

160   Move to Gerrard Street. Osborn, p. 196.

160, l. 18   Squib. Scott-Saintsbury, Vol. I, p. 295.

Chapter 11

162, l. 9ff.   Letter from Earl of Nottingham. Christie, p. lxiii.

162, l. 23f   " I must ever acknowledge." *Discourse concerning Satire.*

165, l. 7   G. N. Clark : *The Later Stuarts*, 1660-1714 (1939).

167   Dryden's songs. For a sensitive study of these, see *The Poetry of John Dryden* by Mark Van Doren (published in New York in 1920, and by the Minority Press, Cambridge, England, 1931, with introduction by Bonamy Dobrée).

167-168   St. Evremond. Article in D.N.B. and Scott.

168, l. 26   Character of St. Evremond. Scott-Saintsbury, Vol. XVIII, pp. 13-17

171, l. 9ff.   " A reverend grisly elder." Scott-Saintsbury, Vol. XVIII, p. 306

172, l. 17   "He was of a nature . . ." Congreve, op. cit.

176, l. 28   Defoe. *Daniel Defoe* by Francis Watson (1952)

179, l. 3ff.   Letter to Tonson. Scott-Saintsbury, Vol. XVIII, pp. 110-111.

179, l. 32   Letter to Dennis. Scott-Saintsbury, Vol. XVIII, p. 115f.

180-181   Trip with Tonson. Scott-Saintsbury, Vol. XVIII, pp. 110-111.

181   D'Urfey story. Scott-Saintsbury, Vol. I, p. 383.

181-182   Walsh. Letters to Walsh, Scott-Saintsbury, Vol. XVIII, p. 180ff. Osborn, p. 210ff.

183   Dennis. Scott-Saintsbury, Vol. XVIII, p. 113f.

188, l. 24-25   Swift. " The Epistle to Prince Posterity ", prefixed to *Tale of a Tub*. In *The Battle of the Books*, Swift also draws unfavourable comparisons between Dryden—who, he says, " soothed the good ancient by the endearing title of ' father ' "—and Virgil.

191-192   Thomas Burnet. *State Papers and Correspondence*, ed. Kemble, 1857, p. 193.

Chapter 12

196, l 4-5   " Up all night." Scott-Saintsbury, Vol. I, p. 341.

196, l. 13   Bridgman. Letter (to his sons in Rome), Scott-Saintsbury, Vol. XVIII, p. 133f.

197, l. 9f.   Marlay. Malone, op. cit., pp. 476, 477.

199, l. 5f.   Montagu (afterwards Earl of Halifax). Scott-Saintsbury, Vol. XVIII, p. 158ff.

200–201   Pepys. Scott-Saintsbury, Vol. XVIII, pp. 154-155.

204, l. 17f.   C. S. Lewis. *Rehabilitations* (1939), p. 13.

210, l. 13f.   Mrs. Shaw. Osborn, p. 236.

216   Mrs. Creed. Words recorded on the monument at Titchmarsh (Christie, lxxix)

217   Epilogue.

217, l. 3f.   Sir John Shadwell. Scott-Saintsbury, Vol. xviii, p. 161.

217–218   Funeral. Christie. lxxx.

219, l.34-35   " Be Kind." *To my dear friend, Mr. Congreve* (1693).

220, l. 27   Not " Henry " but Thomas Howard : Mrs. Creed's memory failed her.

Select Bibliography

The Poetical Works of Dryden, ed. George R. Noyes. Houghton Mifflin, Boston (The Riverside Press, Cambridge, Mass.). Second Edition. 1950.

The Works of John Dryden, ed. Sir Walter Scott. Revised and Corrected by George Saintsbury. Vols. I-X VIII, 1882. (William Peterson, Prince's Street, Edinburgh).

Samuel Johnson, Lives of the Poets. 2 Vols. (Oxford. World's Classics).

John Dryden : Some biographical Facts and Problems, by James M. Osborn. (Columbia University Press). 1940.

The Intellectual Milieu of John Dryden, by Louis M. Bredvold. (University of Michigan Press). 1934.

The Poetical Works of John Dryden, ed. with a memoir by W. D. Christie. (Macmillan, London). 1875.

The Poetry of John Dryden by Mark van Doren (Harcourt, Brace and Howe, New York, 1920 ; Gordon Fraser, The Minority Press, Cambridge, 1931.

The Poems of Edmund Waller, 2 Vols., ed. G. Thorn-Drury. (Muses' Library, Routledge). 1893.

Dramatic Essays by John Dryden. (Dent, Everyman Library). 1912.

Letters of John Dryden, ed. Charles E. Ward. (Duke University Press). 1942.

John Dryden, by George Saintsbury. (Macmillan, London. English Men of Letters series). 1893.

Lectures on Dryden, by A. W. Verrall. (Cambridge University Press). 1914.

John Dryden : A Bibliography, by Hugh Macdonald. (Oxford University Press). 1939.

John Dryden : A list of Critical Studies, published from 1895-1948, by Samuel Holt Monk. (University of Minnesota Press). 1950.

The Seventeenth Century Background, by Basil Willey. (Chatto and Windus). 1939.

Cross-Currents in English Literature of the XVIIth century, by Prof. H. J. C. Grierson. (Chatto and Windus). 1929.

From Donne to Dryden. The Revolt against Metaphysical Poetry. By R. L. Sharp. (University of North Carolina Press). 1940.

Critical Essays of the 17th Century, 3 Vols., ed. J. E. Spingarn. (Oxford University Press). 1908-9.

The Laureateship : a Study of the Office of Poet Laureate in England, by E. K. Broadus. (Oxford University Press). 1921.

Elkanah Settle, by F. C. Brown. (Chicago University Press). 1910.

The Commonwealth and Restoration Stage, by Leslie Hotson. (The Riverside Press, Cambridge, Mass.). 1928.

Thomas Shadwell, by A. S. Borgman. (New York University Press). 1928.

Collected Works of John Wilmot, Earl of Rochester, ed. Hayward. (Nonsuch Press). 1928.

The Critical and Miscellaneous Prose Works of John Dryden. ed. Edward Malone. (Cadell and Davies). 1800.

The Complete Works of Thomas Shadwell, ed. Montague Summers. (Fortune Press). 1927.

The Life of Joseph Addison, by Peter Smithers, M.P. (Oxford University Press). 1954.

The Mourning Bridge, Poems and Miscellanies, by William Congreve, ed. Prof. Bonamy Dobrée . (Oxford Univ. Press, World's Classics series). 1928.

William Congreve, the Man, by Prof. John C. Hodges (Columbia University Press, New York). 1941.

Restoration Tragedy, by Prof. Bonamy Dobrée. (Oxford University Press). 1928.

The Senecan Amble : A Study of Prose form from Bacon to Collier, by Prof. George Williamson. (Faber and Faber). 1951.

Samuel Pepys, by Dr. Arthur Bryant, 3 Vols. (Cambridge University Press). 1933-1942.

Aphra Behn, by V. Sackville-West. (Gerald Howe, Ltd.). 1927.

John Milton, by Prof. E. M. W. Tillyard. (Chatto and Windus). 1934.

NOTE.—A definite three-volume edition of all Dryden's poetry, including the translations, but not the plays, is to be published by the Oxford University Press in the Oxford Texts series in 1955. The editor is Prof. James Kinsley.

Index